THE DEATH OF ROCK 'N' ROLL

THE DEATH OF ROCK 'N' ROLL

Untimely Demises, Morbid Preoccupations, and Premature Forecasts of Doom in Pop Music

JEFF PIKE

Faber and Faber

BOSTON • LONDON

Library of Congress Cataloging-in-Publication Data

Pike, Jeff.
    Death of rock 'n' roll : untimely demises, morbid
preoccupations, and premature forecasts of doom in
pop music / by Jeff Pike.
        p. cm.
    ISBN 0-571-19808-2 (paper)
    1. Rock music—History and criticism.   2. Rock
musicians—Death.   3. Death in music.   I. Title.
ML3534.P55   1993
781.66—dc20   93-12040
                                                       CIP
                                                       MN

Cover design by Mary Maurer
Printed in the United States of America

This book is dedicated to God
and to Satan—with a tip of
the hat to Thorstein Veblen,
wherever you are.

CONTENTS

ACKNOWLEDGMENTS

*T*HESE DAYS there is much knowledge in pop music reference books, many of which stood me in good stead during my work on this dreadful project. In particular I found much of my factual material and the answers to many questions in *The Penguin Encyclopedia of Popular Music,* ed. Donald Clarke; *The Rolling Stone Encyclopedia of Rock & Roll,* eds. Jon Pareles and Patricia Romanowski; *The Billboard Book of Top 40 Hits,* 5th edition, Joel Whitburn; *Rock On,* Volumes 1 and 2, Norm N. Nite; *The Billboard Book of Number One Hits,* Fred Bronson; *One-Hit Wonders,* Wayne Jancik; and *Rock Movers & Shakers,* ed. Barry Lazell.

I would also like to thank my friends who stood by me and tolerated me during this past year, offering advice, sharing information, and holding my hand: Carol Allin, Bart Becker, John Beckwith, Jim Greenwald, Mike Phillips, Joel Pike, Jeff Reid, Brent Rucker, Neal Skok, Pat Towle, and Mary Truscott. Thanks also to my editor, Betsy Uhrig, who helped me in pulling this from the fire, such as I did; and to my agent Jeremy Solomon, who works very hard and earns every penny he gets.

I would especially like to thank my father, who made this possible. Thanks, Dad.

INTRODUCTION

Untimely Demises . . .

"Rock 'n' roll is here to stay," Danny Rapp sang with his sock-hop band, the Juniors, in 1959. "It will never die." In the midst of payola scandals and other serious troubles that year—including the sudden deaths in an airplane crash of the Big Bopper, Buddy Holly, and Ritchie Valens—Danny Rapp wanted to offer something like a call to arms, an anthem for a generation. What he came up with, however, was more a statement of pure puppy-dog faith, a product of its high-school ponytail times marked as much by innocence as by ardor.

But twenty-four years later, in 1983, the innocence was gone, and so was the ardor. Danny Rapp locked himself in a motel room in Arizona and put a gun to his head. And the beat went on. Irony rarely comes so painfully rich. There's hardly a point in discussing the death of Danny Rapp, it's so obvious. Rock 'n' roll had claimed another one, and made a truth so striking it's a cliché just that much more evident. Along with sex, drugs, and haircuts, death has set the tone for rock 'n' roll since its earliest days. As much as anything, it's what ties Elvis Presley to the Rolling Stones to the Sex Pistols to Slayer.

And here it comes again: If it's likely that rock 'n' roll will continue to live on, an arguable point, it's guaranteed that its adherents will not. Many will die young and, sad to say, some under ludicrous circumstances: victims of drug and alcohol abuse, auto and plane accidents, severe depression, and from causes we can't even imagine. Certainly it's a long-standing tradition by now. Bluesman Robert Johnson and country singer Hank Williams, perhaps the two most influential figures in everything rock 'n' roll was to become, never even saw the age of thirty, and both died years before Bill Haley had ever urged anyone to rock around a clock. (The lights went out for Bill Haley in 1981, by the way: heart attack.)

And, oh yes, there is Elvis Presley, too, who certainly put the finishing touches to what Johnson and Williams started, arriving as the Son to complete a kind of holy Trinity among them. If Elvis inherited rock 'n' roll, and he did, he inaugurated practically everything that came in its wake. Without Elvis, there could never have been a Bryan Ferry or a Prince, let alone a John Lennon or a Bruce Springsteen. And if Elvis did make it past thirty, he still died early—in the process turning the age of forty-two into nearly as much of a mythical hurdle as thirty-three.

One wonders what in hell is going on here. Is there something about the trappings of rock 'n' roll—the drugs and alcohol, the obsessions of the fans, the life on the road—that is inherently fatal or dangerous? Or is it that those people attracted to rock 'n' roll already have a lifeline that peters out approximately at their middle finger, and are destined for early death no matter what their career choice?

Well, yes and yes. After nearly half a century of rock 'n' roll there is a feast of deaths to sort through—one for every occasion, and a few for some occasions we didn't know existed. If politicians, film celebrities, models, wrestlers, and even race-car drivers and stunt pilots are liable to the same dangers and death rates as rock 'n' roll stars, and that's a big *if,* their contexts have never provided the same sort of thrilling shout at the devil, that chilling gesture of challenge not just to physical limitations, but to metaphysical limitations as well.

Face it. There just is no escaping the death of rock 'n' roll. What else can we possibly do but catalog this litany of disasters, the better to gape at it in wonder?

Morbid Preoccupations . . .

Speaking of Robert Johnson, it's long been speculated, and taken quite seriously, that Johnson struck a bargain with Satan at about the time Franklin Roosevelt was ousting Herbert Hoover for the U.S. presidency. Presumably, in exchange for his enormous talent, Johnson traded away his immortal soul. In one way—a very weird one—that explains his abrupt, overpowering appearance as a giant of the blues, the unearthly authority of his music, and the quaking terror at its heart. But he died so young, and left relatively so little—just a few dozen tunes. You'd think he could have at least, like Jerry Lee Lewis, seen the terms out to the end, or, like Mick Jagger, hired a good celestial attorney to find a loophole and renege on the deal altogether.

Still, the point remains. Dedicating one's life to rock 'n' roll has always involved an essentially religious decision, and has led to lives full of ritual and mystery. So many thank God on their album sleeves, and so many are accused of worshipping Satan. Alice Cooper got his stage name from a ouija board, Bob Dylan is deathly afraid he will burn in hell, the Grateful Dead play the Egyptian pyramids, Deicide dunks itself in pigs' blood, Little Richard is ordained as a minister in the Seventh Day Adventist church, Sinéad O'Connor creates waves of scandal by tearing a photo of the Pope in half on live television.

Since its earliest days rock 'n' roll has been shot through with intimations of death and visions of the great beyond — and many times a lot more than just shot through. If you don't want to start with Robert Johnson, consider Hank Williams's "I'll Never Get Out of This World Alive," a hit in 1952 shortly before his death. If that won't do, try Elvis Presley's "Mystery Train." Or Screamin' Jay Hawkins's "I Put a Spell on You." Or Jerry Lee Lewis's "Great Balls of Fire."

That weird, obsessive fascination with death and supernatural power in rock 'n' roll runs along under the surface, yet traces through pretty easily, until about 1968 — at which point it breaks wide open. What had once been darkly hinted, not least because of powerful taboos, suddenly became a focal point and chief feature, or at least a prevailing image, of whole groups and careers: the Rolling Stones, the Doors, Iggy Pop, the Velvet Underground, and countless more.

By 1971, the Buoys could have a novelty hit, "Timothy," about cannibalism, while Bloodrock (and note that name) could have a hit, "D.O.A.", that was anything but a novelty about a grisly accident. A few years later the Sex Pistols turned genuine self-mutilation (borrowed from Iggy Pop) into viable shtick and fashion statement. By 1981, the death obsessions of such figures as Joy Division's Ian Curtis, who hanged himself, had come to be seen as romantic. By 1991, death metal act Gwar was enacting scenes of gore onstage, with blood spewing from the gaping wounds left behind by arms and heads lopped off with single mighty blows.

Goodness — what is the meaning of all this? Are we faced with a chicken-and-egg dilemma? Are rock 'n' roll musicians obsessed with death because they've witnessed so much carnage in what is supposed to be an entertainment industry? Or is it death-obsessed people who are attracted to rock 'n' roll in the first place?

As the millennium approaches, let us together consider the meanings of the death of rock 'n' roll.

Premature Forecasts of Doom . . .

As for the death of rock 'n' roll, that has happened a few times now—once in about 1959, around the time of Buddy Holly's plane accident; again in about 1970, as part of the post-Woodstock morass that included Altamont and the deaths of Jimi Hendrix, Janis Joplin, and Jim Morrison; and again in about 1977, and this time for real, when the Sex Pistols and punk-rock not only declared it dead, but effectively destroyed it.

Of course, the first two deaths of rock 'n' roll were something of staged media events, with a good deal of public hand-wringing in print—much, in fact, as this book itself is intended to be. The end of rock 'n' roll makes a good, dramatic story, and, incidentally, has served the interests of the industry as well. At the time of the first death of rock 'n' roll, it was an opportunity to sanitize what had come to be seen as a dangerous youth activity—a view that, with government agencies beginning to take action, clearly threatened sales. At the time of the second death, it was an opportunity to shift the focus from songs on AM-radio to album tracks on FM-radio, thus opening up the market permanently for the more lucrative LP format.

The last death of rock 'n' roll, of course, which happened almost silently—inevitably raising questions of trees crashing to the ground in uninhabited forests—is a different case. There was nothing for the industry to gain by it, so they ignored it. Punk-rock was a nonevent, a false alarm, a meaningless blip. In the year that the Sex Pistols went international, 1977, Fleetwood Mac and Debby Boone blew out the top of the charts, single *and* album, and the year finished with the release of *Saturday Night Fever*. How do *you* read that? Does it really add up to rock 'n' roll being more vital than ever?

Consider what critic Rick Shefchik, writing in the *Village Voice* in 1988, had to say: "Although I don't really remember what it was like when the Dorseys and the Glenn Miller Orchestra and Benny Goodman and even Duke Ellington and Count Basie were passing from mass popularity, I feel as though we're entering a similar phase of pop culture. Rock and rollers have proven they can get old and still make good music, but so did the big band leaders. I hear rock and roll being refined, expanded, colorized and in some cases even improved, but it ceased being invented a long time ago. The pros have taken over, the scene is as mainstream as the big bands ever were, and it will wither and die just as inevitably. I no longer wait for the Next Big Thing as though I could possibly have any hand in discovering it; my three-year-old daughter will tell me what it is when she discovers it."

Here's hoping she tells us all. Meanwhile, let me tell you a little about the Last Big Thing.

This book is organized into four sections that coexist in space and time like all good things, with chapters that list dead rock stars linked by the type of music they made, set in rough chronological order, and noting their influence in condensed biographies; chapters that discuss themes of death raised by various figures in rock 'n' roll; three chapters that examine the great falls of rock 'n' roll, followed by chapters listing the great fallen heroes associated with those eras; and snapshot lists that provide a cross-referenced overview of who died and how—whether by cancer, at the age of thirty-three, or on December 8.

Please, don't anyone reading this kill yourself.

Seattle, 1993

1

Hellhound on His Trail

BLUESMAN ROBERT JOHNSON stands as one of the most significant players in both blues and rock 'n' roll. But his story and his life raise a crucial question: how did it happen? He played country blues and slide on an acoustic guitar, recorded only a few dozen tunes in 1936 and 1937, never performed outside of the South, and died in 1938 when he was twenty-seven. Still he is credited, and rightly so, with shaping the entire course the blues has taken since his time, including every piece of it that went into rock 'n' roll. How? Why?

The force of his music only begins to tell the story. Robert Johnson operated, musically and historically, in the brutal passageway between the hardships of rural living and the horrors of urban survival. His simple, evocative accompaniment on guitar provided the perfect complement to his voice, a bleating instrument that intimated anguish beyond knowing, and to his songs, exercises in bravado and dread that have, almost all of them, become blues standards: "I Believe I'll Dust My Broom," "Love in Vain," "Sweet Home Chicago," "Cross Road Blues," "Stones in My Passway," "Terraplane Blues," "Hellhound on My Trail," "Me and the Devil Blues," and more, covered by Elmore James, Cream, the Rolling Stones, Captain Beefheart, and others.

The details of Johnson's life remain sketchy and confusing, as perhaps they should, given that much of his success has been whispered as deriving from the black arts. They, a vague *they*, say that Johnson turned to voodoo. With the room to speculate afforded by the obscurity of Johnson's life and the unearthly power of his music, which has endured down the years despite its shoddy recording quality, many have wondered if Robert Johnson did not strike a bargain with Satan.

It certainly goes a distance toward explaining the mysterious events of his life—an endless litany of painful difficulties, for centuries merely the norm for a black man in the South. But somehow Johnson transformed all of it into a spectacular triumph that almost as quickly collapsed in on itself. There was always *something* insidiously powerful and mysterious at work in his life. Even his origin is marked by complexity—he was born in 1911, the offspring of a brief affair that his mother had after her husband, Charles Dodds, left her to live with his mistress in Memphis (Dodds was also fleeing a personal vendetta). Both rejoined Dodds for a time, but first Johnson's mother, and then Johnson, when he was seven, left to live in Robinsonville, Mississippi.

There he started playing music in his teens, learning what he could from local bluesmen Charlie Patton and Willie Brown. He married when he was seventeen, in 1929, but his wife died in childbirth the following year. After that he threw himself into his music, learning what he could from Son House, a recent arrival in Robinsonville. Johnson was no prodigy, by all accounts. In fact, he was not considered very good at all.

Shortly after the death of his first wife, Johnson, until then a farmer, took to drifting. He ended up in Hazlehurst, Mississippi, the town of his birth, searching for his father, Noah Webster. Johnson didn't find Webster but he did meet his mentor, an obscure bluesman named Ike Zinnerman. Zinnerman liked to say he'd learned to play guitar at night in a cemetery, with only tombstones for company; some believed him to be Satan. Whoever he was, he taught Johnson well. After a year or two, Johnson returned to Robinsonville, where Son House and the others were amazed at his development. Johnson then played continually for the rest of his life, traveling around the South and gradually building a reputation for music and for boozing and womanizing.

His name was becoming known throughout the South by the time he began recording in 1936, but only "Terraplane Blues" won him any kind of notice outside the region while he was still alive, and that, of course, was as a "race" artist. But it did catch the attention of John Hammond, who wanted to book him in late 1938 for his "Spirituals to Swing Concert" in Carnegie Hall. By then, however, it was already too late. Robert Johnson had died on August 16, 1938. The best evidence indicates it was from poisoning by a jealous husband, when Johnson drank from a glass he'd left unattended, though other versions claim it was a stabbing, by the jealous husband or by the woman herself.

In any event, the die seemed cast. Through Robert Johnson, Satan had deeply insinuated himself into the heart of the music that would become rock 'n' roll and had already begun to demand his unholy terms. Many shuddered, and rightly so, at what Satan had required of Robert Johnson, as they had shuddered and shudder still at the fearsome power of his music.

And all those who followed Johnson and made themselves students of his work found themselves paying on his account, from Elmore James to Brian Jones to Eric Clapton. By 1938, the year before German forces marched into Poland and the year after heroin and marijuana were made illegal in the United States, the spiritual force of rock 'n' roll was upon the land.

2

Tombstone Blues

BLUES MUSIC is a huge part of the rock 'n' roll equation, indeed a huge part of American popular music. It contributed many of its lyrical concerns and much of its musical style to rock 'n' roll—but not before it had already made an enormous impact on jazz and then a significant one on country music. The curiously enduring appeal of the "blue note" and its associated arrangements and chord progressions, along with the resigned attitude of stubborn survival in its most characteristic lyrics, originated in the black South and have been developed over the course of a century. It has less influence now, but it is far from over.

The impact of blues on rock 'n' roll is most obvious in the fixations of rock culture, whose players tried to co-opt blues whole and were gauged critically by their ability or inability to do so. Remember the great white wonders—Cream, Johnny Winter, Canned Heat, Ten Years After, Fleetwood Mac, Savoy Brown? All had been anticipated in early-sixties Britain, when John Mayall and Alexis Korner conducted seminars in blues proficiency, providing lasting results with their ongoing projects—the Bluesbreakers and Blues, Inc., respectively—and all they spawned, including the Yardbirds, the Rolling Stones, and the Animals.

Yet the inherent weakness was already there. As with the folk boom of a decade earlier, too many were judged by how faithfully they aped already existing sounds. (At the same time, authentic players unearthed for the occasion, such as Fred McDowell, John Hurt, Furry Lewis, Mance Lipscomb, and dozens more, were often patronized and, by implication, expected to show gratitude for the favor of attention.) The more that pure replication was demanded and provided, the more it was necessarily doomed to the status of cliché. Sadly enough, much of the blues that emerged then sounds suffocatingly stale now.

But the most profound pattern of influence the blues had on rock 'n' roll was never that obvious. That pattern was set in the fifties, when rock 'n' roll was still tearing away from it. Such figures as Chuck Berry, Elvis Presley, and Jerry Lee Lewis, along with many vocal groups (including the Clovers, Cadets, and Flairs), had absorbed the blues and consciously abandoned it for something called rhythm and blues and the prospects of pop success. But unconsciously the blues still had a grip, emerging in subtle embellishments, style, and tone: Berry's guitar licks, Presley's vocal tics, the Clovers' raucous attack. For nearly thirty years, that tension of trying to escape the blues but finding it still present time and again, provided much of the impetus for rock 'n' roll to continually reinvent itself.

The pattern never disappeared for long. By 1968 the Rolling Stones had also absorbed the blues and abandoned it, as they proceeded to invent a whole new rock 'n' roll. To satisfy market requirements of the time, they paraded "authentic" blues covers on their albums. But the Stones' best music was something else entirely, though always shot through with ineffable blues touches ("Street Fighting Man," "Jumpin' Jack Flash," "Brown Sugar"). Jimi Hendrix also had a background in blues, and, when he showed it, was astonishingly proficient; but he too transcended it while never really getting far from it. The same pattern held later for Jimmy Page and Led Zeppelin, and holds now for Robert Cray.

Many of the blues' best practitioners are now dead, of old age and natural causes as often as anything. Below is a list of those who made significant and specific contributions to rock 'n' roll; it is for reasons of space only a partial list of a sweeping and powerful music's best players.

Willie Dixon, died January 29, 1992, age 86
From Vicksburg, Mississippi. With Howlin' Wolf and Muddy Waters, Dixon was a major figure in the development of Chicago's urban version of Mississippi delta blues. As an instrumentalist, playing bass in small groups and then with the Chess label's house band, he was negligible. But as a songwriter he was a giant. He wrote "Back Door Man," "I Just Wanna Make Love to You," "Little Red Rooster," "Wang Dang Doodle," "You Shook Me," "Spoonful," "I'm Your Hoochie Coochie Man," "I Ain't Superstitious," "I Can't Quit You, Baby," and others, all standards, since covered by black and white artists alike, including Muddy Waters, Howlin' Wolf, Bo Diddley, Otis Rush, Cream, Sam Cooke, the Rolling Stones, the Doors, Led Zeppelin (against whom Dixon fought and won a lengthy and complex copyright battle), and the Jeff Beck Group. Sadly, he sold many of his songs outright, at about thirty dollars a shot, missing out on a fortune in royalties. Even so, he lived a long, happy, and active life. In the eighties he wrote and

published his autobiography, *I Am the Blues*. When he died of heart failure, he was survived by eleven children and thirty grandchildren.

Lightnin' Hopkins, died January 30, 1982, age 69
From Centerville, Texas; born Sam Hopkins. Like John Lee Hooker, Hopkins continued working through a series of mid-century waves of blues popularity, eventually emerging as an imposingly prolific figure. To rock 'n' roll, like John Lee Hooker, he lent a potent aura of brooding, violent menace seemingly born of experience beyond ken. Hopkins came of age during the Depression playing in the streets with Blind Lemon Jefferson. Because he signed no contracts and insisted on being paid cash at his sessions (relinquishing most of his rights to royalties), his output is difficult to track. But it's been estimated that he recorded over a thousand songs, most delivered in his characteristic style, with stripped-down arrangements creating a charged atmosphere over which Hopkins mutters and chuckles through lyrics as often as not improvised on the spot. He was a direct influence on Texas-based rock players Johnny Winter, Tony Joe White (you can hear it in "Polk Salad Annie"), and Doug Sahm of the Sir Douglas Quintet, among others. Throughout his career Hopkins toured widely and released new material at a clip of two or three albums a year. In 1972 he appeared on the soundtrack of the heavily relevant *Sounder*. He died of cancer.

Howlin' Wolf, died January 10, 1976, age 65
From West Point, Mississippi; born Chester Arthur Burnett. Howlin' Wolf was an enormous influence on rock culture, rivaled only by B.B. King, Muddy Waters, and John Lee Hooker. His weird, raw singing voice was the source of his name and inspired figures as diverse as Mick Jagger, Captain Beefheart, and Tom Waits. His offbeat arrangements and approach deeply influenced the most innovative blues-rock players, and the pure presence of his sound created a sensation everywhere, most particularly in Chicago. As a boy working on a Mississippi plantation, he preferred the yodeling of country giant Jimmie Rodgers. By the time he was in his teens, however, he was playing guitar and studying at the feet of masters such as Robert Johnson and Rice Miller (aka Sonny Boy Williamson), who taught him to play harmonica. In 1948, already nearing forty, he formed his first band in Memphis with James Cotton and Junior Parker. His subsequent bands were unique, often with two harmonica players and no bass. In 1952, Ike Turner, then a kind of talent scout at large, had Howlin' Wolf record for Sam Phillips's Sun label. Eventually those recordings found their way to Leonard Chess, who made Howlin' Wolf a key part of the Chess Records roster. Howlin' Wolf then moved to Chicago, making it his permanent

home base. He enjoyed some notice on the rhythm and blues charts with a series of releases from the late fifties through the sixties and played briefly with Muddy Waters until their relationship degenerated into bitter rivalry. Then, as white blues-rock became popular, the pillaging began, by the Yardbirds, the Jeff Beck Group (with Rod Stewart), Cream, the Doors, Led Zeppelin, and others. But Howlin' Wolf was always revered, performing constantly at blues and rock festivals. He recorded *The London Sessions* in 1972, featuring support from Eric Clapton, Bill Wyman, Charlie Watts, Steve Winwood, and Ringo Starr. Toward the end of his life he suffered a series of heart attacks and kidney failures, but continued to perform. He gave his last concert in November 1975 with B.B. King. Within weeks he was hospitalized again. He died the next month of kidney disease.

Elmore James, died May 24, 1963, age 45
From Richland, Mississippi. Elmore James was perhaps the single most important figure in translating the acoustic slide guitar of Robert Johnson into the amplified Chicago setting. His version of Johnson's "I Believe I'll Dust My Broom" became his signature song and was a significant influence on British blues players in the early sixties. Brian Jones borrowed his slide-guitar stylings practically whole from James, and James's tunes and style have been covered by Eric Clapton, Fleetwood Mac (in their first incarnation as a blues band), John Mayall, and others. Duane Allman became another disciple of the sound later in the decade. James made his mark after moving to Chicago in the fifties but recorded some of his best work even earlier. He performed with Robert Johnson and Rice Miller (aka Sonny Boy Williamson) in Mississippi during the thirties. He died of a heart attack in Chicago.

Blind Lemon Jefferson, died December, 1930, age 33
From Couchman, Texas; named Lemon, born blind (the source, very incidentally, of Jefferson Airplane's name). An enormously influential Texas bluesman in the first decades of this century, at one time or another Jefferson played with and taught Lightnin' Hopkins, T-Bone Walker, Big Bill Broonzy, and Leadbelly; through them, his influence extends to nearly every bluesman who lived and played in this century. His repertoire ran wide and deep, from blues to field hollers to moans to spirituals to chain-gang songs, and he wrote as well as performed in many of these styles. He began recording in the mid-twenties and until his death was, along with Bessie Smith, one of the most popular "race" artists in what was considered at the time an exotic, almost decadent form of music. His "Booger Rooger Blues" gave the world the term "booger rooger" for wild party, which was eventu-

ally corrupted into "boogie woogie," later a specific musical idiom. In 1930, just before Christmas, he reportedly suffered a heart attack, and died of exposure on the streets of Chicago.

Robert Johnson, died August 16, 1938, age 27
See Hellhound on His Trail.

Muddy Waters, died April 30, 1983, age 68
From Rolling Fork, Mississippi; born McKinley Morganfield. Perhaps no other single figure was as instrumental as Muddy Waters in transforming blues from the acoustic, folk-tinged sound originating in the Mississippi delta to the amplified, driving sound it took in Chicago. This spirit in turn anticipated and defined much of rock 'n' roll — and gave particular shape to the Monterey/Woodstock generation's fascination with blues. Waters, whose name came from his penchant for fishing and swimming in a muddy creek near his home as a boy, formed a band in his teens — a departure from the prevailing style of solo players. He modeled his singing on Son House and taught himself to play guitar by listening to Robert Johnson records. In 1940 he moved to St. Louis, where he was recorded by archivist Alan Lomax in a tent show. He moved to Chicago in 1943. Already accomplished on slide, within a year he acquired an electric guitar and started to establish his trademark sound, an unyielding assault that emphasized a crunching beat with Waters's rough-hewn vocals growling and muttering across the top. He was signed to Chess (then still called Aristocrat) in 1946 and released his first single in 1948, "Rollin' Stone," later the name of a rock band, a rock song, and a rock magazine. His band during this period included Willie Dixon, Little Walter, Otis Spann, Junior Wells, James Cotton, and Buddy Guy. His most enduring and memorable hits came in the early and mid-fifties, all as a rhythm and blues artist: "Honey Bee," "She Moves Me," "Hoochie Coochie," "I Just Want to Make Love to You," "I'm Ready," "Rollin' and Tumblin'," "Got My Mojo Working," "Mannish Boy," and others. Almost immediately they became blues standards. During the sixties he began to appear at jazz, folk, and blues festivals, and recorded with the white kids who idolized him, including Paul Butterfield and Mike Bloomfield, on the albums *Fathers and Sons* and *London Muddy Waters Sessions*. During the seventies he appeared at the Band's farewell concert in 1976 and in the film *The Last Waltz*, and worked with Johnny Winter toward the end of the decade on two releases for Blue Sky. In the early eighties he returned to Chess. He died of a heart attack.

Bessie Smith, died September 26, 1937, age 43

From Chattanooga, Tennessee. Bessie Smith was one of a small handful, including Blind Lemon Jefferson, who found sudden and overwhelming success with the blues in the twenties. She reached the highest point of them all. In her prime and beyond it, Bessie Smith gave voice to songs and a style that influenced such disparate figures as Billie Holiday, LaVern Baker, Janis Joplin, the Band, and others. After years on the vaudeville circuit, with Ma Rainey providing guidance, Smith's breakthrough came in 1923 when she was signed to Columbia's Race subsidiary. "Downhearted Blues," her first release, sold nearly a million copies in six months. From then on she was the "Queen of the Blues" (or the "Empress of the Blues"), a prominent feature of the decade, and the highest paid black performer of her time. But it was a triumph that dissipated as quickly as it appeared. With the onset of the Depression, public taste ran more toward country and folk forms and the popularity of the blues evaporated; her last hit was 1929's "Nobody Knows You When You're Down and Out." With John Hammond producing, she recorded her last sides in 1933 but continued performing until the end of her life. She died in an auto accident in Mississippi, and was buried in a grave that remained unmarked until 1970.

T-Bone Walker, died March 16, 1975, age 64

From Linden, Texas; born Aaron Thibeaux Walker (nickname derived from his mother's corruption of his middle name). Along with his boyhood friend Charlie Christian, he was a pioneer of the electric guitar. But where jazz player Christian's innovations were primarily musical, Walker's also involved performance. Without Walker, it would be hard to imagine B.B. King, Chuck Berry, Bo Diddley, Jimi Hendrix—even, to some degree, Elvis Presley. At age ten, Walker played the streets of Dallas with Blind Lemon Jefferson. He moved to the West Coast in 1934 and began experimenting with early models of what would become the electric guitar. By 1942, shortly after the death of Charlie Christian, he was making an indelible impression on his peers. While his playing often looked to jazz phrasings, like Christian's, his performances were wild: he did the splits, played the guitar behind his head, ground it into his groin, aimed the neck at his audience. His biggest hit came in 1943 with "Call It Stormy Monday," now a blues standard. Walker maintained his popularity right along. He continued to record and perform and make TV appearances into the seventies. He died of bronchial pneumonia.

Sonny Boy Williamson, died May 25, 1965, age 65

From Glendora, Mississippi; born Rice Miller. Sonny Boy Williamson was the name taken by two men who both played blues harmonica. John Lee Williamson, from Jackson, Tennessee, died in 1948 in Chicago at age thirty-four in a mugging. He wrote and recorded "Good Morning, Little Schoolgirl," played with Big Bill Broonzy, Joe Williams, and Muddy Waters, among others, and was a significant influence on Little Walter. But the more famous and influential of the two was Rice Miller, who came from Mississippi and was some fifteen years older than John Lee. Miller claimed to have invented the name himself, but more likely plucked it from the "race" chart to fortify his reputation as a blues harpist—a reputation that, as it turned out, needed little fortification. During his long career he played sessions with Robert Johnson, Howlin' Wolf, Elmore James, Arthur "Big Boy" Crudup, Otis Spann, and others. He hosted a popular radio show in the early forties in Arkansas, "King Biscuit Time," and began recording for regional labels in the early fifties. He moved to Chicago in 1955 and recorded for Chess, occasionally backed by Muddy Waters's band. Already a favorite among British blues players—his "Eyesight to the Blind" was covered by the Who, who normally shied away from blues—Miller was a big hit when he toured Britain in 1963. He made appearances on "Ready, Steady, Go" and recorded live albums with the Yardbirds and the Animals. Back in the United States, he also played sessions with Levon and the Hawks, who later became the Band. He died of tuberculosis.

Faces of Death 1:
Tuberculosis

Charlie Christian, died March 2, 1942, age 25
See Guitar Heroes.

Jimmie Rodgers, died May 26, 1933, age 35
See Country Corpses.

Sonny Boy Williamson, died May 25, 1965, age 65
See Tombstone Blues.

3

Country Corpses

COUNTRY MUSIC is the second part of the rock 'n' roll equation, an equation complicated by the fact that the blues influenced country music nearly as much as the blues influenced rock 'n' roll. Jimmie Rodgers, the founding father of country music along with the Carter Family, always included blues numbers in his repertoire, and many consider his yodels simply a more exuberant, European folk-inflected version of blues moans. Hank Williams, a towering figure in country music, perhaps the greatest of them all, also sang the blues—as, indeed, have all country artists of any stature, including the best of the batch just emerging to commandeer the pop charts, Garth Brooks and Mary-Chapin Carpenter among them.

Thus, striving to avoid pat racial categorizing, and with a nod to Charley Pride in passing, it may as well be said that the identifying qualities of country music are its general preference for guitars and other stringed instruments, the elegant architecture of its song structures, the cloying sincerity of its lyrics, and its overwhelming practice by white people. With the exception of the cloying sincerity and the structure of its songs, these are also country music's most significant contributions to rock 'n' roll.

Unlike the blues, though, country music discourages innovation. The names that appear below belong, by and large, to one of three camps: faithful practitioners of the form who somehow wandered, blinking, onto the pop chart to make their mark on rock 'n' roll; giants who cannot be denied; and alienated experimenters. Perhaps the only thing they have in common is not that they played country music, which I'm sorry to say must be considered almost as vague a term as rock 'n' roll, but that they are dead.

Johnny Bond, died June 12, 1978, age 63
Singer, songwriter, movie star. Born Cyrus Bond; from Enville, Oklahoma. In the movies, he was a guitar-strumming sidekick to Gene Autry, Tex Rit-

ter, Roy Rogers, and Hopalong Cassidy. In 1960 he landed in the top thirty of the pop charts with the catchy, boogie-driven mutterfest "Hot Rod Lincoln," which was covered by Commander Cody and His Lost Planet Airmen in 1972, their version went to number 9. Bond died of a heart attack.

Boudleaux Bryant, died June 25, 1987, age 67
Songwriter; from Shellman, Georgia. Boudleaux was the husband half (with wife Felice) of the prolific country songwriting team who contributed a handful or so of rock 'n' roll standards, chiefly through the Everly Brothers: "Bye Bye Love," "Wake Up Little Susie," "Problems," "Bird Dog," and "All I Have to Do Is Dream" (perhaps the greatest rock 'n' roll song ever about masturbation). He also cowrote Buddy Holly's "Raining in My Heart," Bob Moore's instrumental "Mexico," and Bob Luman's "Let's Think About Living." He died of cancer.

The Carter Family
Formed 1926, dissolved 1943; from Virginia. The original trio consisted of A.P. Carter, Sara Dougherty Carter, and Maybelle Addington Carter. A.P. and Sara were married; Maybelle was Sara's cousin and married to A.P.'s brother, hence their "Family" designation and common surname. Headed up by A.P., they almost single-handedly invented the idea of taking folk songs and arranging them for country instruments. They added the folk element to country music at the same time Jimmie Rodgers was pulling the blues into it. Maybelle's guitar playing—picking melody on the bass strings while strumming rhythm on the treble, known as the "Carter" style—influenced hundreds of folksingers and country music players that followed. The Carters' repertoire, made up exclusively of traditional numbers, was also influential: "Wabash Cannonball," "Wildwood Flower" (which sold over a million copies as a 78), "Will the Circle Be Unbroken," "Worried Man Blues" (not a blues song), and more. After the group broke up in 1943, Maybelle worked with her daughters, June (who married Johnny Cash), Helen, and Anita, as Maybelle Carter and the Carter Sisters. A.P., meanwhile, formed a group with his children, and worked with them until he died in 1960, aged sixty-nine. Maybelle then adopted the name of the Carter Family for her group, a good group but not as good as the original. In 1967 she performed with Sara at the Newport Folk Festival, which produced the LP *An Historic Reunion*. Sara, however, who had divorced A.P. in the thirties, remained mostly inactive until her death in 1979, aged eighty. Maybelle continued to perform and record in the sixties, traveling with Johnny Cash's revue and appearing on his TV show. She sang "Will the Circle Be Unbroken" for the Nitty Gritty Dirt Band's project of that

name in 1971, but was not particularly active after that. She died in 1978, aged sixty-nine. Members of the Carter family continue to work in the music industry, but none has achieved the kind of recognition, let alone lasting influence, of the first generation.

Patsy Cline, died March 5, 1963, age 30
Country/pop singer; from Winchester, Virginia. Patsy Cline was an affecting singer who seemed destined for pop success but was the victim all too often of troubles in which she had no hand. Her sound, backed often by the Jordanaires and only the sparest instrumentation, was as slick as it was pure, anticipating by a good ten years what would eventually be called "countrypolitan." Few before or since have matched her ability to project a vulnerability unencumbered by affectation. In 1961 she made her first break into the pop top ten with "Crazy," which reached number 9, but shortly after she was badly hurt in an auto accident. For all her promise, it was her only pop top ten hit. Bad luck struck again two years later. Returning from a Kansas City engagement with Cowboy Copas and Hawkshaw Hawkins—a benefit for the widow of a DJ who had died in an auto accident—their chartered plane crashed into a mountaintop near Camden, Tennessee. Everyone aboard was killed.

Lew DeWitt, died August 15, 1990, age 52
Singer and songwriter with the Statler Brothers; from Staunton, Virginia. An enormous presence in country music in the seventies and eighties, the Statlers (who weren't brothers) hit the pop charts in a big way only once, in 1966, with the number 4 "Flowers on the Wall," a monotonously catchy ode to boredom written by DeWitt. With the rest of the group he went on to spend the remainder of his career indulging in corny humor, collecting awards, and cashing checks. He died from Crohn's Disease.

Pete Drake, died July 29, 1988, age 65
Pedal steel guitar player; from Augusta, Georgia. Drake was an innovative Nashville sessioneer whose work did much to popularize the pedal steel guitar among rock players. He recorded with Elvis Presley, Bob Dylan (*John Wesley Harding*), George Harrison (*All Things Must Pass*), and many more. Another of his claims to fame was the invention of the "talking guitar," a weird sound that anticipated the vocoder by about fifteen years. He used it to get a number 25 pop hit in 1964, "Forever."

Tennessee Ernie Ford, died October 16, 1991, age 72
Country/pop/gospel singer, TV personality; from Bristol, Tennessee. Af-

ter recording nimble bluesy fare in the early fifties, Ford was the first country singer to breach the pop charts in a big way, largely the result of his televised variety show. First came the 1955 number 5 "Ballad of Davy Crockett," then "Sixteen Tons," which spent eight weeks at number 1 that year. Then he turned to hymning. He died of liver problems.

Lefty Frizzell, died July 19, 1975, age 47
Singer, born William Orville; from Corsicana, Texas. Lefty Frizzell was one of the greatest country artists ever in the honky-tonk style. He was nicknamed for his strong suit as a boxer. His hard-edged baritone warble was an enormous influence on later country music generations, in the line descending from Jimmie Rodgers, and including Merle Haggard, Willie Nelson, and John Anderson. John Doe of X also ranks as an heir. Frizzell's hits, all country, include "Saginaw, Michigan" and "Long Black Veil." He died of a stroke.

Stuart Hamblen, died March 8, 1989, age 80
Singer, songwriter, actor; from Kellyville, Texas. Hamblen started out as a singing cowboy in the late twenties and went on to star in westerns, usually wearing the black hat. During the fifties Billy Graham converted him and he became a gospel singer, replacing his popular numbers "I Won't Go Hunting with You Jake (But I'll Go Chasin' Wimmin)" with such fare as "It Is No Secret," which Elvis Presley covered on his 1957 EP *Peace in the Valley*. Hamblen even ran for president on the Prohibition ticket in 1952. In 1955 he scored a number 8 hit with "Open Up Your Heart (And Let the Sunshine In)," recorded by a group of kids called the Cowboy Church Sunday School. He died during surgery for a brain tumor.

Johnny Horton, died November 5, 1960, age 33
Country-pop singer; from Tyler, Texas. Johnny Horton scored high on the pop charts in 1959 and 1960 with a series of patriotic novelties, including the number 1 "The Battle of New Orleans" (everybody now: "Well we fired our guns and the British kept a-comin'/Fired once more and they began to run"), the number 3 "Sink the Bismarck," and the number 4 "North to Alaska," the theme for a John Wayne movie. Oddly enough, his could be considered the first occult rock 'n' roll death. A lifelong believer in the dark forces, Horton suffered premonitions of his own death early in 1960 and began to behave erratically, canceling engagements and refusing to fly anywhere. He died with his guitar player Gerald Tomlinson in a head-on auto collision, returning home from Austin's Skyline in foggy conditions. His

widow Billie Joe was also the widow of Hank Williams, who had also played his last date at the Skyline.

Bob Luman, died December 27, 1978, age 41
Rockabilly artist; from Nacogdoches, Texas. Bob Luman was the first, if you want to debate it, to discover guitar legend James Burton. Ricky Nelson wooed Burton away from Luman's band when they came to Los Angeles to record in the late fifties. Luman scored a number 7 pop hit in 1960 with the uncharacteristically topical "Let's Think About Living" and afterward did well as a country artist, eventually becoming a regular on the Grand Ole Opry. He was hospitalized for nearly six months in 1976 for a blocked artery; Johnny Cash lent him moral support after his recovery, producing the album *Alive and Well*. Luman died of pneumonia in Nashville.

Roger Miller, October 25, 1992, age 56
Country/pop singer, songwriter; from Fort Worth, Texas. Roger Miller spiked to popularity in 1964 and 1965 with a series of droll country novelties that earned him a couple of fistfuls of Grammy awards and the undying enmity of anyone who has heard "Dang Me" (number 7 in 1964) first thing in the morning and had it rattle around the brain the rest of the day. His best, the 1965 number 4 "King of the Road," ranks with "Fever" and "Yesterday" as one of the most covered pop songs of all time, and his 1965 number 8 "England Swings" remains a curious artifact of those early British Invasion times. Otherwise it was dang-me type fare such as the 1964 number 9 "Chug-A-Lug" and "Do-Wacka-Do," or bathetic outings like "Husbands and Wives" and "Little Green Apples." Miller was off the pop charts by 1970, but continued to record country albums for a series of labels. In 1985 he returned to notice when he scored the Broadway musical "Big River," based on Mark Twain's *The Adventures of Huckleberry Finn*. He died of cancer.

Moon Mullican, died January 1, 1967, age 57
Piano player; from Corrigan, Texas. Called "King of the Hillbilly Piano Players," Moon Mullican's left hand pumped, walked, and otherwise boogied furiously, making a huge impact on Jerry Lee Lewis. His nickname came from an early stint in Houston, playing a brothel at night. He never hit the pop charts, but his "Jose Blon," from 1947, and "I'll Sail My Ship Alone," from 1951, were sizeable country hits, and he appeared regularly on the Grand Ole Opry during that period. He died of a heart attack.

Jim Reeves, died July 31, 1964, age 39
Singer; from Galloway, Texas. Jim Reeves was among the first to take the twang to the pop charts with authority, starting in 1957 with the number 11 "Four Walls." His biggest hit was 1960's somnolent number 2 "He'll Have to Go." He was not able to capitalize much on the momentum of that, however, though he remained extremely popular as a country performer, continuing to chart beyond his death into the seventies. His last country top ten, in fact, came in 1981 with the macabre "Have You Ever Been Lonely?" Producer Owen Bradley's brainchild, it was a duet between Reeves and Patsy Cline accomplished electronically, long after both had died; the two never recorded together while alive. He died in a plane crash, perhaps the only thing he really had in common with Patsy Cline.

Tex Ritter, died January 3, 1974, age 67
Singer, movie star, politician; from Panola County, Texas. Ritter was mostly famous as a star of western movies—he appeared in nearly a hundred of them with his horse Whiteflash. Pop attention came in 1956 with a top thirty showing of "The Wayward Wind" (Gogi Grant later took it to number 1), and then, in 1961, with the number 20 spoken-word "I Dreamed of a Hill-Billy Heaven," in which Ritter narrates a trip to heaven to visit some of the dead country stars mentioned in this chapter. In the seventies Ritter ran for U.S. senator from Tennessee and for the governorship of Tennessee, losing both times. He is also the father of TV's John Ritter ("Three's Company," "Hearts Afire")—but try not to think of that in terms of loss or victory. He died of a heart attack.

Marty Robbins, died December 8, 1982, age 57
Singer; from Glendale, Arizona. Marty Robbins, like Elvis Presley, was a hugely successful singer capable of many styles, including country, rock 'n' roll, teen pop, and more. He went to the pop charts with the 1957 number 2 "A White Sport Coat (And a Pink Carnation)," the 1960 number 1 story-song "El Paso," and the 1961 number 3 "Don't Worry," and for much of his early career he stood as a kind of disquieting shadow figure to Elvis, covering "That's All Right" in late 1954, and striking the same pose as Elvis for the cover of his debut album—Robbins's came first. But Robbins's label clearly preferred him to sing country, and thus he spent much of his career as a mainstay of the country charts, with some fifty top ten country hits, fourteen of them reaching number 1. For fun he raced stock cars, which he continued against all medical advice after major heart surgery in 1969. He did finally die of a heart attack, but it wasn't until over thirteen years later.

Jimmie Rodgers, died May 26, 1933, age 35
Singer, songwriter; from Meridian, Mississippi. Along with the Carter Family, Jimmie Rodgers is the most important figure in the development of country music during the first half of this century. Often called the father of country music, he drew on the blues to transform traditional folk music into a new musical form at once intimate and dramatically powerful. He was an enormous influence on the honky-tonk strain of country music— which has provided both structure and sensibility to rock 'n' roll—standing as a model to such as Hank Williams, Lefty Frizzell, and Merle Haggard. He was also an early influence on Howlin' Wolf. Nicknamed "The Singing Brakeman" for his railroading job, Rodgers established himself with his trademark yodels, an eerie keening derived in part from the blues moans to which he was exposed by his fellow railroad workers, who were black. His use of Hawaiian guitar prefigured the introduction of pedal steel guitar to country music. He catapulted to fame in late 1927 on the strength of his first "Blue Yodel," which sold a million copies. Even before his breakthrough his health had begun to deteriorate from tuberculosis, but with his family's welfare in mind he churned out the tunes while there was time, including "When the Cactus Is in Bloom," "In the Jailhouse Now," "Mule Skinner Blues," a series of blues yodels, and more; 113 tunes in all between 1927 and 1933. TB finally got the best of him while he was in New York City to record.

B.W. Stevenson, died April 28, 1988, age 38
Singer, songwriter; from Dallas. B.W. Stevenson came up in the early seventies from the "outlaw" school of country music, typified by Willie Nelson and Waylon Jennings. But RCA wanted him to take a pop direction, and he tried. In 1973 he almost had a hit with "Shambala" but Three Dog Night covered it and took the prize. Stevenson came back quickly, with "My Maria," which kind of sounded like a Tony Orlando song and went to number 9 that year. But that was his only hit and he soon faded from view. He died fifteen years later after heart surgery.

Merle Travis, died October 20, 1983, age 65
See Guitar Heroes.

Keith Whitley, died May 9, 1989, age 33
Singer; from Kentucky. Keith Whitley broke in playing bluegrass but returned to his honky-tonk origins toward the end. His talent was vastly promising; he doubtless would have benefited from the country resurgence of the early nineties, but drinking problems stopped him cold. He died of

alcohol poisoning in a reportedly isolated but nonetheless sizable spree (blood-alcohol level: .47).

Hank Williams, died January 1, 1953, age 29

Singer, songwriter; from Georgiana, Alabama. Hank Williams was perhaps the greatest country artist who ever lived—certainly he was one of the most prolific, contributing handfuls of standards: "Hey, Good Lookin'," "Your Cheatin' Heart," "I'm So Lonesome I Could Cry," "My Bucket's Got a Hole in It," "Cold, Cold Heart," "Jambalaya (On the Bayou)," and more, covered by many, from Tony Bennett to Elvis Costello. He cut a figure both tragic and pathetic, anticipating the dimensions and trajectory of the most significant rock 'n' roll personalities: Elvis Presley, John Lennon, Jim Morrison, Marvin Gaye, even Sid Vicious. Williams's homely, penetrating voice, instantly recognizable and setting a country standard, may be the way many know and remember him, but it's his strength as a songwriter that keeps his work alive. Spinning soulful tales out of the painful life from which he emerged, his songs accurately relate the defeats, joys, and cruel ironies of a life committed to love in the midst of violence and privation, the same sources and strategies on which the vast majority of great rock 'n' roll draws. He paid his dues during the forties in rough Southern honkytonks known throughout the region as "blood buckets." In 1949 he scored the first of many country number 1s with "Lovesick Blues," and fame was upon him. When he debuted at the Grand Ole Opry that year he was called back for six encores. Hank Williams's star had risen, and for the brief duration of his life it shone brightly, as he turned out a series of country hits covered to pop success by the usual parasites.

But things were not really so good for Williams. A congenital back disorder, spinal bifida, produced a debilitating dependence on painkillers, worsened by the desperate excesses of his drinking, a lifelong problem. His first marriage ended after eight years and he became a notoriously unreliable performer, eventually barred altogether from the Grand Ole Opry for missing too many dates. Williams died on New Year's Day 1953, of a heart attack in the back seat of a Cadillac, or of alcohol and drug complications in a hotel room. Reports conflict. Either way, after his death his career—safe from the damage that could be wreaked by a living maniac—took off in huge fashion and included two more country number 1s, "Kaw-Liga" and "Take These Chains from My Heart," as well as his last hit "I'll Never Get Out of This World Alive."

Bob Wills, died May 13, 1975, age 70

Bandleader, fiddler; from Kosse, Texas. During the Depression Wills pioneered western swing, a radical merging of country music and jazz that anticipated rock 'n' roll's merging of country music and blues in the fifties. Combining country fiddle and cornball twang with the rhythmic drive and improvisatory strategies of big band music in such hits as "San Antonio Rose," it was a sound fresh, vital, and resilient, still popular today, though it must have seemed pretty weird fifty years ago. It still seems kind of weird now. Partly from a lifetime of drinking, Wills's health began to fail in the early sixties and he suffered a series of heart attacks. A stroke in 1973 resulted in a coma, and he died two years later.

Faces of Death 2: Pneumonia

Jim Backus, died July 3, 1989, age 76
See Last Laughs: Novelty Artists.

Chan Daniels, died August 2, 1975, age 35
See Just Us Dead Folk.

Miles Davis, died September 28, 1991, age 65
See Sha Na Na, Inc.: The Second Death of Rock 'n' Roll.

Guitar Slim, died February 7, 1959, age 32
See Necro-Orleans.

Jim Henson, died May 16, 1990, age 53
See Last Laughs: Novelty Artists.

Little Willie John, died May 27, 1968, age 30
See Twitch and Shout: Rhythm and Blues Deaths.

Bob Luman, died December 27, 1978, age 41
See Country Corpses.

Jerry Nolan, died January 14, 1992, age 45
See I Wanna Destroy: The Final Death of Rock 'n' Roll
(The New York Dolls).

T-Bone Walker, died March 16, 1975, age 64
See Tombstone Blues.

4

Twitch and Shout:
Rhythm and Blues Deaths

WHEN ROCK 'N' ROLL first began to emerge in the early fifties it was impossible to tell it from rhythm and blues, because most of it essentially was rhythm and blues — that is, black pop music. In a passing fit of genius, DJ Alan Freed called it something else to allay the fears of white parents. That was all. Racial lines then began to blur in a most alarming fashion; Buddy Holly's first label thought him black from the demos he sent; many thought, from listening to "Maybellene," that Chuck Berry was white. Nobody knew what Elvis Presley was. In the era of the Supreme Court's landmark 1954 *Brown v. Board of Education* ruling, the kids of the day seemed unconsciously ready for everything. Many adults were not (nor, sadly, were many of the white kids after they became adults — but by then it was already too late).

Once again it might be nice to avoid the issue of race altogether. But rock 'n' roll tranformed pop music into the meeting ground of races. The debate over the origins of rock 'n' roll (one that can never be resolved) stems partly from the fact that musical developments tend to be uninterrupted, but also from the fact that rock 'n' roll, unlike rhythm and blues, was primarily a sociological phenomenon. Rhythm and blues, with its adaptations of both jazz and blues, was a natural musical development that can be, and has been, succinctly mapped by talking about arrangements and song structures and vocal styles. The earliest rock 'n' roll is subject to the same interpretations, because, basically, it is the same music.

But it is clearly more as well, something other. Rock 'n' roll was the point where southern American white culture, with its roots in European folk music, stolid hymnody, the recent country music, and various permutations of political power and powerlessness — having fought and lost a war to hold slaves — met American black culture, with its roots in blues, gospel, jazz, and political powerlessness. While gospel and jazz had previously marked similar meeting points between the races, they were often furtive and blemished by guilt, judgment, justification, and condescension.

Rock 'n' roll was full of joy and power and rebellion; in rock 'n' roll the races embraced as equals. That flashpoint of connection was powerful and lasting, transforming American culture into something more than it had been—but also annihilating something of what it was. If the liberation of rock 'n' roll was acknowledging the truth (something as banal as "we all must live in this world together"), it was also the death knell for what had gone before (including, incidentally, the previous belief that all wars fought by northern whites are just).

At this point in the life of rock 'n' roll, I am arbitrarily marking Freed's 1951 radio show as its birth, the point of no return. I call all rhythm and blues that followed it rock 'n' roll; all rock 'n' roll that preceded it I call rhythm and blues. The people on the list below fall in the gray area—they played rock 'n' roll before 1951, or rhythm and blues after. They are dead but their music is as vitally alive as ever.

Johnny Ace, died December 24, 1954, age 25
See The Ghost of Johnny Ace.

Bill Brown, date of death unknown
Bass singer, with the Dominoes; from New York (not to be confused with Bill Brown of the Harptones, see Death's Ululating Maw: Vocal Group Deaths). Normally relegated to the usual supporting role of the bass singer, Brown stepped forward to deliver the goods on the timelessly lewd "Sixty Minute Man," a number 1 rhythm and blues hit in 1951, and probably the best remembered Dominoes song today from an impressive catalog. Brown, like many in that group, was shown the door shortly after his moment, however, and obscurity then enveloped him like a thick fog. We don't even know when he died, or what killed him.

Roy Brown, died May 25, 1981, age 55
See Little Elvis Deaths.

Cecil Gant, died February 4, 1951, age 37
Singer, piano player; from Nashville. Breaking in as a World War II soldier playing War Bond rallies (billed as "The G.I. Sing-sation"), Gant pumped up a fine-sweat boogie on the piano or, alternately, laid back for potent supper-club croons with an unworldly baritone. But he was out of step with whites on both counts, five years too early for either. He died of pneumonia, related to heavy drinking.

Wynonie Harris, died June 14, 1969, age 54
See Little Elvis Deaths.

Ivory Joe Hunter, died November 8, 1974, age 60
Singer, songwriter, DJ, piano player; from Kirbyville, Texas. Hunter brought a gutbucket feel to his smooth balladeering that anticipated Ray Charles's country music phase and set him apart from supper-club crooners. With his own labels and on others, he scored steady hits on the "race" charts beginning in 1947. But, victim of the usual parasites (Pat Boone took his "I Almost Lost My Mind" to number 1 in 1956), he hit big on the pop charts only once, with the nice and easy 1956 number 12 "Since I Met You Baby," as good an example of his strong suit as any. Reportedly Hunter wrote thousands of songs. Late in his career he sang country music at the Grand Ole Opry. He died of cancer.

O'Kelly Isley, died March 31, 1986, age 48
Singer, with the Isley Brothers (later dropped the "O'"); from Cincinnati. For the Isley Brothers, an incredibly flexible and long-lived family group, musical aspirations were part of their lives from the beginning, thanks to their father's ambitions. But they made little impression until 1959 when, signed to RCA and produced by Hugo and Luigi, they released "Shout," now a rhythm and blues standard and a favorite at sporting events, though Joey Dee and the Starliters got the pop hit with it. The Isleys did score a number 17 pop hit in 1962 with their version of "Twist and Shout," covered more famously two years later by the Beatles (whose version charted again in 1986 because of its appearance in movies of the day). Later the Isleys made the transition to soul with their 1969 number 2 "It's Your Thing," and still later to funk and disco with the 1973 number 6 "That Lady (Part 1)" and the 1975 number 4 "Fight the Power (Part 1)," and they continued releasing albums that sold well right on into the eighties. In the mid-sixties, while the Isleys were relegated to the chitlin' circuit for a time, a then-unknown Jimi Hendrix backed them. Kelly was with them all the way, until the day he died of a heart attack.

Little Willie John, died May 27, 1968, age 30
Singer, songwriter, born John Davenport; from Camden, Arkansas. Little Willie John was a gifted, expressive singer discovered by Johnny Otis in 1951 at a talent show that also included Hank Ballard and Jackie Wilson. He put together a wholly original style that drew on the same orientation to gospel and pop as Sam Cooke and Ray Charles (his sister Mable was later a Raelette), salted liberally with jazz inflections and whatever else he could

throw in, which given the scope of his talent was a lot. Eventually he would prove a huge influence on soul music, but for himself he went searching for pop success and found it with the 1956 number 24 "Fever" (which he cowrote; later it was covered by both Peggy Lee and the McCoys), the 1958 number 20 "Talk to Me, Talk to Me," and the 1960 number 13 "Sleep." He was not the most stable person, however, often packing a gun even on stage, and in 1966 he was convicted (perhaps wrongly) of stabbing a man to death in a Seattle tavern. Sent to prison, he died there of pneumonia.

Louis Jordan, died February 4, 1975, age 66
Singer, bandleader, alto saxophone player; from Brinkley, Arkansas. As slick and savvy of his own powers as anyone ever, Louis Jordan made music that was smooth, electrifying, and funny all at once. It was composed of irresistible boogie rhythms delivered with unexpected savoir-faire, made palatable for whites by the humor of the lyrics and, for better or worse, by the clarity of Jordan's diction—many had been put off by the slurred vocals of most rhythm and blues material. They call it jump blues now but it was rock 'n' roll from the git. Jordan was wildly successful for a time, virtually ruling the "race" charts. At one point in late 1946 he held down the top three positions and was tied for the fourth. His song titles say it all: "Choo Choo Ch'Boogie," "That Chick's Too Young to Fry," "Somebody Done Changed the Lock on My Door," "What's the Use of Gettin' Sober," "Saturday Night Fish Fry," "Beans and Corn Bread." (Yes, I did say savoir-faire—and meant it.) But by the early fifties it was over. Jordan spent the next two decades moving from label to label attempting to engineer a comeback that never happened. He died of a heart attack.

Percy Mayfield, died August 11, 1984, age 63
Singer, songwriter, piano player; from Minden, Louisiana. An overlooked balladeer in the dog-faced Charles Brown vein, Percy Mayfield warbled, but so atmospherically and softly that he brought a shivery ethereal quality to his croon that sets it quite apart, much like Billie Holiday's eerie coos. He shied away from performing after a 1952 auto accident disfigured him. Mayfield was the writer of Ray Charles's 1961 number 1 "Hit the Road, Jack." He died in Los Angeles the day before his sixty-fourth birthday.

Stick McGhee, died August 15, 1961, age 44
Singer, guitar player, songwriter, born Granville McGhee; from Knoxville, Tennessee. The nickname derived from pushing his more famous brother Brownie, stricken with polio, around in a wagon with a stick when they were both boys. Stick wrote and recorded "Drinkin' Wine Spo-Dee-O-Dee,"

the first hit for the Atlantic label in 1949. Later it became a standard covered by Lionel Hampton, Wynonie Harris, Johnny Burnette, Jerry Lee Lewis, and many others. Stick McGhee died of cancer.

Clyde McPhatter, died June 13, 1972, age 38

Singer, with Billy Ward and the Dominoes, the Drifters, solo; from Durham, North Carolina. Clyde McPhatter was an innovative, powerfully expressive, deftly economical singer. He sang lead on a number of hits for Billy Ward and the Dominoes ("Have Mercy, Baby," "The Bells," and more) but was unhappy with his lack of credit in that group—Ward was the arranger, not the lead singer. He left in 1953 after training his replacement, Jackie Wilson. Signed to Atlantic later that year, McPhatter formed the Drifters and enjoyed phenomenal success for a year before he was drafted, spending nineteen weeks in 1954 at number 1 on the rhythm and blues charts with "Money Honey" and "Honey Love." After his tour of duty he returned for a solo career, scoring the biggest with the 1959 number 6 "A Lover's Question" and the somewhat less effective 1962 number 7 "Lover, Please." He spent the rest of the decade at a succession of major labels, chasing the pop grail and wandering ever further into the wilderness of orchestral arrangements. Toward the end, he spent a year in England trying to foster a comeback before returning to the United States to die in obscurity of heart, liver, and kidney ailments.

Amos Milburn, died January 3, 1980, age 52

Piano player, singer, songwriter; from Houston. With his thundering, pumping piano, Milburn emerged in the forties setting forth the great themes of rock 'n' roll: sex, booze, and parties. But mostly he drank and sang about it: "Let Me Go Home, Whiskey," "One Bourbon, One Scotch, One Beer" (covered by George Thorogood), and "Vicious, Vicious Vodka," to scratch the surface. In the sixties the hits, all of which had been on the rhythm and blues charts, ended, and a lifetime of bad habits caught up with him when he suffered two strokes within months of each other, leaving him an invalid. Too late, he gave up drinking and turned to religion. In 1979 a leg was amputated. Six months later he died.

Little Junior Parker, died November 18, 1971, age 44

See Little Elvis Deaths.

Esther Phillips, died August 7, 1984, age 48

Singer, piano player; from Galveston, Texas. With Johnny Otis, she broke in as Little Esther Phillips at age fifteen, one of the best teen singers ever.

Her early hits include "Double Crossing Blues" (backed by the Robins, who later became the Coasters), which went to number 1 in 1950 on the rhythm and blues charts. She developed drug problems almost right away, however, which quickly put her out and, even after her return, haunted the rest of her career. When she showed up again over ten years later she was no longer "little." Inspired by Ray Charles, she gave the uptown treatment to the country-style "Release Me," which went to number 8 in 1962. She hit the top twenty for the last time in 1975 with a disco version of "What a Diff'rence a Day Makes," which was followed by obscurity and illness. She died of kidney and liver failure.

Piano Red, died August 1, 1985, age 73
Piano player, singer, songwriter, born William Perryman, brother of Speckled Red; from Hampton, Georgia. Also known as Dr. Feelgood, Piano Red hit big in the early fifties with the two-sided single "Rockin' with Red" b/w "Red's Boogie," which sold a million and occasionally gets fingered as the first rock 'n' roll record. His "Mr. Moonlight" was covered weirdly by the Beatles in 1965. He died after a protracted illness.

Louis Prima, died August 24, 1978, age 66
Trumpet player, singer, bandleader; from New Orleans. Prima, a white man who became a Las Vegas staple in the fifties after years of paying dues in jazz clubs, was a pioneer of "gleeby rhythm," which is basically idiotically infectious jive and must be heard to be believed. Says critic Nick Tosches: "Long before there was a Little Richard, there were people sitting around listening to Louis Prima records, asking one another, 'What was that? What did he say?'" Unknown causes put him into a coma in 1975, and he stayed in that condition for three years before dying.

Willie Mae "Big Mama" Thornton, died July 25, 1984, age 57
See Little Elvis Deaths.

Tommy Tucker, died January 22, 1982, age 49
Piano player, singer, born Robert Higginbotham; from Springfield, Ohio. With the Bob Woods Orchestra in the late forties Tucker played with Big Maybelle, Billie Holiday, Little Willie John, Jimmy Reed, and others. He scored a pop hit in 1964 with the number 11 "Hi-Heel Sneakers." The recording was originally intended as a demo for Reed, but the people at Chess subsidiary Checker liked it just the way it was and released it as a single. Jose Feliciano covered it in 1968. Tucker later returned to college. He eventually died of poisoning, but details are scant.

Big Joe Turner, died November 24, 1985, age 74

Blues shouter; from Kansas City. Perhaps the greatest in the style, in the early fifties Turner also recorded what later came to be considered among the most characteristic rock 'n' roll songs: "Shake, Rattle and Roll" (cleaned up and covered by Bill Haley, Elvis Presley, and Arthur Conley), "Flip, Flop and Fly," and "Corrine, Corrina." All were sizable hits for Turner on the rhythm and blues charts, and all were pop hits for others. But Turner never really wanted to be a rock 'n' roll star, which allowed him to relax and make the huge imprint on it that he did. He died of a heart attack.

Jackie Wilson, died January 20, 1984, age 49

See Souls.

5

The Ghost of Johnny Ace

JOHNNY ACE was a rhythm and blues singer and piano player who enjoyed a phenomenal string of hits in the early fifties on the rhythm and blues charts, and appeared poised for pop success. Born and raised in Memphis as John Alexander, Jr., in 1952 he signed to Duke, chiefly to play piano on their sessions. The roster at Duke also included Bobby "Blue" Bland, Rosco Gordon, and Junior Parker. On a recording session, Bland was having trouble with the vocals on one number. Producer James Mattis asked Alexander to give it a shot. The result was "My Song," which against all expectations (except, perhaps, Alexander's) catapulted to number 1. His father was a preacher and to save him embarrassment Alexander adopted the name Ace from the Four Aces, a popular white vocal group of the era.

For the duration of his life Ace and his homely baritone displayed a Midas touch, with everything he released entering the rhythm and blues top ten: "Cross My Heart," "The Clock," "Saving My Love for You," "Please Forgive Me," "Never Let Me Go," and, finally, "Pledging My Love," a posthumous number 1 hit in 1955, which, again against expectations, "crossed over" to the pop charts and went to number 17.

On Christmas Eve of 1954, after a show at Houston's Civic Auditorium with Big Mama Thornton and others, Johnny Ace and members of his band were playing Russian roulette, reportedly a regular practice of theirs—although the story and nearly all its details have been recounted and refuted equally and in general it's all a little flimsy and murky. Thornton was there but never told all that she saw. Ace, according to the commonly accepted story, shot himself in the head and died instantly. He was twenty-five.

Hank Williams, a couple of years earlier, may have been the first to show the wisdom of death as a career move; Johnny Ace was the first to have it bear fruit on the pop chart. "Pledging My Love" was a fine song, an effective ballad marked by a basset hound declaration of fealty and haunting if corny piano graces. But it didn't warrant all the fuss, and the gushingly sentimental tribute records that followed—"Johnny Has Gone" by Varetta Dillard, "Why, Johnny, Why" by Johnny Moore's Blazers, the A-side of a single with "Johnny Ace's Last Letter" by Frankie Irwin as the B, and others—served only to emphasize that fact by overkill. They were only pieces in a puzzle, the first and among the best examples of rock 'n' roll's incipient fascination with its own bad ends.

That spectacular posthumous success was hardly the result of nationwide grief—Johnny Ace was a Negro, a rhythm and blues singer and piano player, and it was 1955. No, it was something else entirely, something to do with the way he died and the way his records were sold afterwards: a resonant shard of the forbidden and the horrific was tapped and then pushed hard by athletic marketing (Robey released the final Johnny Ace single in tandem with one by someone named Buddy Ace, encouraging listeners to "Complete your collection with this *last* record on the late great *Johnny Ace*. Start your collection with the *first* record release on this up and coming artist").

In retrospect, the meaning of Johnny Ace's life, his sudden run of unexpected hits and the subsequent elevation to star status, has been overwhelmingly defined by his death. There is something extraordinary about the whole thing, something weirdly prophetic, coming as it does at the very brink of the rock 'n' roll explosion. The details of Johnny Ace's story anticipate many that followed: the deeply religious background; the steeping in blues; the lucky break; the change of name (and implied confusion of identity); the sudden wild success, seemingly at odds with the actual accomplishment; and the pointlessly violent end, shrouded in mystery.

That pattern has endured since the day he died until now, with Queen records flying off the shelf, the fate of Elvis Presley's postal issue relying on national election, and a book like this being written and published. But here's the rub. It's just a little unnerving how often the name of Johnny Ace comes up first, chronologically or alphabetically or both, in any history that includes him, as if it belongs there. As if even now, nearly forty years later and from well beyond the grave, he's still striving hard to be number 1 forever. And succeeding.

Faces of Death 3:
Meet John Death

Johnny Ace, died December 24, 1954, age 25
See The Ghost of Johnny Ace.

John Belushi, died March 5, 1982, age 33
See Last Laughs: Novelty Artists.

John Bonham, died September 25, 1980, age 32
See Drummed Out.

Johnny Bond, died June 12, 1978, age 63
See Country Corpses.

Johnny Burnette, died August 1, 1964, age 30
See The Day the Music Died: The First Death of Rock 'n' Roll.

John Cipollina, died May 29, 1989, age 45
See Guitar Heroes.

"Sleepy" John Estes, died June 5, 1977, age 74

John Hammond, Sr., died July 10, 1987, age 76
See Sha Na Na, Inc.: The Second Death of Rock 'n' Roll.

Johnny Horton, died November 5, 1960, age 33.
See Country Corpses.

Little Willie John, died May 27, 1968, age 30
See Twitch and Shout: Rhythm and Blues Deaths.

John Kennedy, died November 22, 1963, age 46

Johnny Kidd, died October 7, 1966, age 26
See Sha Na Na, Inc.: The Second Death of Rock 'n' Roll.

John Lennon, died December 8, 1980, age 40
See Beatles Bugouts.

Johnnie Ray, died February 25, 1990, age 63
See Oozing Crooners.

John Rostill, died November 26, 1973, age 31
See Beatles Bugouts.

Johnny Shines, died April 20, 1992, age 76

Johnny Thunders, died April 23, 1991, age 38
See I Wanna Destroy: The Final Death of Rock 'n' Roll
(The New York Dolls).

6

Death's Ululating Maw:
Vocal Group Deaths

VOCAL GROUPS of the fifties, now commonly, condescendingly called "doo wop" groups, created rock 'n' roll that was as exciting and important as anything by Elvis Presley, Chuck Berry, or Little Richard. Pioneered by urban blacks, chiefly in New York and Los Angeles, it is perhaps the most distinct, self-enclosed rock 'n' roll sound of all, the least related to country music, and the most dependent on the renaming of rhythm and blues for pop success. It held sway from the late forties—when the Clovers, the Orioles, and the Ravens transformed the jazzy uptempo barbershop quartet approach of the Ink Spots and the Mills Brothers into something infinitely more vital—until the early sixties, when it was supplanted first by the advent of the producer-auteur and then by the British Invasion. During that time literally thousands of vocal groups came and went, most of them from big cities on the coasts of the United States. The style was also picked up and inflected to good effect by some ethnic whites, perhaps best by Italian-Americans in New York and Philadelphia.

It remains a sad fact that the rash of white covers that became a pop chart norm in the mid-fifties robbed many of the greatest vocal groups of the success due them. Unlike the appropriations of white blues players in the following decade, whose work is all too often constricted by its worried, self-absorbed adulations, or the pop song covers by seventies punks and eighties postpunks, which functioned as a kind of coded identity register, the covers of the mid-fifties were strictly business moves, made with an eye blind to all but the bottom line. Most are ham-handed, wrong-headed, and insipid. The painful truth, of course, is that most people, given the opportunity to hear both versions of a hit, generally preferred the original. But few listeners had that opportunity, as the labels producing the covers made it a point to be in the better position to pressure radio stations to play their records.

Girl groups, Phil Spector productions, and other factors in the early six-ties blurred the decline of vocal group rock 'n' roll, and after the British In-vasion it was irrelevant. At that point it fossilized either as Aht, with the advent of such essentially non-hit practitioners as the Persuasions, or, more often (and worse), as cheap nostalgia ripe for caricature from such groups as Sha Na Na. Even in its heyday the music boasted few stars. The most popular groups survived as faceless self-contained units, for the most part, enjoying only a passing vogue with one or two hits: the Penguins ("Earth Angel"), the Marcels ("In the Still of the Nite"), the Rays ("Silhouettes"), the Silhouettes ("Get a Job"), Maurice Williams and the Zodiacs ("Stay"), Little Caesar and the Romans ("Those Oldies but Goodies"), and countless more. If they were lucky, one hit was enough to land them on the oldies cir-cuit. If they were not, and many of these groups were anything but lucky, you might find them on the casualty list below. Enough time has passed that old age has claimed some of them as well.

Jesse Belvin, died February 6, 1960, age 26
Singer, songwriter, with many groups and solo; from San Antonio, Texas. Belvin was a promising Los Angeles-based vocal group figure steeped in the ways of the studio. He cowrote the Penguins' 1955 number 8 "Earth An-gel." In 1956, he recorded four separate vocal tracks to create the illusion of a group, the Cliques, for "Girl of My Dreams," a minor pop hit. Perhaps his most familiar hit also came in 1956, the smooth "Good Night, My Love," which DJ Alan Freed used as his closing theme. He was signed to RCA a few years later with aspirations to croon, but died soon after in an auto accident that also killed his manager/wife.

Bill Brown, died 1956, age 20
Bass, with the Harptones; from New York (not to be confused with Bill Brown of the Dominoes, see Twitch and Shout: Rhythm and Blues Deaths). Formed in 1953, the Harptones' rich, church-heavy harmonies, gloriously captured on "A Sunday Kind of Love," "My Memories of You," "Life Is But a Dream," and others, followed in the pioneering footsteps of the Orioles, deepening and enriching the sound of inexpressibly anguished ennui. Brown's death marked only one of many personnel changes endured by the group. Their leader, Willie Winfield, went on to become a funeral director but kept versions of the group alive over the years. In 1982 they reappeared with the album Love Needs.

The Coasters
Originally the Robins; from Los Angeles, the source of their name. The

Coasters were one of the greatest rock 'n' roll vocal groups, striking a perfect balance between smooth, nimble melody and arrangement and impeccable comic timing. Already with illustrious credits by the mid-fifties (not the least of which was their association with songwriters/producers Jerry Leiber and Mike Stoller, with whom they had hooked up in 1953), their hits included the still impressive "Riot in Cell Block No. 9" and the plain weird "Smokey Joe's Cafe." In 1956 the people at Atlantic heard them, liked them, and signed them, along with Leiber and Stoller, an important part of the deal. In effect, that was the beginning of the independent producer as auteur, one of rock 'n' roll's greatest and most enduring contributions to the modern conception of pop music. Personnel changes followed as half of the original quartet sniffed at the deal, but originals Carl Gardner (lead) and Bobby Nunn (bass) stayed on. Then, in 1957, came "Searchin' " b/w "Young Blood," fixing their characteristically spry, quick, witty sound. But when the group made plans to move to New York, Nunn balked and quit, only to be all too ably replaced by Will "Dub" Jones (formerly of the Cadets). Never again did Nunn enjoy success on the scale he'd known with the Coasters (not for lack of trying, of course); he died of a heart attack in 1986, aged sixty-one. Tenor Leon Hughes also quit with Nunn, for the same reason, and was replaced by Young Jessie, who left too and was replaced by Cornelius Gunter, who was on hand for the rest of the hits ("Yakety Yak," "Charlie Brown," "Along Came Jones," "Poison Ivy"). Are you getting all this? The well finally went dry in the early sixties and the group was basically finished except for sporadic minor hits, reissues, and the omnipresent oldies circuit. The Coasters have, however, hung on through the years in one fashion or another. Since no one has rights to the name, numerous Coasters aggregates, each with slivers from the glory days, have taken their turns at career resuscitation. Gunter was shot to death in 1990, aged fifty-one—specific details are scant. No matter; there's probably a Coasters show coming to your town soon.

Bert Convy, died July 15, 1991, age 52
With the Cheers, later a TV game show host; from Los Angeles. Convy took the same path to syndicated TV eminence as Wink Martindale and Jaye P. Morgan, namely the pop chart. He scored the 1955 number 6 hit "Black Denim Trousers" (a squeaky-clean paean to juvenile delinquency) with the Cheers, a group originally put together by Jerry Leiber and Mike Stoller to record demos. In 1954 Capitol liked their "(Bazoom) I Need Your Lovin' " just the way it was and signed the group. "Trousers," however, and its follow-up, "Chicken" (another squeaky-clean paean, this time to a dan-

gerous auto-racing pastime), were not by Leiber and Stoller. Convy died of a brain tumor.

The Crows
From New York. Formed in 1948, the Crows were one of the classic "bird" groups (along with the Robins, Orioles, Penguins, Ravens, Flamingos, Eagles—wait a minute). Their only hit, the snappy, virtually wordless 1954 number 20 "Gee," was among the first songs by a black group to get airplay on white radio and was the source of the name for what would become Frankie Lymon's label. Lead Sonny Norton and bass Gerald Hamilton are both dead now, circumstances unknown.

The Duprees
Italian-American quintet; from Jersey City. They hit in 1962 and 1963, most successfully with the number 7 "You Belong to Me." First tenor Joe Santollo died in 1981 aged thirty-seven. Lead singer and group leader Joey Vann died in 1984 aged forty. The group was long finished by the time of their deaths.

Carl Feaster, died January 23, 1981
Lead, with the Chords; from New York. The Chords' only hit, the 1954 novelty "Sh-Boom" (on Cat, a subsidiary of Atlantic), is occasionally fingered as the first rock 'n' roll song chiefly because their pop hit was stolen by Toronto's Crew Cuts, whose version was rush-released by Mercury. It was the first of what would become an epidemic of covers by white artists on bigger labels of black artists on smaller. Feaster died of cancer.

John Felten, died 1982
Tenor, with the Diamonds; from Toronto. Felten didn't join the Diamonds, an ever-fluctuating Mercury group of white-cover specialists, until 1959, after they'd already had their biggest hits: the 1957 number 2 "Little Darlin'," covering the Gladiolas; the 1957 number 10 "Silhouettes," covering the Rays; and the 1958 number 4 "The Stroll," covering Chuck Willis. After Felten's death, the lineup switched again and the group went to the country charts in the late eighties. Felten died in a plane crash.

Charles Fizer, died August, 1965, age 25
Baritone, with the Olympics; from Los Angeles. Formed in 1954, the Olympics' biggest hit was the 1958 number 8 shoot-'em-up novelty "Western Movies." Only 1963's number 40 "The Bounce" came close to a follow-up, but for years they never stopped trying, on a variety of labels, until finally

they made the transition to the oldies circuit in the late sixties. By then Fizer was dead, killed in Watts rioting.

Ronnie Goodson, died November 4, 1980, age 33
Lead, with Ronnie and the Hi-Lites; from Jersey City. Goodson was the front man for Ronnie and the Hi-Lites, a Frankie Lymon and the Teen-agers-type vocal group who hit once and once only, with the 1962 number 16 "I Wish That We Were Married." But if their moment in the sun was short-lived, it was thoroughly enjoyed—fifteen-year-old Goodson even got a thing going with Carole King's teen babysitter, Little Eva ("The Loco-Motion"), for a short time. He died of a brain tumor.

Bill Harris, died December 10, 1988, age 63
Guitar player, with the Clovers; from Washington, D.C. Formed in 1946, the Clovers were one of the first and most popular vocal groups, scoring such rhythm and blues hits as "One Mint Julep," "Ting a Ling," "Hey Miss Fannie," "I Played the Fool," and more, but all too often losing the pop hit to lesser white covers. After the group split up in the late fifties, Harris, encouraged by Mickey "Guitar" Baker, played jazz on a variety of labels, including his own Jazz Guitar. He died of cancer of the pancreas.

Corinthian "Kripp" Johnson, died June 22, 1990, age 57
First tenor, with the Dell-Vikings; from Pittsburgh. The Dell-Vikings, an accomplished interracial quintet formed while its members were in the air force together, fell apart after the 1957 number 4 "Come Go with Me" and their discharge from the service. One offshoot, the Dell-Vikings with Johnson and Chuck Jackson, hit number 9 with "Whispering Bells." The other, the Del Vikings, hit number 12 with "Cool Shake." That was the end of the hits. Next, everybody went to court, where commercial oblivion awaited. Johnson died of prostate cancer.

Norman Johnson, died 1970
Bass, with the Jive Five; from Brooklyn. Formed by Eugene Pitt, formerly of the Genies, the Jive Five was indeed a quintet at first but across the shifting sands of time became a quartet, called the Jyve Fyve, among other names. Their biggest hit came in 1961 with the stately number 3 "My True Story." Little is known of Johnson; some sources say his first name is Billy, but most agree he sang bass and is now dead.

Bobby Lester, died October 15, 1980, age 50
First tenor, with the Moonglows; from Louisville, Kentucky. The Moon-

glows are perhaps best known for showcasing Harvey Fuqua, who wrote
(with DJ Alan Freed, according to the label credit) their 1955 number 20
"Sincerely"; the McGuire Sisters took the song to number 1 for ten weeks
that year. (Freed, aware of the group since 1952, helped them keep recording throughout their career.) It was Lester who formed the group originally,
but Fuqua supplied much of their material, a style of singing he called "blow
harmony," and a good deal of ambition, gradually edging Lester for control
of the group. By 1958 and their last hit, the number 22 "Ten Commandments of Love," which featured only nine commandments, they were Harvey and the Moonglows. Fuqua went on to Motown. Lester tried to go solo,
but struggled. He died of cancer in Louisville.

Frankie Lymon and the Teenagers

The story of Frankie Lymon and the Teenages is nothing but tragedy, in the
classic style, with all appropriate elements intact: the astonishing rise to
prominence and subsequent sparkling vogue, followed by the equally rapid
collapse and withering of all gains to dust (in this case white dust). The
group started out in mid-fifties New York as friends singing on street
corners, organized by baritone Joe Negroni. In 1955 they signed to Gee. At
their first session they were slated to record "Why Do Fools Fall in Love?,"
cowritten by Lymon, with tenor Herman Santiago on lead vocals. But that
day Santiago had a bad throat, and the responsibility fell to Lymon, who
positively shone. On the strength of that one brilliant performance they
rechristened themselves Frankie Lymon and the Teenagers (though Lymon,
at thirteen, just barely qualified). The song, as expected, was an instant
winner. (If you need evidence, for God's sake get a copy of it.) Its infectious,
irresistible spunk catapulted it into the pop top ten in 1956 for sixteen
weeks, as well as to number 1 on the rhythm and blues charts and in the
United Kingdom, where no vocal group had made much impact yet. Sad
to say, it proved practically their only hit, and the money they saw from it
was limited.

It's an old story: they hadn't signed a particularly advantageous contract.
Their fortunes began to ebb as fortunes will in the music industry, with little
to cushion their fall. But they lasted a little while longer, appearing in
1956's *Rock, Rock, Rock* to sing the memorably weird and appropriately
defensive, "I'm Not a Juvenile Delinquent"; and they also appeared in
1957's *Mr. Rock and Roll*. Shortly after, on somebody's bad advice, Lymon
left the group for a solo career—he was only fifteen. The Teenagers were
immediately washed up, and Lymon sputtered, due as much as anything to
drug problems already out of control. It didn't help any when his voice
changed. His first single, "Goody Goody," reached number 20 in 1957 but

he never cracked the top forty again. At eighteen his career was over. He spent the remaining eight years of his life battling his addiction to heroin, finding time in there for a stint in the army. In the mid-sixties he appeared on TV's "Shindig," lip-synching the original version of "Why Do Fools Fall in Love?" People who knew the score cried then. By 1968 he was destitute. He died of a heroin overdose in his grandmother's New York apartment February 28, 1968, at the age of twenty-six. Bass Sherman Garnes died in 1977 during open heart surgery, at age thirty-six; baritone Joe Negroni died from an aneurysm in 1978, four days short of thirty-eight. In 1992, after a protracted lawsuit, the dispute over the rights to their one big hit was finally settled in favor of the surviving members. Re-formed, with a female "Frankie" (Pearl McKinnon), they can now be found on the oldies circuit.

The Manhattans
From Jersey City. Formed in 1964 and continuing to this day, the Manhattans are an example of a latter-day vocal group steeped equally in tradition and nostalgia with an overweening focus on technique, all of which diminishes their impact but hasn't prevented occasional hits, including the number 1 "Kiss and Say Goodbye" in 1976. Lead George Smith died in 1970 of spinal meningitis. Baritone Richard Taylor (later Abdul Rashid Talhah), who left the group in 1976, died in 1987, aged forty-seven.

The Monotones
From Newark, New Jersey. Living all the way up to their billing, the Monotones' only hit came in 1958 with the brisk dog-howl "Book of Love," which reached number 5. Brothers John and Warren Ryanes are both dead now, John in 1972; the date of Warren's death is not known.

Nate Nelson, died June 1, 1984, age 52
Lead, with the Flamingos; from Chicago. The Flamingos found their ground between the cool poise of the Harptones and the Orioles and the overwrought bombast of the Platters (see Oozing Crooners). Their biggest and best was the super-ethereal torcher "I Only Have Eyes for You," which went to number 11 in 1959. It is one of the great songs of the era. Accept no substitutes. Nelson went on to try his hand at reviving the failing Platters in 1962, to no avail. The oldies circuit then beckoned. He died of a heart attack.

The Orioles
From Baltimore. The Orioles are among the earliest and most influential black vocal groups, with many and sundry extraterrestrial charms: slower-

than-slow tempos, sparse instrumental accompaniment, softly cooing, moaning vocals. In their first incarnation in the late forties they called themselves the Vibranairs, altogether more appropriate to their sound—but they were from Baltimore, and civic pride (not to mention a group with an almost identical name in New Jersey) dictated the name by which they're known. Somehow they caught on as a rhythm and blues act; their second release, "Tell Me So," went number 1 in 1949. Their guitarist, Tommy Gaither, he of the lightest of all possible strums, died in an auto accident in 1950; their next release, "I Miss You So," marked his passing. Second tenor George Nelson left in 1953 on the eve of their biggest hit, "Crying in the Chapel," which went to number 1 on the rhythm and blues chart again, and also to number 11 pop (one of the first songs to "cross over"). They disbanded shortly after, in 1954, ghostly yet dignified victims of a clamoring for harder, more rockin' and boppin' vocal group sounds from the Dominoes, Drifters, Clovers, Coasters, and all that followed. Five years later, in 1959, tenor Alexander Sharp died of a heart attack. Nelson died in the late sixties, of asthma. And finally, in 1981, lead Sonny Til, who had worked over the years with various groups of re-formed Orioles, died too, of a heart attack, aged fifty-six.

Larry Palumbo, died 1959, age 18
Baritone, with the Earls; from the Bronx. The Earls, an Italian-American vocal group, scored their biggest hit with the 1963 number 24 "Remember Then"—cliché-ridden but not without its charms. Palumbo was dead by then; he met his fate as a paratrooper when his chute failed to open in training exercises.

Janet Vogel Rapp, died February 21, 1980, age 37
First tenor, with the Skyliners; from Pittsburgh. The Skyliners, a lush white vocal group, were unusual in that Vogel, a woman, was included not as the lead but simply as one of the backup harmonizers. Her soaring swoops were put to unusually good effect on their biggest hit, the resplendent "Since I Don't Have You," which went to number 12 in 1959; the follow-up that same year, "This I Swear" was also impressive. But beyond a cover of "Pennies from Heaven" in 1960 there was only obscurity. The group disbanded shortly after, then re-formed again in the eighties for the oldies circuit. By then, however, Vogel was dead. A housewife with two children, she committed suicide by carbon monoxide poisoning. Other details are not known.

Herbert "Tubo" Rhoad, died December 8, 1988, age 44
Baritone, with the Persuasions; from Brooklyn. Formed in 1962, the Per-

suasions have scored no hit singles and typically perform a capella. They are purists, delivering an effective if insulated and overly studied vocal group sound. Their albums are uniformly hailed as classics, particularly *Chirpin'*. They have indeed become legends. Rhoad was an original member.

James "Shep" Sheppard, died January 24, 1970

Lead, with the Heartbeats, Shep and the Limelites; from New York. Sheppard bequeathed to us two vocal group classics, by two different groups. The first was the gorgeous "A Thousand Miles Away," by the Heartbeats, which reached number 5 on the rhythm and blues chart in 1957 but never went pop. The second was the 1961 number 2 "Daddy's Home" by Shep and the Limelites, an answer to the first hit. Sheppard's legendary personal problems (namely his drinking and his temper) ended both groups. His body was found in his car on the Long Island Expressway; the details are somewhat murky, but basically he'd been robbed and beaten to death.

Ted Taylor, died November 22, 1987

Tenor, with the Cadets; from Los Angeles. One of the best groups of their time and place, the Cadets scored only one significant hit, the novelty "Stranded in the Jungle," which reached number 15 in 1956—a cover (of the Jayhawks) but definitely up to snuff. It was covered in turn by the New York Dolls on their 1974 *Too Much Too Soon*. Taylor later enjoyed some solo success as a rhythm and blues singer. He died in an auto accident.

Carl White, died January 7, 1980, age 48

Lead, with the Rivingtons; from Los Angeles. The Rivingtons chipped in one key chant to the pop vocabulary that they have guarded zealously ever since: "Papa-Oom-Mow-Mow," their first release, in 1962. The follow-up? "Mama-Oom-Mow-Mow," of course. "The Bird's the Word" six months later was their last. None came close to the pop top forty. But at the end of that year the Trashmen combined the first and last of those songs for the 1964 number 4 "Surfin' Bird." The Rivingtons sued. Nearly twenty years later, in 1981, the Oak Ridge Boys used the Rivington mantra in "Elvira," and the Rivingtons sued again (thank God somebody could). By then, however, White was dead. The results of neither case are known.

Faces of Death 4:
Heart Troubles

David Blue, died December 2, 1982, age 41
See Just Us Dead Folk.

Bobby Darin, died December 20, 1973, age 37
See Oozing Crooners.

Mama Cass Elliot, died July 29, 1974, age 32
See Just Us Dead Folk.

Andy Gibb, died March 10, 1988, age 30
See Hustled: Disco Deaths.

Bill Haley, died February 9, 1981, age 55
See The Day the Music Died: The First Death of Rock 'n' Roll.

Bob Hite, died April 5, 1981, age 36
See Sha Na Na, Inc.: The Second Death of Rock 'n' Roll
(Canned Heat).

Hollywood Fats, died December 8, 1986, age 32
See I Wanna Destroy: The Final Death of Rock 'n' Roll.

O'Kelly Isley, died March 31, 1986, age 48
See Twitch and Shout: Rhythm and Blues Deaths.

Louis Jordan, died February 4, 1975, age 66
See Twitch and Shout: Rhythm and Blues Deaths.

Mario Lanza, died October 7, 1959, age 38
See Little Elvis Deaths.

Van McCoy, died July 6, 1979, age 35
See Hustled: Disco Deaths.

Nate Nelson, died June 1, 1984, age 52
See Death's Ululating Maw: Vocal Group Deaths.

Roy Orbison, died December 6, 1988, age 52
See The Day the Music Died: The First Death of Rock 'n' Roll.

Vernon Presley, died June 21, 1979, age 63
See Little Elvis Deaths.

Marty Robbins, died December 8, 1982, age 57
See Country Corpses.

David Seville, died January 16, 1972, age 52
See Last Laughs: Novelty Artists.

Sonny Til, died December 9, 1981, age 56
See Death's Ululating Maw: Vocal Group Deaths (The Orioles).

Big Joe Turner, died November 24, 1985, age 74
See Twitch and Shout: Rhythm and Blues Deaths.

Muddy Waters, died April 30, 1983, age 68
See Tombstone Blues.

7

Blow, Big Man

DURING THE fifties a very real battle for the hearts and minds of rock 'n' roll fans was waged between the electric guitar, the piano, and the saxophone. At the time it was anybody's guess which would win. Jerry Lee Lewis, Little Richard, and Fats Domino matched everything on piano that Chuck Berry delivered with the electric guitar. King Curtis, who blew tenor on some of the Coasters' biggest hits (notably "Yakety Yak"), seemed to be defining the rock 'n' roll sound as much as any of them. Eventually, of course, the electric guitar won, thanks to decisive votes cast by British Invasion groups. But the saxophone players listed below, all now dead, each deserve at least a polite round of applause.

Cannonball Adderley, died August 8, 1975, age 46
Alto player, chiefly jazz, born Julian Edwin; from Tampa, Florida. Cannonball Adderley was a busy postbop jazz player who made his career sitting in with Miles Davis, John Coltrane, Bill Evans, and many more. He freakishly went to the pop charts in 1967 with the number 11 soul cry "Mercy, Mercy, Mercy" (written by Weather Report founder Joe Zawinul), and had a few other chart successes during the decade. Accused of selling out by some jazz fans, he merely cashed his checks and arranged the next session. He died of a stroke.

Earl Bostic, died October 28, 1965, age 52
Alto player; from Tulsa, Oklahoma. In the early fifties Bostic went high on the rhythm and blues charts with the number 1 "Flamingo," followed by the number 9 "Sleep." Along with his entire oeuvre, they established him as the master of the gutbucket wailing sax, a legacy heard in the rock and soul playing of three decades, from Junior Walker to Clarence Clemons. Today Bostic stands as perhaps the most influential saxman in all rock 'n' roll,

though after those hits he spent the rest of his career playing jazz. He died of a heart attack.

Stan Getz, died June 6, 1991, age 64
Tenor player, chiefly jazz; from Philadelphia. Starting in the mid-forties, Getz played with Tommy Dorsey, Benny Goodman, Stan Kenton, Woody Herman, and many other jazz players. On his own he was admired for his tone colorations on slow numbers. In the early sixties he embraced the bossa nova, even before Elvis Presley, taking it to the pop charts most famously with "The Girl from Ipanema," which reached number 5 in 1964. A bogus checked-pants-Hugh-Hefner figure to one generation because of that, he was still respected as a jazz player until the end. He died of liver cancer.

Phalon Jones, died December 10, 1967, age 18
See Souls under Bar-Kays.

Louis Jordan, died February 4, 1975, age 66
See Twitch and Shout: Rhythm and Blues Deaths.

Bill Justis, July 15, 1982, age 55
Alto player, arranger; from Birmingham, Alabama. He cut the first big rock 'n' roll instrumental, the 1957 number 2 "Raunchy," with guitar player Sid Manker (also covered by Ernie Freeman and Billy Vaughn, but it was Justis who had the hit). At Sun, Justis was the arranger for Johnny Cash, Jerry Lee Lewis, Charlie Rich, and others. The circumstances of his death are not known.

King Curtis, died August 13, 1971, age 37
Tenor player, born Curtis Ousley; from Fort Worth, Texas. A much respected rhythm and blues session player, Curtis's nimble, stuttering style, perhaps captured best on the Coasters' 1957 "Yakety Yak," made an enormous impact, though it was a style that essentially died with the coming of the British Invasion; still, he ranks with Earl Bostic among the most influential saxman in rock 'n' roll. On his own, he hit number 1 on the rhythm and blues chart in 1962 with "Soul Twist," which also went to number 17 pop. But it was as a behind-the-scenes man that he enjoyed his greatest influence, working with dozens, including the Shirelles, Wilson Pickett, Aretha Franklin, and the Allman Brothers Band. He was stabbed to death in a fight outside his New York home.

Rudy Pompilli, died February 5, 1976, age 47

Tenor player, with Bill Haley and His Comets. Pompilli was not a Comet at the time of "Rock Around the Clock." He joined shortly after and was on hand for most of the afterglow. He was featured on their 1956 number 34 "Rudy's Rock."

Chris Wood, died July 12, 1983, age 39

Tenor and alto, flute, with Traffic, Jimi Hendrix; from England. Chris Wood was overshadowed by all those he worked with—Hendrix, Steve Winwood, Dave Mason, even Jim Capaldi. He foresaw his own death, after a fashion, fifteen years before the fact, playing on Hendrix's "1983 . . . (A Merman I Should Turn to Be)" included in 1968's *Electric Ladyland*. He died of liver failure after years of obscurity.

Faces of Death 5:
Respiratory Failure and Lung Cancer

John Cipollina, died May 29, 1989, age 45
See Guitar Heroes.

Nat King Cole, died February 15, 1965, age 47
See Oozing Crooners.

Ral Donner, died April 6, 1984, age 41
See Little Elvis Deaths.

Ronnie Dyson, died November 10, 1990, age 40
See Super Dead.

Tom Fogerty, died September 6, 1990, age 48
See Sha Na Na, Inc.: The Second Death of Rock 'n' Roll.

Eddie Kendricks, died October 6, 1992, age 52
See The Motown Morgue.

Doc Pomus, died March 14, 1991, age 65
See Little Elvis Deaths.

Allan Sherman, died November 21, 1973, age 48
See Last Laughs: Novelty Artists.

8

Necro-Orleans

THE SOUND of New Orleans transcends time yet remains inextricably bound with rock 'n' roll. Its easy-rollicking drive, pumping piano chords, and complex backbeats have become common currency in American music, for those who can master them, and have emerged continually in rock 'n' roll. Little Richard appropriated the New Orleans sound as the starting point for his unique brand of rock 'n' roll, tossing in gospel shrieks and revving it all up to an impossibly manic pitch. Fats Domino grew up in New Orleans, as indeed have many influential piano players, including Huey "Piano" Smith, Allen Touissant, and Dr. John. Alex Chilton has spent time there and it shows. Johnny Thunders died there.

The list below contains people no longer alive. But on their letters from heaven they probably still absentmindedly scribble a New Orleans zip code on the return. As clichéd as it may sound, New Orleans remains a city no one who spends any time there ever quite leaves.

Roy Brown, died May 25, 1981, age 55
See Little Elvis Deaths.

Clifton Chenier, died December 12, 1987, age 62
Accordion player; from Opelousas, Louisiana. Chenier was known for much of his life as the "King of Zydeco," referring to a black variation on cajun music that mixes up the music of blues, country, New Orleans barrelhouse, and French folk—and plays the whole concoction at breakneck speed. Starting in the mid-fifties Chenier was a regional giant, but he never broke through nationally. After all these years zydeco still has not caught on outside Louisiana—yet it still promises to do so any day now, and just might. This could be its year.

Lee Dorsey, died December 1, 1986, age 61
Singer, boxer, auto mechanic; from New Orleans. Known as Kid Chocolate when he boxed professionally, in the early sixties Lee Dorsey delivered such perfectly charming nonsense hits as "Ya Ya" and "Do-Re-Mi." Then his label folded behind him and he was left fixing cars. But producer Allen Touissant, after returning from a stint in the service, took him on again for another batch of lively, memorable hits, including "Ride Your Pony" and what is perhaps his best known song, the 1966 number 8 "Working in the Coal Mine." Then the string ran out again and he was back to fixing cars. He opened for the Clash on their 1980 U.S. tour, when Joe Strummer rightly called him "the hidden jewel of soul." He died of emphysema.

Guitar Slim, died February 7, 1959, age 32
Guitar player, born Eddie Jones; from Greenwood, Mississippi. Guitar Slim was a dresser and a showman, renowned in the fifties for his audience participation shtick during extended guitar solos, still something of an anomaly at the time. He had only one hit, "The Things That I Used to Do," which went to number 1 on the rhythm and blues chart in 1954 and sold over a million. The memorable rocker, which has since become a standard, was arranged by Ray Charles. Guitar Slim's health worsened as his drinking increased. He died of pneumonia.

Chris Kenner, died January 25, 1976, age 46
Singer, songwriter; from Kenner, Louisiana. Kenner was a New Orleans stalwart who enjoyed just one national hit, the 1961 number 2 "I Like It Like That, Part 1," which was later covered by the Dave Clark Five and went to number 7 in 1965. Kenner also wrote "Sick and Tired" for Fats Domino and "Land of 1,000 Dances" for Cannibal and the Headhunters, later also a big hit for Wilson Pickett. Kenner was sent to prison in 1968 on statutory rape charges. Released four years later a wash-up, he basically spent the rest of his life drinking and died of a heart attack.

George Landry, died August 9, 1980
With the Wild Tchoupitoulas; from New Orleans. The uncle of the Neville brothers (Aaron, Art, Charles, Cyril), Landry took the role of Big Chief Jolly in the Wild Tchoupitoulas, an exuberant "Mardi Gras Indian tribe" whose lone self-titled mid-seventies album on Island stands as a milestone of funk, not least because the Nevilles are all over it.

Leonard Lee, died October 26, 1976, age 41
Singer, Lee of Shirley and Lee with Shirley Goodman. The duo's lively,

much-covered "Let the Good Times Roll," which went to number 20 in 1956, was one of those songs that somehow permanently captures a moment in time and becomes a kind of universal touchstone, like "Gloria" ten years later. They had no other hits close to it. During their run as "The Sweethearts of the Blues," they had a series of answer and answer-back releases ("I'm Gone," "Shirley Come Back to Me," "Lee's Dream," etc.). They split up in 1963. Shirley departed for Los Angeles, and sang back-up with Sonny and Cher, the Rolling Stones, and others; she also had a disco hit in 1975 with the number 12 "Shame, Shame, Shame." Lee stayed in New Orleans to finish college and eventually took a government job. They reunited once, in 1972, on the oldies circuit in New York. Lee died of a heart attack.

Smiley Lewis, died October 7, 1966, age 46
Piano player, singer, songwriter; from New Orleans. Lewis did well on the rhythm and blues charts in the fifties, but his biggest hit, "I Hear You Knocking," fell victim to the white-cover syndrome of the period: in 1955 Gale Storm took a wretched version of it to number 2 on the pop charts. (Fifteen years later British pub-rocker Dave Edmunds took it to number 4 with a much better version.) Lewis wrote "One Night (of Sin)," which Elvis Presley delicately changed to "One Night (of Love)" for a number 4 hit in 1958. Ten years later that song provided some of the best moments on Elvis's TV special. Lewis died of stomach cancer.

Professor Longhair, died January 30, 1980, age 61
Piano player, singer, born Henry Byrd; from Bogalusa, Louisiana. Professor Longhair was a highly influential New Orleans piano player whose boogie-woogie gumbo drew on ragtime, delta blues, rhumba, and much more—he practically invented the style made popular by Fats Domino, Allen Touissant, Dr. John, and others. In the fifties he wrote "Go to the Mardi Gras," which eventually became the theme song for the annual New Orleans festival, and he also hit number 5 on the rhythm and blues chart with "She Ain't Got No Hair," later retitled "Baldhead" for Mercury release. But he was mostly unsuccessful and in 1964 left music altogether to work as a manual laborer. He had a comeback of sorts in 1971, inaugurating what became an annual tradition for him of playing the New Orleans Jazz and Heritage Festival, but as one of the great players of the region he never lived to see his due. The specific circumstances of his death are not known.

Larry Williams, died January 7, 1980, age 44
Singer, songwriter, piano player; from New Orleans. Larry Williams is an

all too often overlooked rock 'n' roll stylist whose biggest and best hits—
"Short Fat Fannie," which went to number 5 in 1957, and the number 14
"Bony Moronie" that same year—linked the freneticism and excitement of
Little Richard with the supple poise of Fats Domino. His background included time in bands with Roy Brown, Percy Mayfield, and Lloyd Price. In
1965 the Beatles covered his "Dizzy Miss Lizzy." Maybe Williams's obscurity came from his decidedly normal name, but more likely it was related
to a lifetime of troubles, which started for him in 1960 when he was imprisoned on drug charges. He spent the rest of his life attempting comebacks,
first as a rock 'n' roller and then as a funk star. His last album, 1978's *That
Larry Williams,* was disco. It failed and, despondent, he committed suicide
by shooting himself in the head.

Faces of Death 6:
Brain Tumors

Bill Black, died October 21, 1965, age 38
See Little Elvis Deaths.

Bert Convy, died July 15, 1991, age 52
See Death's Ululating Maw: Vocal Group Deaths.

Ronnie Goodson, died November 4, 1980, age 33
See Death's Ululating Maw: Vocal Group Deaths.

Stuart Hamblen, died March 8, 1989, age 80
See Country Corpses.

Little Junior Parker, died November 18, 1971, age 44
See Little Elvis Deaths.

Tammi Terrell, died March 16, 1970, age 23
See The Motown Morgue.

9

Jerry Lee Lewis: Apocalypse Now

WITH THE possible exception of Johnny Rotten, no one has brought more howling fury, destructive glory, or netherworldly powers to rock 'n' roll than Jerry Lee Lewis. He is a figure plunged wholly in apocalyptic Christian faith and defined by it like no other in modern popular culture. Jerry Lee Lewis was raised in the Assemblies of God church, a sect that believes a man serves only one master, God or Satan. He took that edict seriously, and still does, and has spent his life torn between them. He considered the ministry, like his cousin Jimmy Swaggart (himself wonderfully felled by Lucifer in the eighties) and Little Richard. But time and again, he has opted for the temptations of the Dark Prince—women, booze, pills, money, and pumping boogie music that is among the best rock 'n' roll.

Consider the circumstances of the birth of Jerry Lee Lewis as detailed in Nick Tosches's remarkable biography of him, *Hellfire:* "On that day, September 29, 1935, at an hour more dark than light, [his mother] Mamie Lewis heard the first scream of her newborn child. A dog no one had ever seen had been howling outside the window near her bed. Her sister Stella had thrown stones to chase it away, but it had come back. Now, finally, it went off into the brush toward Turtle Lake, and Stella Calhoun never saw it again."

If Jerry Lee Lewis has been rent all his life by the agony of choice, Satan has never been slow to draw his boon. Every crumb of hard-won success for Jerry Lee has been followed by a bone-jarring fall to ever lower depths. Perhaps the most spectacular came in 1958, when he was challenging Elvis Presley for the rock 'n' roll throne. The hits, starting in 1957, had been fine and much loved: the number 3 "Whole Lotta Shakin' Goin' On," the number 2 "Great Balls of Fire," the number 7 "Breathless" (well, at least it was much loved), the number 21 "High School Confidential" (well, at least it was fine). Live performance had borne out all his promise and then some.

With Presley donning army khaki, all that lay ahead for Jerry Lee, seemingly, was open road and riches.

But suddenly, poised there, the prize practically in his grasp, Jerry Lee Lewis's career collapsed from a flouting of convention superhumanly thorough: he married his thirteen-year-old cousin Myra, the daughter of his bass player, before his divorce from his second wife (itself a shotgun marriage) was final, and without permission from her parents. It outraged not just the world, which would never have been expected to understand anyway, but also the insulated Louisiana community where he came from—he should have asked her father for her hand. And so full of himself was Jerry Lee at the time that he obviously couldn't have cared less, even after the facts came out. Within six months he was washed up.

Eventually he returned to the limelight as a country singer (still pumping boogie in performance), but that ended in a morass of pills and women and money and liquor. Satan salted down the wounds well: Elvis Presley never lost his momentum and another cousin, the bland Mickey Gilley, became the more successful country singer in the seventies. In fact, of the three cousins—Gilley, Lewis, and Swaggart, together constituting a kind of neatly contained allegorical cosmology all their own—Gilley is by far the least tortured. He is also the most conventionally successful.

But falling from the graces of a coquettish world has been the least of Jerry Lee Lewis's burdens over the years. Lewis was nicknamed "The Killer" as a youth (no one knows quite where it came from, but he has always hated it). He has been married seven times; the longest, to Myra, lasted thirteen years. They divorced in 1970. His fourth wife, Jaren, drowned in 1982 while awaiting terms of the final settlement of their divorce. He married his sixth wife, twenty-five-year-old Shawn Michelle Stephens, in 1983; after less than ninety days she was taken from his home dead of an overdose of methadone. Witnesses reported seeing blood and bruises on her body, and deep scratches on Lewis's hands, but the death was ruled accidental.

Both of his sons have died untimely deaths: one, Steve Allen Lewis, named for the television host and announced enemy of rock 'n' roll, drowned in a swimming pool at age three in 1962; the other, Jerry Lee Lewis, Jr., was killed in an auto accident at age nineteen in 1973. In addition, Lewis's elder brother Elmo died when still a boy, making Jerry Lee the last remaining male heir to a family name that stretches back nearly to the American Revolution; a proud line of forebears who fought in the Civil War to preserve the Southern way of life, now without sons to bear the name.

But Jerry Lee Lewis is still alive. He will probably outlive you and me. In the early eighties he suffered serious health problems related to a stomach ulcer and looked a goner, but Lucifer, presumably, had no need of him just yet. Throughout it all, he has remained as convinced as Robert Johnson ever could have been that his rock 'n' roll career was not the work of the Lord. In a famous session with Sam Phillips in 1957, he felt constrained to call off a recording of "Great Balls of Fire," suddenly troubled by the Satanic implications of the song and what that boded for his immortal soul.

It was as if it had just dawned on him how deeply evil rock 'n' roll was, and how far—and how eternally—it would take him from the pious and solemn hymnody of his church upbringing. Much of the long debate that ensued between Lewis and Phillips was recorded. "How can the Devil save souls?" Lewis cries at one point, responding to producer Phillips's spurious argument from the Bible—Phillips obviously interested only in getting the track cut. "Man, I got *the Devil* in me! If I didn't have, I'd be a Christian!"

Phillips finally held sway, and late that night Lewis begrudgingly relented and put down a red-hot reading of the song. Early in 1958 it spent four weeks at number 2. But the soul of Jerry Lee Lewis must remain troubled, when he stops long enough to think of it. Four weeks at number 2 was a pittance for Satan compared to all he has claimed in return.

Faces of Death 7:
At Another's Hand

Murders

Carlton Barrett, died April 17, 1987, age 36
See Death inna Babylon.

Shirley Brickley, died October 13, 1977, age 32
See Da Doo Ron Death.

Bobby Fuller, died July 18, 1966, age 22
See The Day the Music Died: The First Death of Rock 'n' Roll.

Samuel George, died March 17, 1982, age 39
See Da Doo Ron Death.

Cornelius Gunter, died February 26, 1990, age 51
See Death's Ululating Maw: Vocal Group Deaths (The Coasters).

Robert Johnson, died August 16, 1938, age 27
See Hellhound on His Trail.

King Curtis, died August 13, 1971, age 37
See Blow, Big Man.

John Lennon, died December 8, 1980, age 40
See Beatles Bugouts.

"Sir" Walter Scott, died circa December 27, 1983
See Death Lite.

James "Shep" Sheppard, died January 24, 1970
See Death's Ululating Maw: Vocal Group Deaths.

Domestic Disputes

Marvin Gaye, died April 1, 1984, age 44
See The Motown Morgue.

Felix Pappalardi, died April 17, 1983, age 44
See Sha Na Na, Inc.: The Second Death of Rock 'n' Roll.

Stacy Sutherland, died August 24, 1978, age 32
See Sha Na Na, Inc.: The Second Death of Rock 'n' Roll.

Surprised an Intruder

Al Jackson, died October 1, 1975, age 39
See Drummed Out.

Sal Mineo, died February 13, 1976, age 37
See The Day the Music Died: The First Death of Rock 'n' Roll.

Peter Tosh, died September 11, 1987, age 42
See Death inna Babylon.

10

The Big Elvis

ELVIS PRESLEY is the most famous American who ever lived. After Jesus Christ and Mickey Mouse, in fact, there is no name in the world more familiar. But how he managed it, and how he sustained it, remain among the great mysteries of rock 'n' roll. In the beginning he just wanted to sing and be an entertainer, like Dean Martin, but in the end he was vastly more. The story of Elvis Presley combines the elements of every great American story—from Horatio Alger to Malcolm X, from Moby Dick to Crazy Horse, from Henry Ford to Richard Nixon—in a life that embodied and consumed American myths like so many french fries chased back with chocolate shakes.

Like Jay Gatsby, the figure of Elvis Presley only looms larger in death. His life and career partook of none of death's untidy obsessions. But somehow, like everything else that came into his orbit, Elvis Presley finally embodied and consumed the dark side of life too, including death itself, leaving behind like some smudge from the ash of a great fire this gnawing conundrum: Did Elvis go to heaven, or did he go to hell?

Let us consider the familiar facts together and then quickly, like Elvis himself, depart this all too disturbing forty acres of the mortal realm.

On January 8, 1935, in Tupelo, Mississippi, Elvis Presley was born in a shotgun shack—literally a shotgun shack. He was the only son of a poor white Mississippi couple, the first of a pair of twins. His brother, named Jesse Garon, was stillborn. All his life Elvis felt close to his mother Gladys and distant from his father Vernon, but by and large they were a tight-knit family. He was raised in the faith of the First Assembly of God, a pentecostal sect. At the age of ten he won a state fair competition for singing "Old Shep."

At thirteen he moved with his family to Memphis. As a high school student, Elvis was quiet and polite, yet different. He wore his hair longer than others, and grew sideburns, and maintained as flashy a wardrobe as his allowance would afford. His favorite colors, appropriately enough, were pink and black. But his budding sense of style made him an outcast as a teen. Still, he already knew what he wanted: to sing and to entertain, like Dean Martin, and to be rich and famous. Memphis was a hotbed of rhythm and blues music at the time, and Elvis spent as much of his spare time as he could on Beale Street, absorbing it all. Blues shouter Wynonie Harris would later claim that Elvis learned everything from him, and he was probably right.

After he finished high school, Elvis drove a truck for the local electric company. One day in 1953 he stopped at the Memphis Recording Service, which was owned by Sam Phillips as a sideline to his Sun label. There he recorded two songs for a do-it-yourself acetate: "My Happiness" and "That's When Your Heartaches Begin." Legend has long had it that he recorded them as a birthday gift for his mother, but, given that her birthday was months away, it's doubtful. More likely it was a fumbling career move—fumbling, but it worked. Phillips's assistant, Marion Keisker, liked what she heard, surreptitiously caught part of it on tape, and convinced Phillips to give the boy a try. (That original acetate resurfaced, by the way, and was authenticated in 1988, and those two songs are now available in the RCA catalog.)

Phillips did, of course, give the boy a chance, and though the sessions were not without their troubles, after many long hours they finally got something. It was July of 1954, and with Scotty Moore accompanying him on guitar, and Bill Black on bass, Elvis launched into a loose, impromptu reading of Arthur "Big Boy" Crudup's "That's All Right." After they got that track, they got another, "Blue Moon of Kentucky." Sam Phillips suddenly knew that he had found his pop grail: "a white man with the Negro sound and the Negro feel."

He began to work it hard. At first the country stations to whom he pitched the single told him it was too Negro, and the rhythm and blues stations told him it was too hillbilly. But everywhere it was played in the South it created a sensation and an instant demand. More singles were recorded and released, and Elvis, ready for everything, took his act to the road, where he worked out an electrifying, astonishingly obscene act. His eerie rapport with audiences helped him create a series of legendary shows on which he built a reputation. No matter what names he was packaged with —including some of the biggest, such as Webb Pierce and Hank Snow— Elvis inevitably closed the show. No one wanted to go on after him.

Eventually this new sensation caught the attention of veteran promoter Colonel Tom Parker, title honorary, who had previously served as the manager for Eddy Arnold and Hank Snow. Now the Colonel liked the looks of this Presley kid and, in the second half of 1955, stepped on in to manage him. He negotiated the sale of Elvis's Sun contract to RCA in November for some $25,000, the biggest deal of its kind at the time. Elvis also received a $5,000 bonus, which he used to buy his mother a pink Cadillac.

In 1956 Elvis broke wide open, and became the biggest thing ever in show business. Some claim the Beatles were bigger, but forget it. In terms of practically any criteria you want to use—chart action, record sales, name familiarity, lasting influence—Elvis was the biggest. Period. You need a degree in math to talk about it he was so big. Here's just one piece of it: He spent nearly half of 1956, twenty-five weeks, with a record in the number 1 position on the pop chart, with "Heartbreak Hotel" (number 1 for eight weeks), "I Want You, I Need You, I Love You," "Don't Be Cruel" b/w "Hound Dog" (number 1 for eleven weeks, a feat not matched until 1992's "End of the Road" by Boyz II Men, which had an incredible thirteen-week run), and "Love Me Tender." Then he repeated the stunt in 1957 (yes, that's right, another twenty-five weeks at number 1) with "Too Much," "All Shook Up," "(Let Me Be Your) Teddy Bear," and "Jailhouse Rock" b/w "Treat Me Nice."

Television appearances, especially on the Ed Sullivan show, played their part too. Parker, who by this time was reportedly taking an unprecedented 25 percent of Presley's earnings, sought to consolidate their gains by putting Elvis in the movies. It worked, of course. Elvis's first movie, *Love Me Tender,* shot and released in 1956, earned back its $1 million investment in three days. (For that matter no Elvis movie, not *Clambake,* not *Charro!,* not *Harum Scarum,* not even *Paradise, Hawaiian Style,* ever lost money.)

Elvis was the first and is still the most powerful incarnation of what would later be called the generation gap. He was always far more than an entertainer (all "Love Me Tender"-type sops notwithstanding) in spite of anything Elvis himself had to say about it. He was the face of a massive revolution, and everybody knew it. Critic Greil Marcus has previously noted that Texas singer/songwriter Butch Hancock put the fine point to it when he said, struggling to talk about the impact of Elvis: "Yeah, that was the dance that everybody forgot. It was the dance that was so strong it took an entire civilization to forget it. And ten seconds to remember it."

Kids worshipped him, adults reviled him—it was almost as simple as that. On a profoundly nonverbal level, Elvis proclaimed liberation. It finally took the U.S. Army to stop him, but by then it was too late. The box had been opened and could never be shut again. Drafted late in 1957, the millionaire Elvis quietly served his two-year hitch driving jeeps around Germany. There he met his future wife, Priscilla Beaulieu, then thirteen. And that was also when his mother died, an enormous personal loss for him. It marked the beginning of an isolation that, except for a brief period in late 1968 and 1969, lasted the rest of his life.

Released from the army in 1960, Elvis spent the decade making bad movies and toss-off records and unthinkable piles of money, trying to distance himself from the revolution he had initiated while only wanting to be rich and famous, like Dean Martin. Mindful of Jerry Lee Lewis, he held off marrying Priscilla until she was fully twenty-one, finally wedding her in 1967. Their only child, Lisa Marie, was born nine months later to the day, in 1968. After the stunning "Elvis TV Special" aired late in 1968—the only time when we might have seen the real Elvis—he switched his focus from movies to concert appearances, playing Vegas every year and continually mounting small tours. In 1969 he enjoyed his first number 1 hit in seven years, "Suspicious Minds," which has turned out to be his last (so far).

Life seemed good but somehow it wasn't. Adulation and insulation from the world damaged Elvis in countless ways. Paranoid and emotionally impoverished, he succumbed to ever-worsening drug and eating problems in the seventies. He was divorced in 1973. And, finally, on August 16, 1977, he died, alone in the master bathroom of Graceland, his Memphis mansion, tottering off the toilet in a drug-induced stupor while trying to focus his dimming eyes on a book about sex and astrology. The cause of his death was congestive heart failure; an autopsy revealed advanced arteriosclerosis, enlarged liver, and evidence of drug abuse.

11

Little Elvis Deaths

ELVIS PRESLEY'S death in 1977 came as a resounding shock that rang down the curtain on rock 'n' roll for a whole generation. It is perhaps no accident that far more people now honor and remember the day of his death—and it's also a little weird that the day of his death coincides with that of bluesman Robert Johnson and baseball player Babe Ruth. What is it about August 16 that fells kings? Like Johnny Ace, Elvis Presley's life must now be defined in terms of his death. Like Jim Morrison's death, Presley's transcends tragedy and ultimately seems a feeble lie in the face of his continuing, mocking, restless existence. Elvis has clearly ascended the Olympian heights of the gods, and taken his appointed role as Zeus. The only surprise, really, is that more tabloid reports of his sightings do not include visions of ravishing swans.

Here is a list of some of the mortals touched by Elvis who are now dead. Many fell into the orbit of his career and as a result were at least partly subsumed by him. Some were grateful for this boon, others not. Most of their names bring Elvis almost immediately to mind.

Bill Black, died October 21, 1965, age 38
Bass player, Elvis's first; from Memphis. Bill Black played with Elvis and guitar player Scotty Moore on the Sun sessions, and with Moore and drummer D.J. Fontana behind Elvis, on sessions and live dates in 1956, until Elvis was drafted in late 1957. Then they never played together again. It was Black who instinctively laid down the easy, seductive walking line when Elvis started goofing between takes on "That's All Right," which many claim as the ultimate big-bang moment of rock 'n' roll. In 1959 he formed the Bill Black Combo, a five-piece sax and piano instrumental group whose sound, called "The Untouchable Sound," took root somewhere between country and the incipient soul of Booker T. and the MG's. They cov-

ered the hits of the day. Their biggest was the 1960 number 9 "White Silver Sands"; they also covered "Don't Be Cruel." Poor health forced Black's retirement from the group in 1962, which with personnel changes carried on into the eighties. Black died after surgery for a brain tumor.

Roy Brown, died May 25, 1981, age 55
Blues shouter; from New Orleans. Brown, credited with originating the "crying" style of the blues shout, was a major influence on the singing of B.B. King, James Brown, Little Richard, and others. But he may be best remembered now for writing the oft-covered "Good Rockin' Tonight," which he also recorded in 1947. In the mid-fifties it became practically a signature song for Elvis while he was still at Sun. Like many rhythm and blues players of the time, including Wynonie Harris, Louis Jordan, and even Big Joe Turner, Brown virtually disappeared from view in the late fifties, though he continued to perform and record. He died in Los Angeles of a heart attack.

Arthur "Big Boy" Crudup, died March 28, 1974, age 70
Bluesman; from Forest, Mississippi. Crudup is probably most famous for writing "That's All Right," Elvis's milestone first single. He emerged during the Depression with gospel group the Harmonizing Four and moved with them to Chicago. His unethical manager, Lester Melrose, helped Crudup get record deals but took advantage of him and never paid out his royalties. Crudup quit him after discovering the fraud in 1947. Bitter about his experience, Crudup returned South to raise sweet potatoes. During the sixties blues promoter Dick Waterman took up Crudup's cause and secured some $60,000 in back royalties for him. Crudup then resumed his career. Although he was a big fan, for some reason Elvis avoided him, and they never met. Crudup died of a heart attack.

Ral Donner, died April 6, 1984, age 41
Pop singer; from Chicago. Donner adopted Presley's early smoldering style just as Presley was sinking into his heavy three-movies-a-year schedule. Donner's biggest hit came in 1961 with the number 4 "You Don't Know What You've Got (Until You Lose It)." He spent the rest of his life going from label to label looking for another hit. In 1981 he supplied narration for the documentary *This Is Elvis*. He died of lung cancer.

Wynonie Harris, died June 14, 1969, age 54
Blues shouter; from Omaha, Nebraska. Wynonie Harris was one of the greatest of all the blues shouters, growing to prominence along with the mu-

sical style in the forties. There are perfectly credible claims that Elvis learned much of his singing and all his stage moves from seeing Harris in Memphis, and that what raised a ruckus with Elvis was merely a mild version of Harris. The late forties and early fifties were Harris's peak period, as he recorded "Drinkin' Wine, Spo-Dee-O-Dee," "Good Rockin' Tonight," "All She Wants to Do Is Rock," and more. But his themes (as in "Bloodshot Eyes," "Sittin' on It All the Time," and "I Like My Baby's Pudding") were often far too "mature" even for teens, let alone their parents. With the advent of rock 'n' roll Harris's fortunes waned and numerous attempts at a comeback failed. He opened a café in New York that failed, then moved to Los Angeles to open another café. He died of cancer.

Mario Lanza, died October 7, 1959, age 38
Opera singer, born Alfred Arnold Cocozza; from Philadelphia. Lanza, an opera singer, scored a series of pop hits in the early fifties (with titles like "Be My Love" and "Vesti la Giubba") that evidently caught the ear of a youthful Elvis, or perhaps it was Colonel Tom Parker. In any event, in 1960, following his discharge from the army and with the determination to win favor as an adult entertainer, Elvis tackled the Lanza-like milestone "It's Now or Never"—adapted from an 1899 Italian opera song "O Sole Mio." It was overpuffed if enjoyable tripe (pure Elvis, after a fashion). It worked, for the most part. The song went to number 1 for five weeks and the teens he'd won earlier stayed with him as adults. By then, Lanza had died in Rome of a heart attack, blamed partly on his penchant (reminiscent of Elvis) for rapidly gaining and losing weight.

Smiley Lewis, died October 7, 1966, age 46
See Necro-Orleans.

Ricky Nelson, died December 31, 1985, age 45
See Oozing Crooners.

Little Junior Parker, died November 18, 1971, age 44
Blues singer, harmonica player; from Clarksdale, Mississippi. Talented Little Junior Parker built his career on fortuitous happenstance. He first emerged in 1948 at a Sonny Boy Williamson show, responding to a request by Williamson for a harmonica player from the audience. From there he caught on with Howlin' Wolf, eventually inheriting his band (which included piano player and arranger Ike Turner) when Howlin' Wolf took a sabbatical in 1951. Next he moved to Memphis and joined the Beale Streeters, whose ranks included Johnny Ace, Bobby "Blue" Bland, Rosco

Gordon, and B.B. King. After Ace died late in 1954, Parker inherited *his* band, re-naming it Blues Consolidated. In 1953 he wrote "Mystery Train," which became a definitive hit for Elvis in 1955. By the end of the decade Parker had established a unique singing style rivaled only by Bobby "Blue" Bland, and enjoyed steady rhythm and blues hits until he died. Al Green dedicated his 1974 "Take Me to the River" to Parker, who died after surgery for a brain tumor.

Jay B. Perkins, died 1958

Guitar player, brother of Carl Perkins; from Tiptonville, Tennessee. Jay B., with Carl and a third brother, bass player Clayton, formed the nucleus of the band that recorded Carl's "Blue Suede Shoes," a sudden number 2 pop hit within weeks of its release in 1956. It was also a big hit on both the rhythm and blues and country charts. It was the first of its kind to score on all three charts. The band was invited to appear on the Perry Como show and the Ed Sullivan show, but the trip to New York resulted in an auto crack-up that killed their manager and sent both Jay and Carl to the hospital. Instead, Elvis was the first rock 'n' roll star to gain widespread national exposure on TV. Carl eventually recovered and went on to a diminished and checkered career, but brother Jay B. was not even that fortunate. Only partially recovered, he returned to recording, appearing on the Million Dollar Quartet session. Then he died of complications from injuries sustained in the accident.

Webb Pierce, died February 24, 1991, age 69

Honky-tonk country singer; from West Monroe, Louisiana. Starting in 1952, Pierce was among the biggest country stars for twenty years. He headlined dates in the mid-fifties with a then unknown Elvis, who continually upstaged him until Pierce finally relented and allowed Elvis to close the shows. Pierce was famous for his guitar-shaped swimming pool at his Nashville mansion, a gesture reminiscent of Elvis. He died of heart failure.

Doc Pomus, died March 14, 1991, age 65

Songwriter, with Mort Shuman; born Jerome Solon Felder, from Brooklyn. With Mort Shuman, Doc Pomus was one of the greatest of the so-called Brill Building songwriters. He was the lyricist for much of Elvis's most appealing sixties work, including "Viva Las Vegas," "Surrender," "Little Sister," "(Marie's the Name) His Latest Flame," "She's Not You," and others. He also cowrote "Lonely Avenue" for Ray Charles, "Young Blood" for the Coasters, "A Teenager in Love" for Dion and the Belmonts, "Save the Last Dance for Me" for the Drifters, and many more. He died of lung cancer.

Gladys Presley, died August 14, 1958, age 46

Elvis's mother, née Smith; from Tupelo, Mississippi. Though the Presley family came from a small dirt town in Mississippi and struggled financially—were poor white trash, in a phrase—Gladys always told Elvis he was as good as anybody else and could do or be anything in life he wanted, lessons he learned well. She also taught him manners, more lessons he learned well. Buying her a house and a pink Cadillac were among the first actions he took upon the arrival of fame and fortune. Chronically overweight and a drinker, she worried if she had her son's approval—unnecessarily. He loved her beyond anything. It was more likely her death and not his army induction that marked the beginning of his withdrawal from rock 'n' roll and from life. She died of heart failure, related to acute hepatitis. Her death shattered him.

Vernon Presley, died June 21, 1979, age 63

Elvis's father; from Tupelo, Mississippi. He met and married Gladys Smith in 1933, when he was seventeen and she was twenty-one. Elvis was born less than two years later, and was given Vernon's middle name. When his son became rich and famous, Vernon was put on the payroll, overseeing expenses. Two years after Gladys died Vernon remarried Davada "Dee" Stanley; they had three sons. Elvis did not attend the ceremony. Though Vernon was well liked by members of the clan that surrounded Elvis, his son remained distant and aloof. Vernon died of a heart attack.

Willie Mae "Big Mama" Thornton, died July 25, 1984, age 57

Rhythm and blues singer; from Montgomery, Alabama. "Big Mama" Thornton was a big belter with a big, bawdy presence, in the tradition of Bessie Smith, Big Maybelle, Etta James, and Koko Taylor. She toured in the early fifties with Johnny Otis, Junior Parker, and Johnny Ace (she witnessed the death of Ace, but kept silent about what she saw all her life). Big Mama was the first to record Leiber and Stoller's "Hound Dog"—it was a number 1 hit for her on the rhythm and blues charts in 1953, and some say her contributions to it warrant a cowriting credit. She sniffed at Elvis's version. Thornton also recorded and performed with Muddy Waters, Otis Spann, and many others, but fell into obscurity toward the end and died alone in her tiny Los Angeles studio.

Faces of Death 8:
Pills

Lester Bangs, died April 30, 1982, age 33
See I Wanna Destroy: The Final Death of Rock 'n' Roll.

Nick Drake, died November 25, 1974, age 26
See Just Us Dead Folk.

Brian Epstein, died August 27, 1967, age 32
See Beatles Bugouts.

Keith Moon, died September 7, 1978, age 31
See Who's Dead.

Elvis Presley, died August 16, 1977, age 42
See The Big Elvis.

The Singing Nun, died March 31, 1985, age 52
See Da Doo Ron Death.

Rory Storm, died September 27, 1972
See Beatles Bugouts.

Dinah Washington, died December 14, 1963, age 39
See Oozing Crooners.

Hank Williams, died January 1, 1953, age 29
See Country Corpses.

12

The Day the Music Died:
The First Death of Rock 'n' Roll

IN THE late fifties one incident after another seemed to bode the end of
rock 'n' roll. Its greatest stars were systematically diminished, as often as
not by their own enthusiastic choice. In 1957 Little Richard, aboard a failing airplane somewhere over Australia, had a vision of the apocalypse and
promised God he would straighten up and fly right if He just got that damn
plane back on the ground safely; He did and he did, entering a seminary
and eventually becoming ordained as a Seventh Day Adventist minister.
Later, much later, Little Richard would divide his energies between that and
"Hollywood Squares."

That same year of 1957, at age twenty-two, Jerry Lee Lewis married his
thirteen-year-old first cousin before his divorce from his second wife was
even close to final; when the facts came out in 1958 his career ended as spec-
tacularly as it had begun, though he has since survived as a kind of Lazarus,
plying his country music skills when he can't get away with rock 'n' roll.
Also in 1958, Elvis Presley went into the army, and after his mother Gladys
died, began a protracted withdrawal from the world which ended in his
own death in 1977.

In 1959 Buddy Holly along with Ritchie Valens and the Big Bopper died
in an airplane crash; his spirit, however—as we shall see—has never
departed rock 'n' roll. And, at the end of that year, Chuck Berry went up
on a morals charge. In one of the uglier chapters of racist U.S. justice, he
was imprisoned, a travesty exceeded only by his imprisonment on tax evasion charges in 1979. Those experiences embittered and corroded—
understandably—perhaps the wittiest and most creative mind in early rock
'n' roll.

Payola investigations, at the behest of music publishers—a corner of the
industry grown surly over the rise of rock 'n' roll because their royalty struc-

tures had been challenged and upset by the upstarts—were launched in 1959 by self-interested arbiters of the public weal in the U.S. Congress. Investigators solemnly looked into business practices that arose naturally from the conflation of broadcast radio and the rise of recorded commercial music in the late forties. Despite the grandstanding of that investigation, these practices have never gone away, likely never will, and can probably be judged only on the basis of taste—if you like what's being played on the radio, they aren't so bad; if you don't, you're ready to take the bastards to court yourself. That has been the pattern now for nearly fifty years.

In response to the payola investigation, religious zealots continued their practice of record-smashings with renewed vigor—a public ritual that had begun on a nationwide scale with the rise of Elvis Presley in 1956. If the intention of the congressmen was to rid the music industry of certain business practices, the result was a bleach of vital music, ushering in an era of parent-safe prefab teen idols. Where once there had been Elvis Presley, now there was Ricky Nelson. Where once there had been Buddy Holly, now there was Bobby Vinton. Where once there had been Alan Freed and "Moondog Rock 'n' Roll Party," now there was Dick Clark and "American Bandstand."

At the same time white liberal intellectuals had begun to mask their patrician distaste for (and fear of) rock 'n' roll by championing folk music. The heroes of the folk boom, which surfaced in the late fifties, tended to be such pasty types as the Kingston Trio, the Limeliters, the Highwaymen, and Joan Baezzzz; or, alternately, black blues players from the South such as Brownie McGhee and Sonny Terry, and Big Bill Broonzy, made safe by their advanced ages and the gratitude they were expected to show for the boons of fame and fortune bestowed upon them.

While there is much to be said in favor of the folk music of the time (and much to be said against it), devotees clearly made the concept of "authentic" an excluding totem. By and large "authentic" could be applied only to music played on acoustic instruments, or delivered with vocal harmonies, or both, with songs that uniformly expressed a highly specific politically inflected social consciousness. The Dominoes' "Sixty Minute Man," Little Richard's "Long Tall Sally," and Carl Perkins's "Blue Suede Shoes" never had a chance, of course, but neither did Eddie Cochran's "Summertime Blues," the Coasters' "Riot in Cell Block No. 9," or Chuck Berry's "Brown-Eyed Handsome Man." Go figure.

Somehow, according to the media and the satisfied view of many grownups, all of it—the scandals, the rise of folk music, and the deaths of rock 'n' roll players—meant the death of rock 'n' roll. For the first time the cultural phenomenon begun by Elvis Presley in 1956 was vigorously engaged by white middle-class America, who intended to thwart it if they could, or slow it considerably if they couldn't. They waited until its practitioners had begun to hang themselves, and then moved in with informal campaigns of harassment and propaganda.

For some the death of rock 'n' roll meant an end to an impolite fad that had already overstayed its welcome. In the early and mid-fifties, as always in pop music, there were trends and flashes aplenty, including harmony groups descended from barbershop quartets (the Four Lads, the Four Aces) or wartime jazz (the Chordettes), Chicago blues (Muddy Waters, Howlin' Wolf), Texas blues (Lightnin' Hopkins), honky-tonk country (Hank Williams, Lefty Frizzell), western swing (Bob Wills), and a lot more. Rock 'n' roll was supposed to be just another passing trend, to be succeeded by island dance music—the calypso, or the mambo, or the rhumba, or the cha-cha. It was supposed to be goodbye Elvis Presley, hello Harry Belafonte, but it took longer than many impatient observers had expected.

"We fear," said an anonymous editorial voice in a 1957 issue of *Musical America*, "that rock 'n' roll doesn't live up to its billing. We do not find anything in it to move anybody in any spectacular way, and we suspect that viewers with alarm have been jumping to conclusions and getting the cart before the horse. At best rock 'n' roll is a kind of glorified hillbilly music with a two-beat, the familiar twanging guitar and a grotesquely distorted vocal line picked up from the blues. The insistent rhythm is no different from nor compelling physically or emotionally than . . . any other of the manifestations of evolving jazz which succeed each other almost as rapidly as women's fashions. . . . Tomorrow there will be something else."

But for others, those who had taken rock 'n' roll seriously and loved it, this first death of rock 'n' roll meant the passing of an era, withering into supposed inconsequence. The difference between Elvis Presley in 1956 and in 1960, between Chuck Berry and Bobby Darin—the unmistakable loss of vitality and raw spirit, the transmutation from immediate tribal celebration to distant cynical sophistication—was the death of rock 'n' roll for many. Robert Palmer, writing in *Rolling Stone* in 1990, said, "It is a measure of Fifties rock's genuine revolutionary potential . . . that while Sixties rock eventually calmed down, was co-opted or snuffed itself out in heedless excess, Fifties rock & roll was *stopped*. Cold."

It's not hard to understand the perception. If "Mack the Knife" and the studio-bound productions of Phil Spector, Leiber and Stoller, and the Beach Boys ultimately require as much commitment and deliver rewards as vast as "That's All Right," "Whole Lotta Shakin' Goin' On," and "Johnny B. Goode"—and they do, a fact evident from the subsequent rise of glam-rock alone—Percy Faith's "Theme from 'A Summer Place' " does nothing of the sort, nor does anything by Connie Francis, Frankie Avalon, Fabian, and a host more. But then, Pat Boone, the McGuire Sisters, Kay Starr, Nelson Riddle, Roger Williams, and other hit-makers of the mid-fifties also had little to offer.

For still others, rock 'n' roll did die—with Buddy Holly. His death was one of the most emotionally felt extinguishments of the era and the first of its kind to loom larger than life (after Johnny Ace's death, but Johnny Ace has always taken up quarters in more subterranean regions of the pop consciousness). Like Ace, Holly's death spawned a deluge of tributes, most notably Tommy Dee's "Three Stars," along with an attendant list of ghoulish ironies: Holly's last hit was "It Doesn't Matter Any More," Eddie Cochran recorded a version of "Three Stars" shortly before his own death, Holly's birthplace in Lubbock, Texas, was condemned and an order passed for its demolition on the anniversary of his death in 1978. But Holly's death was also a moment of genuine sadness for many of his admirers, including John Lennon and Paul McCartney. McCartney, in fact, was later instrumental in establishing a number of Buddy Holly memorials and events.

Buddy Holly and his death in 1959, even more than Johnny Ace in 1954, cut a wide swath through pop consciousness. His image as an unfathomable, almost mocking icon reappeared at the time of the two subsequent deaths of rock 'n' roll in 1970 and 1977. He showed up as the motivating star and centerpiece of Don McLean's ham-handed "American Pie," which declared the late fifties *and* the early seventies, as writ small in Holly's death, "The Day the Music Died." Five years later, Holly showed up as Elvis Costello, a punk-rock figure who annihilated Bob Dylan even as he suggested the tie between them. Nobody, on first seeing Costello, did not think of Holly; few, on first hearing him, did not think of Dylan.

But the first death of rock 'n' roll, of course, was not really a death; rock 'n' roll emerged triumphant again in just a few years, thanks immeasurably to the efforts of America's cultural colony, Britain. Still full of blues mood and country structure, but now with an element of pop imagery, this new incarnation was music richer and more complex than what had come before, and eventually it spawned its own culture—called simply "rock"—circa 1967. For all that, however, it was not necessarily more effective than what Little Richard, Elvis Presley, Jerry Lee Lewis, Chuck Berry, and Buddy Holly had pioneered. They breathed life into rock 'n' roll with such force that their music today still sounds as fresh and vital as traffic, riots, and summer.

Perished

Jesse Belvin, died February 6, 1960, age 26
See Death's Ululating Maw: Vocal Group Deaths.

The Big Bopper, died February 3, 1959, age 28
See Last Laughs: Novelty Artists.

Johnny and Dorsey Burnette

From Memphis. Singer Johnny Burnette formed the Rock 'n' Roll Trio in Memphis in 1953 with his brother Dorsey, who played bass, and the astonishing guitar player Paul Burlison, a former Howlin' Wolf sideman. The group recorded such impressive rockabilly non-hits as "Train Kept a-Rollin' " and "Tear It Up," later covered by the Yardbirds, Rod Stewart, and others. During the mid-fifties, the Burnettes worked for the same electric company in Memphis as Elvis Presley. After the group broke up in 1957 the Burnettes moved to Los Angeles and wrote "Believe What You Say," "Waitin' in School," and others, for Ricky Nelson. Then Johnny became a teen idol himself, scoring with the 1960 number 8 "You're Sixteen" and the top twenty "Little Boy Sad," "Dreamin'," and "God, Country, and My Baby," all in 1960 and 1961. Almost as quickly, he fell from favor but continued plotting comebacks for the rest of his brief life. In 1964, he fell off a boat while fishing and drowned, aged thirty. Dorsey had his own top thirty hit in 1960 for Era, "(There Was a) Tall Oak Tree," before going on to a career in country music. He died of a heart attack in 1979, aged forty-six. Johnny's son Rocky and Dorsey's son Billy (try to guess where their names came from) both went on to make careers in music. Rocky had a number 8 hit in 1980 with "Tired of Toein' the Line" and Billy became a member of Fleetwood Mac in 1987.

Eddie Cochran, died April 17, 1960, age 21
Rockabilly artist; from Bell Gardens, California, born in Oklahoma City, raised in Albert Lea, Minnesota. Eddie Cochran was a naturally gifted guitar player with a perfect rock 'n' roll voice, at once raw, surly, and joyful. He contributed at least one classic to the rock lexicon, the 1958 number 8 "Summertime Blues," cowritten by Jerry Capehart, which has since been covered by the Who, Blue Cheer, and many others. It stands as one of the great laments of teen life. Cochran was also one of the first musicians to turn the studio into a one-man playground through overdubbing—both "Summertime Blues" and "C'mon Everybody" are entirely solo efforts. He appeared in one of the greatest rock 'n' roll movies, 1956's *The Girl Can't Help*

It, performing "Twenty Flight Rock," and in a Mamie Van Doren vehicle, *Untamed Youth* (1957). His brooding good looks, in the vein of James Dean, promised the potential for a film career. A memorable performer, he was originally scheduled to appear on the 1959 Winter Dance Party bill with Buddy Holly, Ritchie Valens, the Big Bopper, and others, but canceled at the last minute because of other obligations. After the plane crash that killed Holly and the others, Cochran recorded a version of Tommy Dee's tribute, "Three Stars," and told friends he felt like he was living on borrowed time. His feeling was not far wrong. Just over a year later, after a breakthrough tour of England, on his way to the airport with his girlfriend Sharon Sheeley and Gene Vincent, a tire on his limo blew and the car careened into a lamppost. He died within hours from multiple head injuries. His last single, released just before he died, was "Three Steps to Heaven," which subsequently stayed near the top of the British charts for two months.

Bobby Darin, died December 20, 1973, age 37
See Oozing Crooners.

Bobby Day, died July 15, 1990, age 58
Singer, songwriter, born Robert Byrd; from Fort Worth, Texas. With his bell-like, nimble voice and his undeniable knack for songs, Bobby Day should have been a rock 'n' roll star of the first rank, but somehow his only hit was "Rockin' Robin," which went to number 2 in 1958. The flip, "Over and Over," did all right, but when the Dave Clark Five covered it seven years later it was a number 1 hit. Day's career was full of that kind of luck. Marked by a lifelong bird obsession, perhaps the result of the many vocal groups named after birds in the mid-fifties along with his own real name, Day also performed as "Baby Face" Bird, and with the Birds, the Birdies, the Daybirds, etc. He was with the Hollywood Flames for their 1957 number 11 "Buzz-Buzz-Buzz," which he wrote, and he also wrote "Little Bitty Pretty One," which reached number 6 in 1957 for Thurston Harris, and was covered by many others, including Frankie Lymon. Day died of cancer.

Lee Dorsey, died December 1, 1986, age 61
See Necro Orleans.

Esquerita, died October 23, 1990
Piano player, singer, songwriter; from New Orleans. Not much is known about the life and death of Esquerita, aka Eskew Reeder and S.Q. Reeder. He wrote "The Green Door," a number 1 hit for Jim Lowe in 1956 (and later, much later, covered by the Cramps), and was planted squarely in the

Little Richard vein, a wild man delivering raucous goods in a hysterical atmosphere—from all reports he outdid even Little Richard himself. Critic Charlie Gillett: "If a producer or arranger was deputed to the sessions, he must have been bound and gagged and put in a corner. . . . Few of the records sounded as if the band had ever played the songs before, and frequently most of the musicians took off on searing solos whose key and tempo were only vaguely connected to those of others in the band."

Alan Freed, died January 20, 1965, age 42
DJ, concert promoter; from Johnstown, Pennsylvania. In 1951 he dubbed rhythm and blues music "rock 'n' roll"—if he was not the first to use the term, he was the most effective. It stuck. On his late-night radio show in Cleveland, "Moondog Rock 'n' Roll Party," Freed played rhythm and blues tunes, drank scotch, and howled across the airwaves, delivering strange new music into the ears of white teens. He made enemies in the industry by refusing to play white covers, playing only the black originals. Soon he was booking rock 'n' roll acts on stacked, racially integrated bills. To everyone's surprise 25,000 showed up to vie for 10,000 seats at his first extravaganza, in Cleveland in 1952. In 1954 New York's WINS wooed him from Cleveland with a $75,000 salary. He made the movies *Rock Around the Clock; Don't Knock the Rock; Rock, Rock, Rock;* and *Mr. Rock 'n' Roll.* His radio show went into national and then international syndication. If his business practices were questionable, they were not unusual and there was never a doubt that he loved the music he championed. His motto? "Anyone who says rock 'n' roll is a passing fad or flash in the pan has rocks in his head, dad!"

In the anti-rock 'n' roll atmosphere of the late fifties, however, Freed finally became touchable and his enemies took their revenge. In 1957, a TV show hosted by Freed was abruptly canceled when Frankie Lymon was shown dancing with a white girl. In 1958, he was arrested for "anarchy and incitement to riot" after fights broke out at one of his shows in Boston. When the payola investigations started, late in 1959, Freed became a prime scapegoat and was subsequently blackballed. It never got better. Unemployed and increasingly unemployable, he was brought to trial on two counts of commercial bribery late in 1962. In March 1964, living in Palm Springs and doing little more than drinking, he was indicted again, on charges of tax evasion. He did not survive that one. Before the case went to trial, he contracted uremia, was hospitalized, and died.

Bobby Fuller, July 18, 1966, age 22
Singer, songwriter, guitar player; from Baytown, Texas. Fuller mixed up

strains of Buddy Holly and country with his own set of Tex-Mex inflections, and rocked the whole brew hard. His biggest hit was the 1966 number 9 "I Fought the Law," a terrific howl of teen rebel outrage later covered by the Clash among others. Its follow-up was the top thirty Buddy Holly song, "Love's Made a Fool of You." Fuller's posthumous album, a surprisingly well-realized effort, conveyed the scope of his loss to the music scene. Reportedly his body was discovered in his parked car in front of his home in Hollywood. He had been beaten and gasoline was found in his stomach. Friends speculated it was related to Fuller's suspected mob ties. Los Angeles police ruled it a suicide.

Bill Haley, died February 9, 1981, age 55
Singer, guitar player; from Highland Park, Michigan. Bill Haley ranks among the primary innovators of rock 'n' roll, chiefly on the strength of "(We're Gonna) Rock Around the Clock," which went to number 1 for eight weeks in 1955 and is commonly taken as the official arrival of rock 'n' roll. Whether or not that's true must be a debate for another time and place. What's certain is that he belongs to rock 'n' roll.

Haley rose to prominence in the early fifties after years of playing western swing, all the while working out his fresh, peculiar sound, a countrified adaptation of the riff-heavy Kansas City-style dancehall blues. With His Comets, he covered Jackie Brenston's amazing "Rocket 88" circa 1951 and, though he didn't do particularly well with it, saw what it did for the kids. His wild 1952 B-side, "Rock the Joint," continued to capitalize on the sound, and then 1953's "Crazy, Man, Crazy" was a number 15 pop hit, launching him for real. "Rock Around the Clock" was initially released in the spring of 1954 and stiffed. The follow-up, a bleached if boppin' cover of Joe Turner's "Shake, Rattle and Roll," did better, reaching number 7 and setting the scene for a re-release of "Rock Around the Clock" (along with the song's powerful appearance in 1955's *Blackboard Jungle*). This time it clicked; and it has since returned to the charts on seven occasions, most recently in 1974 when it went to number 39 on the heels of *American Graffiti* (1973) and TV's "Happy Days." But if "Rock Around the Clock" was Haley's biggest moment, it was also practically his last. By 1955 he was thirty, losing his hair, and a little beefy. After the follow-up "Burn That Candle" went to number 9 that year, only one more sizable hit came his way, the 1956 number 6 "See You Later, Alligator." He was never able to keep up with Elvis Presley, Little Richard, Chuck Berry, and the rest—they just looked too good. By 1960 he was practically nobody, relegated to the oldies circuit, though he remained popular in Europe and his records always sold (some sixty million by the time of his death, and who knows what by now). Toward the end a brain tumor was diagnosed and his behavior, partly also the result of his drinking, became erratic, paranoid, and bizarre. Reportedly he painted the windows of his Texas home black and installed floodlights to ward off tormentors. He died of a heart attack.

Thurston Harris, died April 14, 1990, age 58
Singer; from Indianapolis. Harris's career was dampened and frequently interrupted by a lifetime of troubles with drugs and mental illness. He recorded for a time in the mid-fifties with the Lamplighters, an impressive vocal group that scored no hits but recorded some lively tunes. On his own, Harris had his only hit in 1957, with Bobby Day's "Little Bitty Pretty One," which he took to number 6. (Later Frankie Lymon and many others covered it.) Harris died of a heart attack.

Buddy Holly, died February 3, 1959, age 22
Rock 'n' roll songwriter, singer, guitar player, with the Crickets, born Charles Holley; from Lubbock, Texas. Buddy Holly was among the most important figures in the first wave of rock 'n' roll—if he looked like a nerd he was anything but. Had he lived he likely would have made the best transition from the original rock 'n' roll to the innovations of the British Invasion groups, if only because his work largely provided their orientation in the first place. Following his lead, they looked to the resources, yet respected the strictures, of a classic four-piece rock 'n' roll band (two guitars, bass, drums). Besides that, Holly always was the most flexible of the early rock 'n' rollers. He proved that a rock 'n' roll band writing its own material could be practically boundless in their versatility. John Lennon and Paul McCartney had a particularly firm grasp of his achievement, one of the reasons their group's name paid homage to him.

Holly literally did it all. He used cutting-edge techniques such as double-tracking in the studio. He incorporated strings into rock 'n' roll without sacrificing its vivid punch. And he wrote astonishing music, quick and tough, or gorgeous and moving, just as he wanted it, and always brimful with hooks. He recorded "That'll Be the Day" in 1957 with the Crickets, which, by a confusion of circumstances, was released before the group was signed, by Brunswick—a label that thought, sight unseen, they were black. Everyone involved watched the song climb to number 1 on the pop charts with something like shock. It was not what anyone (except perhaps Holly) had expected. Decca had nixed the song years earlier, as had Roulette, Columbia, RCA, Atlantic, and other labels. In the song, based on a catch phrase uttered by John Wayne in John Ford's 1956 *The Searchers,* Holly went Wayne one better, taking an attitude of complete self-assurance, fearless of commitment, knowing he wants the woman but also knowing if she leaves him he's better off, and she's not. This was not the work of a nerd. Two years of hits followed—for mystifying contractual reasons some were released as by Buddy Holly, some as by the Crickets.

In late 1958 Holly split from his producer and manager Norman Petty and also from the Crickets, who retained rights to the name. He elected to stay in New York's Greenwich Village (which raises a number of interesting what-ifs related to the later developments there of Bob Dylan and other folkies) and married Puerto Rican native Maria Elena Santiago. Tangled legal problems with Petty tied up Holly's money and forced him to accept a spot on the bill of the Winter Dance Party, a package tour of the midwest in early 1959. There, tired of the grueling conditions imposed by the tour bus, and eager to arrive at the next stop with enough time to do his laundry, Holly chartered a small plane to make the jump from Mason City, Iowa, to Moorhead, Minnesota. Waylon Jennings, backing Holly on the tour, gave up his seat on the plane to the Big Bopper; Ritchie Valens decided to ride along too. The weather, a midwestern winter storm, was bad and getting worse when the plane took off at 2:00 A.M. In short order it crashed near Clear Lake, Iowa, killing all on board.

Ivory Joe Hunter, died November 8, 1974, age 60
See Twitch and Shout: Rhythm and Blues Deaths.

Little Willie John, died May 27, 1968, age 30
See Twitch and Shout: Rhythm and Blues Deaths.

King Curtis, died August 13, 1971, age 37
See Blow, Big Man.

Leonard Lee, died October 26, 1976, age 41
See Necro-Orleans.

Frankie Lymon, died February 28, 1968, age 25
See Death's Ululating Maw: Vocal Group Deaths.

Sal Mineo, died February 13, 1976, age 37
Actor, singer; from New York. Sal Mineo, a Broadway child actor who played a troubled teenager supporting James Dean in *Rebel Without a Cause,* was tabbed by Epic in the mid-fifties as an Elvis Presley-type singer for the kids. Accordingly, he was shuffled into the studio to record "Start Movin' (In My Direction)," which reached number 9 in 1957, and "Lasting

Love," a top thirty hit later that year. Then he returned to his primary interest, acting. He was rehearsing a Los Angeles stage production, *P.S. Your Cat Is Dead,* when he returned home one night and surprised a burglar. He was stabbed to death.

Ricky Nelson, died December 31, 1985, age 45
See Oozing Crooners.

Roy Orbison, died December 6, 1988, age 52
Singer, songwriter, guitar player; from Vernon, Texas. Orbison, like Elvis Presley, Carl Perkins, Johnny Cash, and Jerry Lee Lewis, originally recorded for Sun. But if he was capable of delivering credible rockabilly, it was the melodramatic narrative song that best suited Orbison's painfully introverted personality and huge operatic voice. He attended college with Pat Boone and recorded in 1955 with Norman Petty before coming to Sun in 1956. Though he stayed there three years little came of it. In Nashville in the late fifties, as a songwriter, he contributed a song he'd written for his wife, "Claudette," to the Everly Brothers. Then, in 1959, he signed to Monument—and there, teamed with Bob Moore's Orchestra and Chorus, he started reeling off his most powerful and characteristic hits, starting in 1960 with "Only the Lonely (Know How I Feel)." Too inhibited to pitch the song in meetings with Elvis Presley (who had overslept anyway) and then with the Everly Brothers, Orbison went ahead and recorded it himself. It went to number 2, and was followed by such towering giants of quivering emotion as the 1961 number 1 "Running Scared," the 1961 number 2 "Crying," and the 1964 number 1 "Oh, Pretty Woman," among many others.

Orbison left Monument for MGM in 1965, but a daunting series of personal tragedies followed, all of whose emotional nuances had been articulated, in one way or another, in the hits. First his wife Claudette was knocked from the motorcycle they were riding and killed in 1966. Then, two years later, his two oldest sons died in a house fire, leaving him with only his youngest son Wesley in all this world. In 1969 he remarried and began to pick up the pieces, touring Britain where he was always well loved. He spent the seventies performing regularly, but his profile remained low, perhaps by choice; by then his repertoire was mostly limited to country. Open-heart surgery at the end of the decade slowed him some, but in 1980 he enjoyed a country hit on a duet with Emmylou Harris, "That Lovin' You Feelin' Again." He also opened the West Coast leg of an Eagles tour that year. But Roy Orbison did not go gently into that rock 'n' roll night—his last hurrah was among the most resiliently impressive of anyone in rock 'n' roll. In 1987 he signed to Virgin and released a concert film with performances and support from Elvis Costello, Bruce Springsteen, Tom Waits, and others. The next year he chipped in on George Harrison's Traveling Wilburys project, as "Lefty," with Bob Dylan ("Lucky"), Tom Petty ("Charlie T., Jr."), ELO's Jeff Lynne ("Otis"), and Harrison ("Nelson"). The marvelous album *Volume One* resulted from it. He played his last show in Cleveland at the end of that remarkable year and then died suddenly of a heart attack. Two months later his last album, *Mystery Girl,* was released. Its single, "You Got It," went to number 9, his first big hit in twenty-three years.

Jay B. Perkins, died 1958
See Little Elvis Deaths.

Norman Petty, died August 15, 1984, age 57
Producer; from Clovis, New Mexico. Starting as a jazz-oriented keyboardist, Norman Petty went on to open a recording studio in Clovis, New Mexico, which became a famous stopping point for many rock 'n' roll players in the fifties and sixties, including Buddy Holly and the Crickets, Jimmy Bowen, Buddy Knox, and Jimmy Gilmer and the Fireballs. There Petty produced Knox's "Party Doll," a number 1 hit in 1957, Jimmy Bowen's top twenty "I'm Stickin' with You," also from that year, and Jimmy Gilmer and the Fireballs' number 1 "Sugar Shack" in 1963. Petty is probably most famous, however, for his association with Buddy Holly, producing his hits and serving as his manager until late in 1958. Petty's collaboration with Holly has been much derided as coattailing, but he opened up a whole world to Holly in that studio. Their work together includes the 1957 number 1 "That'll Be the Day," the number 3 "Peggy Sue," also from that year (a very big one for Petty), and many more. Even after Holly's death, Petty continued working with the Crickets, running his studio until the day he died.

Elvis Presley, died August 16, 1977, age 42
See The Big Elvis.

Danny Rapp, died April 8, 1983, age 41
Singer, founded Danny and the Juniors; from Philadelphia. Danny and the Juniors came to prominence in the late fifties with a boppin' sound, heard best on their 1958 number 1 "At the Hop." The top twenty follow-up later that year, "Rock and Roll Is Here to Stay," is practically its equal, making up in spirit what it lacks in originality, which is a great deal. Still, as a response to nationwide record-smashing by religious zealots, its heart was in

the right place. Later, however, it became something of an overripe irony when Rapp shot himself in the head, alone in a motel room in Arizona, after, presumably, too many years on the oldies circuit. "Rock and roll is here to stay," sadly enough, had become his worst nightmare.

Del Shannon, died February 8, 1990, age 50
Singer, songwriter, born Charles Westover; from Coopersville, Michigan. Del Shannon's biggest and most memorable hits both came in 1961 — the number 1 "Runaway" and the number 5 "Hats Off to Larry," both of which feature Shannon's trademark cheesy organ and falsetto. But in fact the body of his work, most of it steeped in country and hard-bitten rock 'n' roll, amounts to much more than that. He worked over the years (sometimes as a producer) with such figures as Andrew Loog Oldham, Brian Hyland, Jeff Lynne, Dave Edmunds, Nick Lowe, and Tom Petty. In his prime he was considered an industry troublemaker because he watched his royalty returns like a hawk and went to court whenever they smelled wrong. There should always be more like him, but on the other hand look what the industry did to him. Long prone to severe mood swings, he ended up taking his life by shooting himself in the head.

Ritchie Valens, died February 3, 1959, age 17
Guitar player, singer, songwriter, born Richie Valenzuela; from Pacoima, California. Valens's only hit was the two-sided "Donna" b/w "La Bamba," which went to number 2 in 1959, shortly after his death. He died far too young to map out any sort of would-have-been scenario (and, contrary to the 1986 movie, he never saw it coming). But "La Bamba" remains a song felt all through rock 'n' roll by virtue of its chord changes, which Valens himself borrowed from Bobby Freeman's 1958 "Do You Wanna Dance." For decades they were called "those 'La Bamba' changes," likely because their roots go directly to Latin music. Listen for them in "Twist and Shout," "Louie, Louie," "You've Lost That Lovin' Feelin'," "Hang On, Sloopy," Neil Diamond's "Cherry, Cherry," Tommy Roe's "Dizzy," Bob Dylan's "Like a Rollin' Stone," the Kinks' "You Really Got Me," Iggy and the Stooges' "No Fun," and the Ramones' "Blitzkrieg Bop." (For a fun game to play at home, find more examples.) In 1987 something like justice prevailed when the legendary southern California band Los Lobos covered "La Bamba" and took it to number 1, largely on the strength of the movie. Valens died in the same plane crash that also killed Buddy Holly and the Big Bopper.

Gene Vincent, died October 12, 1971, age 36

Rockabilly singer, guitar player, born Eugene Vincent Craddock; from Norfolk, Virginia. Gene Vincent is best remembered for his 1956 cross-breeding of "Little Lulu" comics with the Drifters' "Money Honey," which resulted in the number 7 "Be-Bop-A-Lula," establishing him as a rockabilly peer equal to Eddie Cochran and just a shade behind Elvis Presley. He sounded so much like Presley that Elvis's mother reportedly congratulated her son on his new hit when she first heard "Be-Bop-A-Lula." Yet Vincent had his own unique sound, sinuous and smoldering and far more deliberate than Presley's or Cochran's, and one that reportedly was best appreciated in performance. In 1953 Vincent suffered a serious motorcycle accident during a navy hitch in Korea, the cause of his lifelong limp, which became a mannerism affected by those who idolized him. Out of the service he formed a band with guitar player Johnny Meeks (the Blue Caps, named for Eisenhower's golfing tam) and in 1956 landed a contract with Capitol, which was desperate for its own Elvis Presley. Against all medical advice, he toured in support of "Be-Bop-a-Lula," still in a plaster cast, and appeared in one of the greatest rock 'n' roll movies, 1956's *The Girl Can't Help It.* By decade's close, his band had left him to get away from the grueling, non-stop touring, and Vincent was becoming something of an anachronism in the United States, though he was much loved in Europe, Australia, and Japan. After the auto crack-up that killed his close friend Eddie Cochran and worsened his own old injuries, he began drinking hard. Throughout most of the sixties he remained in London, where his popularity held. In 1969 he appeared at the Toronto Rock 'n' Roll Festival, which also featured Chuck Berry, Jerry Lee Lewis, the Doors, and John Lennon's Plastic Ono Band, but all attempts to consolidate a comeback fizzled. He died of internal hemorrhaging from bleeding ulcers.

Thomas Wayne, died August 15, 1971, age 30

Singer, born Thomas Wayne Perkins; from Battsville, Mississippi. Thomas Wayne's one and only hit was "Tragedy," which reached number 5 in 1959 (the Fleetwoods covered it and took it to number 10 two years later). Wayne's older brother was Luther Perkins, Johnny Cash's guitar player who died in 1969 in a house fire (see Guitar Heroes). Wayne attended Humes High School in Memphis, which Elvis Presley also attended. It was Scotty Moore, Elvis's first guitar player and manager, who helped Wayne get his hit recorded. Moore also released it on his own label, Fernwood. Wayne never had another hit—he never even came close. He just moved on over into a music industry job. Then, finally, he was killed in a head-on car collision. It was a real you-know-what.

Larry Williams, died January 7, 1980, age 44
See Necro-Orleans.

Chuck Willis, died April 10, 1958, age 30
Singer, songwriter; from Atlanta. Initially Willis wandered into rock 'n' roll as part of a fad—his 1957 number 12 hit "C.C. Rider" turned him into the beturbaned "Sheik of the Stroll," referring to a lethargic dance of the period. Willis also made an impact as a songwriter with such chestnuts as "I Feel So Bad," recorded by Elvis Presley and others, and the anthem "It Will Stand," recorded by the Showmen, with Norman Johnson, who later went on to form the Chairmen of the Board and record "Give Me Just a Little More Time" in 1970. Willis's biggest hit, the two-sided single "What Am I Living For" b/w "Hang Up My Rock and Roll Shoes," which reached number 9 in 1958, came shortly after his death in an auto accident. How many ironies can *you* find in this story?

Faces of Death 9: In the Air

Plane Accidents

The Bar-Kays, December 10, 1967
See Souls.

The Big Bopper, died February 3, 1959, age 28
See Last Laughs: Novelty Artists.

Bill Chase, died August 9, 1974, age 40
See Death Lite.

Patsy Cline, died March 5, 1963, age 30
See Country Corpses.

Jim Croce, died September 20, 1973, age 30
See Death Lite.

Buddy Holly, died February 3, 1959, age 22
See The Day the Music Died: The First Death of Rock 'n' Roll.

Lynyrd Skynyrd, October 20, 1977
See Sha Na Na, Inc.: The Second Death of Rock 'n' Roll.

Dean Martin, Jr., died March 21, 1987, age 35
See Da Doo Ron Death.

Ricky Nelson, died December 31, 1985, age 45
See Oozing Crooners.

Otis Redding, died December 10, 1967, age 26
See Souls.

Jim Reeves, died July 31, 1964, age 39
See Country Corpses.

Randy Rhoads, died March 19, 1982, age 25
See Munching the Corpse: The Utter Assurance of Death's Future

Kyu Sakamoto, died August 12, 1985, age 43
See Da Doo Ron Death.

Jud Strunk, died October 15, 1981, age 45
See Death Lite.

Ritchie Valens, died February 3, 1959, age 17
See The Day the Music Died: The First Death of Rock 'n' Roll.

Helicopter Accidents

Bill Graham, died October 25, 1991, age 60
See Sha Na Na, Inc.: The Second Death of Rock 'n' Roll.

Stevie Ray Vaughan, died August 27, 1990, age 35
See Guitar Heroes.

Heart Attack on an Airplane

Albert Grossman, died January 25, 1986, age 59
See Sha Na Na, Inc.: The Second Death of Rock 'n' Roll.

13

Just Us Dead Folk

THE HOARIEST aspects of folk music—that is, music made by the working or lower classes to amuse and express themselves—predate everything in this book except death. The direct impact of folk music on rock 'n' roll has been felt only dimly, and mainly second-hand, through folk's influence on country music and reggae, and, in recent years, in the art-damaged inflections of postpunk avatars (such as Talking Heads' David Byrne) gobbling culture wherever they find it.

The kind of neo-troubador songody in vogue in the late fifties, using plaintive warbling or vocal harmonies accompanied by acoustic guitar in the service of a set of received political attitudes, is very far from being authentic folk music. The fifties variety often presented itself in opposition to rock 'n' roll: authentic instead of calculated, sincere instead of phony, thoughtful instead of hedonistic, compassionate instead of cynical, involved instead of self-serving, sensitive instead of brutal. That is all nonsense, of course. The fact is that rock 'n' roll *is* folk music—and a good case can be made that all crimes charged against rock 'n' roll can also be leveled at contemporary folk music, which as we understand it now should really be termed "singer/songwriter music."

Certainly much singer/songwriter music has been phony, calculated, and cynical from the beginning, parading a remarkable series of self-serving self-deceptions. Consider the Kingston Trio and all who followed in their image. Or, more specifically, go figure the connection between the Weavers, who unearthed "Wimoweh," and the South African Zulu culture that produced the song. Personally, I will take the Tokens' "The Lion Sleeps Tonight" any day, or, even better, Brian Eno's later cover of the Tokens—even acknowledging that neither would have happened without the Weavers. At least the Tokens and Eno implicitly concede their distance from the source of the song. Sadly enough, alienation and distance remain for the most part a lot more convincing than cross-cultural embraces (a situation equally true of the fifties, when the Cold War was at its height and the civil rights movement was just beginning). One of the great strengths of rock 'n' roll is that it expresses the experience of alienation and distance so immediately and intimately.

Most of the squabbles between devotees of rock 'n' roll and singer/songwriter music have found their focus in one person, now a totem—Bob Dylan—who has stayed remarkably free of death and its obsessions throughout his long, checkered career. (In this context, I don't count the mid-life crisis represented by Dylan's Christian period, which was closer to the self-pity everyone privileged enough to reach their forties may be allowed to indulge than a genuine fascination with death.) Van Morrison and Neil Young serve nearly as well as Dylan as markers in this battle. Many (notably Christians) have tried to claim them, but in the end they belong most of all to the singer/songwriter tradition, which is otherwise all too often destitute of their fury, vision, and intuitive intelligence.

Their legacy—particularly Dylan's, inherited from Woody Guthrie and Pete Seeger—remains among the most vital aspects of the best singer/songwriters: respecting, adhering to, *reclaiming* rather than reviling their American and European sources, and understanding that most contradictions residing therein come from conditions imposed by life, not by some flaw of political structure that may or may not be solved by paying obeisance to others. It is a legacy that continues as a significant stream of postpunk today in such derivations as Billy Bragg and the Mekons.

Just about everybody on the list below picked up a guitar and strummed it, or at least loved that sound, citing "authenticity" as a prevailing, overriding concern. They did admirable battle with phoniness. Some were wildly successful (often paradoxically taken as a sign in itself of phoniness—see the reaction to Dylan's switch to rock in the mid-sixties). Most of them, though not all of them, were not phony. Now that they are dead, let us sort them out.

Moses Asch, died October 19, 1986

Record company executive, formed Folkways in 1948. The roster at Folkways at one time or another included Leadbelly, Woody Guthrie, Pete Seeger, Burl Ives, Josh White, Mississippi John Hurt, Brownie McGhee and Sonny Terry, the Carter Family, Blind Lemon Jefferson, and many more. Dedicated to keeping the music available, Asch saw to it that albums by his artists stayed in print. After his death Folkways' responsibilities were, appropriately, assumed by the Smithsonian Institution.

Joe Bauer, died 1985, age 43
Drummer, with the Youngbloods; from Memphis. Bauer was a jazz drummer looking for work in Boston in 1965 when he hooked up with singer/songwriter Jesse Colin Young (born Perry Miller—really), whose sensibility gave the world "Get Together." The song, released in 1967, was not a hit until picked up for a TV public service announcement and subsequently re-released in 1969, when it reached number 5. Young eventually went solo and Bauer faded into obscurity.

David Blue, died December 2, 1982, age 41
Singer/songwriter; from New York. Known primarily for his friendship with Bob Dylan, Blue did have his partisans. The Eagles covered his "Outlaw Man" and many sat in with him, including Graham Nash, Dave Mason, and Glenn Frey. In the mid-seventies he toured with Dylan's Rolling Thunder Revue. He died of a heart attack while jogging.

Jacques Brel, died October 9, 1978, age 49
Singer/songwriter; from Brussels, Belgium. Much loved in New York, Brel wrote dozens of sensitive songs covered by many, including "I'm Not Afraid" (Frank Sinatra), "If You Go Away" (Ray Charles, Dusty Springfield), and others; on some, English lyrics were supplied by Rod McKuen. One Brel song, "Le Moribund" ("The Dying Man"), was first recorded by the Kingston Trio in 1964. Ten years later Terry Jacks took a version of it to number 1 as the sing-songy death-fixated "Seasons in the Sun." Four years after that Brel died of cancer, kind of like in the song.

Big Bill Broonzy, died August 15, 1958, age 60
Bluesman; from Scott, Mississippi. In 1939 Big Bill Broonzy appeared at John Hammond's Spirituals to Swing Concert at Carnegie Hall when Robert Johnson could not make it, due to his death (don't talk to me about Buddy Holly and Bobby Vee). Folk fans loved Broonzy, and so did Elvis Presley. He appeared often with Pete Seeger and Brownie McGhee and Sonny Terry, though he never made a living from his music until he was over fifty. He died of cancer.

Tim Buckley, died June 29, 1975, age 28
Singer/songwriter; from Washington, D.C. Though he never quite went over the top, Buckley exuded promise and always seemed to have a contract with one record company or another. He recorded more than half a dozen albums all told, some of them (such as 1972's *Greetings from L.A.*) a marked departure from typical singer/songwriter fare. The most successful

was 1967's *Goodbye and Hello*, which found its way into the top twenty albums chart. Almost a cliché "free spirit," Buckley experimented with jazz, Swahili lyrics, funk, and more, but always displayed a knack for solid song structure. He died of an accidental opiate overdose (thinking it was cocaine).

Chan Daniels, died August 2, 1975, age 35

Baritone singer, with the Highwaymen; from Brazil. The folk-harmony quintet the Highwaymen, masterminded by Dave Fisher, took the nineteenth-century slave song "Michael" to number 1 in 1961, followed it with the 1962 number 13 "Cottonfields," and then hung it up in 1963. Both, particularly "Michael," became favorites of church youth groups everywhere, along with "Kumbaya, My Lord" and "Marching to Pretoria." Thank you, Highwaymen. Typical of their time, they came on all Ivy League, with frosh harmonies, matching suits, and hair clipped short. The whole group belonged to the same fraternity at Wesleyan. After the group broke up and Daniels finished college, he landed a job with MGM. He died of pneumonia.

Nick Drake, died November 25, 1974, age 26

Singer/songwriter; from Burma. Nick Drake emerged out of the British folk revival scene of the late sixties, discovered and encouraged by John Martyn and members of Fairport Convention. He never had anything close to a hit, but anyone who has heard any of the haunted, possessed material he recorded on three albums for Island does not soon forget him: his aching voice, his spare instrumentation, the urgency of even his most lethargic songs. It was like Leonard Cohen with a heart and a tenor voice. Drake was a recluse with evident personal problems. He increasingly insulated himself from the world until finally he recorded his third album, *Pink Moon*, entirely by himself in 1972 and mailed in the tapes rather than deliver them personally. Then he entered a psychiatric rest home and announced his retirement from music. In 1973 he found work as a computer programmer but he never stopped writing and recording his music. He died in bed at his parents' home of an overdose of antidepressant medication. Suicide seems likely, but has been denied by family and friends.

Mama Cass Elliot, died July 29, 1974, age 32

Singer, born Ellen Naomi Cohen, nicknamed Cassandra by her father, with the Mamas and the Papas, solo; from Baltimore. Mama Cass Elliot was the big voice of the Mamas and the Papas, the Los Angeles harmony group built from transplanted Greenwich Village folkies and classed folk-rock for their amplified backing. Starting in 1966 they enjoyed an impressive eighteen-month run of hits: "California Dreamin'," "I Saw Her Again" (obliquely detailing infidelities within the group), a remake of the Shirelles' "Dedicated to the One I Love," and many others, most written by Papa John Phillips. Drug addiction, divorce, and label disputes got the best of them; then the public suddenly lost interest completely—the Mamas and the Papas were already attempting to stage "reunion comebacks" by 1970. Elliot went solo in 1968, scoring with "Dream a Little Dream of Me"; she went on to bomb in Vegas, then repaired to Europe where she found greater acceptance. The screamingly funny rumor has long persisted that she died choking on a ham sandwich. It probably stems from her chronic weight problem and native Judaism, coupled with the approved vomit-choke rock star exit, then in vogue. Actually, she had a heart attack, in the same hotel suite from which Keith Moon would pass out of this world four years later.

Fairport Convention
Formed 1966, in London. Traditionalists Fairport Convention made an indelible impression on the British folk movement and on rock players on both continents. Members fluctuated constantly (you need a program and visual aids to chart it all; see Pete Frame), but included Ian Matthews, who hit in 1971 with a cover of Joni Mitchell's "Woodstock" and then again in 1979 with "Shake It," and Richard and Linda Thompson, who together and apart since 1972 have released albums as impressive and influential as anything by their mother group. Folksinger Sandy Denny signed on in 1968 to replace the departing Judy Dyble. Responsible wherever she went for furthering traditional British folk, Denny was perfectly capable of rocking too, as she later proved with Led Zeppelin ("The Battle of Evermore") and others. She fell down the stairs at a friend's house in 1978, after she had already been in and out of Fairport Convention two or three times, and died from a brain hemorrhage, aged thirty-one. Martin Lamble, who showed up at the group's first gig in 1967 and won the job of drummer by demanding it, was killed in an auto accident in 1969, aged twenty. Surviving members (there are many of them) periodically regroup for yet another hurrah.

Richard Fariña, died April 30, 1966, age 29
Singer/songwriter, novelist; from New York. Fariña spent many years in a folk duo with his wife Mimi, the younger sister of Joan Baez. The two were among the first, on *Reflections in a Crystal Wind*, to heavy up with a rock rhythm section. Close friends with Thomas Pynchon, Fariña is probably best remembered for the novel *Been Down So Long It Looks Like Up*

to Me. He died in a motorcycle accident on the way home from a promotional party for the book, on Mimi's twenty-first birthday.

Dave Guard, died March 22, 1991, age 56
Singer, banjo player, with the Kingston Trio; from San Francisco. Dave Guard was an original member of the Kingston Trio, perhaps the most commercially successful of all the fifties folk groups with their "Tom Dooley," which went to number 1 in 1958, and very steady album sales. Sometimes wrongly pegged as originators of the folk movement, at least they were the source of its collegiate image. Guard left for a largely unsuccessful solo career in 1961 and was replaced by John Stewart. Guard eventually died of lymphoma.

Woody Guthrie, died October 3, 1967, age 55
Singer/songwriter; from Okemah, Oklahoma. Woody Guthrie was a genuine giant of folk music and among the most significant artists of the century, contributing the vastly misunderstood "This Land Is Your Land" along with "talkin' blues," a style uniquely adapted to a radical political stance in the United States, masking earnestness with irony. Nobody missed the point, however, and thanks to anticommunist hysteria in the fifties, Guthrie became an illicit commodity. But his influence was already evident in Bob Dylan, whose "Talkin' New York" upped Guthrie's ante and then some; Dylan was destined to move light-years beyond even that with a series of songs laconically designated "dreams." Guthrie died of Huntington's disease, a degenerative disorder of the nervous system.

Tim Hardin, died December 29, 1980, age 39
Singer/songwriter; from Eugene, Oregon. Bob Dylan once called Tim Hardin the country's greatest living songwriter, shortly before renaming his ancestor (nineteenth-century outlaw John Wesley Hardin) on his 1968 album *John Wesley Harding.* Hardin is best remembered now for writing "If I Were a Carpenter," covered by the Four Tops, Johnny Cash and June Carter, and Bobby Darin; he also wrote "Reason to Believe," "Misty Roses," and many more. He died of a heroin overdose.

Lee Hays, died August 26, 1981, age 67
Bass singer, songwriter, cofounded the Weavers; from Little Rock, Arkansas. Lee Hays and Pete Seeger formed the original Weavers in 1948, convinced that folk music could be commercially successful. They were right and proved it in 1950 with "On Top of Old Smokey" and "Good Night, Irene." But anticommunist hysteria and blacklisting forced the

group to disband in 1952. They regrouped in 1955, however, and continued what they'd started, playing an influential role among singer/songwriters mostly by writing hits for others, including "Kisses Sweeter than Wine," which went to number 3 in 1957 for the pop Jimmie Rodgers, and "If I Had a Hammer," which went to number 10 in 1962 for Peter, Paul and Mary, and number 3 in 1963 for Trini Lopez. Hays died of a heart attack, shortly after the Weavers regrouped one more time for the occasion of a PBS documentary about them.

Leadbelly, died December 6, 1949, age 60
Bluesman, born Huddie Ledbetter; from Mooringsport, Louisiana. Raised in Texas, Leadbelly was a violent man but a gifted twelve-string guitar player and songwriter, and a hero to followers of fifties folk. He contributed some of their most characteristic songs: "Good Night, Irene," "The Rock Island Line," "The Midnight Special," and others. He played with Blind Lemon Jefferson for a time in Dallas, and then, often in trouble for fighting, assaulting men and women alike, he was sent to prison for seven years in Texas in 1916 for murder. He was released when he played a song for visiting Texas Governor Pat Neff, who granted him a pardon. In prison again in Louisiana in 1932 for assault, he met folklorists John and Alan Lomax, who recorded him, vouched for him, and, sure enough, got Louisiana Governor O.K. Allen to commute the sentence. Leadbelly then moved north to New York and his career took off, though those around him remained wary of him. In the late thirties he spent time in prison again for assault, this time in New York. But by this time he was tight with Woody Guthrie and Pete Seeger, and the beginnings of singer/songwriter music were underway in earnest. Leadbelly died of amyotrophic lateral sclerosis (Lou Gehrig's disease).

Phil Ochs, died April 9, 1976, age 35
Singer/songwriter. Phil Ochs was born in Texas, raised in Queens, attended military school (like all the men in his family), studied journalism at Ohio State, and moved to Greenwich Village in 1961. Perhaps even more than Bob Dylan, Phil Ochs was the prototypical angry sixties folksinger, getting over chiefly on bravado and attitude despite basically weak, obvious material. He was frequently compared with Dylan, but never accomplished anything close to Dylan's level, though he never stopped trying. His 1971 album *Gunfight at Carnegie Hall* showed Ochs in gold lamé and trumpeted "50 Phil Ochs Fans Can't Be Wrong." Even the boos and catcalls from the concert were included. Prone to depression and bothered by physical trou-

bles, including damage to his vocal cords after being assaulted in Africa, he finally hanged himself.

Lynne Taylor, died 1982

Singer, with the Rooftop Singers; from New York. Taylor was the female vocalist in former Weaver Erik Darling's early sixties trio the Rooftop Singers, whose beatnicky "Walk Right In" went to number 1 in 1963, the biggest hit ever for the Vanguard label. But that was about it for the group. Taylor's background was as a jazz singer with Tommy Dorsey and Benny Goodman, though she spent many years singing with Darling.

Sonny Terry, died March 12, 1986, age 74

Bluesman; from Greensboro, North Carolina. Like Leadbelly and Big Bill Broonzy, Terry was a bluesman who won favor among fifties folk followers. He played John Hammond's Spirituals to Swing Concert in 1938, but didn't break through in any significant way until 1950, when he played a memorial for Leadbelly with Brownie McGhee. He performed continually, with McGhee and solo, until his death.

Faces of Death 10:
Cancer

Jacques Brel, died October 9, 1978, age 49
See Just Us Dead Folk.

Wynonie Harris, died June 14, 1969, age 54
See Little Elvis Deaths.

Corinthian "Kripp" Johnson, died June 22, 1990, age 57
See Death's Ululating Maw: Vocal Group Deaths.

Smiley Lewis, died October 7, 1966, age 46
See Necro-Orleans.

Bob Marley, died May 11, 1981, age 36
See Death inna Babylon.

Murray the K, died February 21, 1982, age 60
See Beatles Bugouts.

Minnie Riperton, died July 12, 1979, age 31
See Super Dead.

Steve Wahrer, died January 21, 1989, age 47
See Last Laughs: Novelty Artists.

Mary Wells, died July 26, 1992, age 49
See The Motown Morgue.

14

Oozing Crooners

CROONING HAS little to do with rock 'n' roll, in which vocal styles tend to be either self-invented, such as Elvis Presley's and Little Richard's, or draw on sources like the blues shout, honky-tonk country yellers, gospel's call-and-response, or various jazz inflections. Perhaps the closest musical ties crooning has to rock 'n' roll came with the onslaught of teen idols in the late fifties and early sixties. Such singers as Paul Anka, Ricky Nelson, and the many Bobby's (Vee, Vinton, Rydell, Darin) gently warbled what are sometimes called "rockaballads," while the music industry desperately tried to pacify outraged parents and still make a buck off the kids.

Originating with Bing Crosby and carried forward by Frank Sinatra, Tony Bennett, and a host more, crooning is a singing style that emerged from jazz, anticipating and then coexisting with lounge music, that slithery favorite of the cynical. Like rock 'n' roll, it was sped by technology— crooners relied on the microphone as rock 'n' roll did on the electric guitar. Yet if the two styles share little else, the impulse to croon and the appreciation of it remains a common feature of many rock 'n' roll figures. Elvis Presley admired Dean Martin above all others. Chuck Berry has said he wants to retire to heaven with only Nat King Cole records. And Marvin Gaye spent nearly twenty years chasing the dream of wowing a supper-club audience (while Sam Cooke and Smokey Robinson actually realized it).

Crooning has never been as fixed on youth as rock 'n' roll; instead it's a soundtrack for the soft and easy life of Cadillacs and graceful aging. Yet many of the people below died young. Perhaps it underlines their peripheral involvement with rock 'n' roll.

Brook Benton, died April 9, 1988, age 56
Soul, songwriter; from Camden, South Carolina. As a songwriter, Benton had a hand in writing "The Stroll" for Chuck Willis and "A Lover's Ques-

tion" for Clyde McPhatter. As a tuxed-up singer in the early sixties, he scored a series of hard-edged easy-listening pop hits, including impressive duets with Dinah Washington. In many ways his duets with her anticipated the suave cool and angular poise of Marvin Gaye's duets with Mary Wells, Kim Weston, and Tammi Terrell. One last glorious gasp came for Benton in 1970 with the haunting number 4 "Rainy Night in Georgia," and then he wanly retired to the supper-club circuit. He died from complications of spinal meningitis.

Nat King Cole, died February 15, 1965, age 47
Jazz, piano player; from Montgomery, Alabama. The smoothie for all time launched pop hit after pop hit in the fifties and early sixties, but was largely shunned by hipsters as an effete supper-club balladeer (for reasons why, hear the 1962 number 2 "Ramblin' Rose," among many others). Yet especially in the forties, when he played with small groups, Cole stayed close to his blues and jazz sources, transforming them into something brilliant and hard with his unique, sensitive phrasing and absolute poise. If he finally sank into tepid gestures, and he did, Ray Charles and Sam Cooke still needed what he gave the world. He died of lung cancer.

Bobby Darin, died December 20, 1973, age 37
Pop; from the Bronx. At times a Vegas staple, at others a Big Sur recluse, Bobby Darin was among the first and most versatile of the teen idols; certainly he was the most arrogant, claiming he'd be bigger than Sinatra by the time he was twenty-five. But give him credit: lounging up a Weill-Brecht number about a street assassin—the 1959 number 1 "Mack the Knife"—is no hapless goof; compare Morris Albert's "Feelings" for how densely humorless great lounge can become. Besides that, Darin also delivered credible rock 'n' roll ("Splish Splash," which went to number 8 in 1958) and, later, singer/songwriter fare (Tim Hardin's "If I Were a Carpenter," which also went to number 8, in 1966). He died of long-standing heart troubles.

Mark Dinning, died March 22, 1986, age 52
Pop; from Drury, Oklahoma. Dinning inaugurated the early sixties spate of limb-rending teen-death hits with the 1960 number 1 "Teen Angel," a pathetic tale of a girl who, trying to retrieve her boyfriend's high school ring from her car stalled on the railroad tracks, is crushed by a train. Mark was the youngest sibling in a family that also produced the Dinning Sisters (who were big in the forties with "Buttons and Bows" and similar fare). But after "Teen Angel," he never hit again and gradually shifted to the lounge circuit and boozing. He died of a heart attack.

Tommy Edwards, died October 23, 1969, age 47
Pop, songwriter; from Richmond, Virginia. Edwards wrote the jumpin'
"That Chick's Too Young to Fry," which Louis Jordan took to number 3
in 1946 on the "race" chart. Then, in the early fifties, Edwards changed
gears and went schmaltz with "Morning Side of the Mountain" and a saccharine "It's All in the Game." Then he floundered until the 1958 remake
of "It's All in the Game," which was big and suave and harder edged, and
went to number 1 for six weeks. He had a handful of top thirty hits after
that, then fell into obscurity. The circumstances of his death are not known.
   (For fans of fun-nee coincidences, there's another dead guy named
Tommy Edwards worth noting in passing. He died in 1981, age fifty-three,
a white DJ from Milwaukee who reached the lower echelons of the pop
charts in 1957 with embarrassing narrative shtick aimed at concerned
parents—first "What Is a Teenage Girl," and then the inevitable "What Is
a Teenage Boy." He died of an aneurysm.)

Janet Ertel, died November 22, 1988
Barbershop, with the Chordettes; from Sheboygan, Wisconsin. The sickly-
sweet Chordettes, a kind of Andrews Sisters hangover, tried but failed mis-
erably to adjust to rock 'n' roll. Their memorable 1954 "Mister Sandman"
(later covered by Emmylou Harris) was a nice effort, however. Ertel died
of cancer.

Mary Ford, died September 30, 1977, age 51
Country, born Colleen Summer; from Pasadena, California. Ford was the
wife and musical partner of guitar player and musical pioneer Les Paul. Together they enjoyed steady hits during the fifties and early sixties, including
"Vaya Con Dios" and their trademark "How High the Moon," before
separating and divorcing in 1963 after fifteen years of marriage. She died
from diabetes in Los Angeles.

Billy Fury, died January 28, 1983, age 41
British pop, born Ronald Wycherly; from Liverpool. He was part of hustler
Larry Parnes's late fifties British teen-idol stable with Tommy Steele, Marty
Wilde, Vince Eager, Dickie Pride, Johnny Gentle (get the point?). Billy
Fury, perhaps the best of them, rocked hard as a rockabilly act until he was
abandoned by his band (led by Georgie Fame), in search of their own pop
grail. Fury then simply warbled on, sadly but successfully, through the mid-
sixties. When his star set, he retired. He made a cameo as Stormy Tempest
in *That'll Be the Day* (1973) with David Essex. He died of heart disease.

Marvin Gaye, died April 1, 1984, age 44
See The Motown Morgue.

Earl Grant, died June 11, 1970, age 38
Pop, keyboardist; from Oklahoma City. The similarity of Earl Grant's voice to Nat King Cole's gave rise to the rumor that he was Cole's brother, but he wasn't. He was just a guy who liked to play the organ and sing. His biggest hit was the nice and easy "The End," which went to number 7 in 1958. His own end was not nearly as gentle—he died on his way home from an engagement in Mexico when his Rolls Royce crashed.

Roy Hamilton, died July 20, 1969, age 40
Gospel; from Leesburg, Georgia. Perhaps Hamilton's greatest contribution was simply in catching the ears of Jerry Butler and Phil Spector—his rich, solemn sound paved the way for Jerry Butler's operatic "For Your Precious Love," and his biggest hit was "Unchained Melody," which became the best-selling rhythm and blues record of 1955, but was more successful on the pop chart as covered by Les Baxter and Al Hibbler. Then, ten years later, Phil Spector and the Righteous Brothers got a hold of it, taking it to number 4 in 1965 and into the top twenty again in 1990 (because it was featured in the movie *Ghost*). Hamilton died of a stroke and a heart attack the day that men first walked on the moon.

Ricky Nelson, died December 31, 1985, age 45
Pop singer; from Hollywood, California. Perhaps the first calculatedly parent-safe teen idol, Nelson (under the direction of his father Ozzie) emphasized the boyishly safe elements of Elvis Presley and scored steady hits with only the faintest vocal presence through 1964, thanks in large part to the built-in promotional opportunities afforded by the long-running "Ozzie and Harriet" TV show. He loved rockabilly and country music but, ever the good son, tended to do as he was told. Thus the warbling dreck: "Young Emotions," "Teen Age Idol," etc., though some of it was not bad ("Lonesome Town") and certainly some of it rocked ("Believe What You Say," "Waitin' in School"). Most of it sold well anyway, until the show was canceled, upon which Nelson nosedived. For his country-rock phase he evinced respectable instincts in musicians, hiring James Burton (later with Elvis Presley, still later with Jerry Lee Lewis) for the early years, and Clarence White (later with the Byrds, he died in 1973, aged twenty-nine, in a hit-and-run accident while loading equipment after a show with his own band, the Kentucky Colonels) and Randy Meisner (later with the Eagles). But Ricky's lack of focus and passive-aggressive resistance to the advice of others (no

doubt a delayed reaction to his father's iron control of his career in its earliest stages) caused him endless problems. Drugs and profound money troubles hounded his last years. He died when his airplane caught fire in mid-flight. The craft was formerly owned by Jerry Lee Lewis who sold it because of its continual problems. Contrary to rumors, the fire had nothing to do with free-basing. Nearly all on board were killed.

The Platters
Vocal group; from Los Angeles. The Platters are frequently lumped in with vocal group rock 'n' roll but listen to them: "Only You (And You Alone)," "The Great Pretender," "Smoke Gets in Your Eyes." Does that sound like a rhythm and blues derivation? No, it's pure fifties pop, put over resoundingly by the impressive, resilient operatic voice of lead singer Tony Williams, who died in 1992, aged sixty-four. Manager Buck Ram got them signed to Mercury in 1955 only as a condition of the Penguins signing, making the then-unknown Platters' signing one of the great flukes of pop. Ram was also managing the group that gave us "Earth Angel" (and only "Earth Angel") at the time. He died in 1991, aged eighty-three. Original tenor David Lynch died in 1981, aged fifty-one. Original baritone Paul Robi died in 1989.

Elvis Presley, died August 16, 1977, age 42
See The Big Elvis.

Johnnie Ray, died February 25, 1990, age 63
Pop; from Rosebud, Oregon. Johnnie Ray heralded a whole new era in 1951 with a rhythm and blues-inflected style he picked up courtesy of LaVern Baker and her manager. His breakthrough hit "Cry" stayed at number 1 on the pop charts for eleven weeks—when he sang it, he did, like clockwork. (The song was produced by Mitch Miller, the self-proclaimed enemy of rock 'n' roll, with backing from the Four Lads.) The emotional style Ray brought to crooning turned out to be no novelty, but a lasting contribution. Ray himself, however, was not particularly lasting. The hits dried up for him in the late fifties. He died of liver failure.

Billy Stewart, died January 17, 1970
Scat; from Washington, D.C. Originally discovered by Bo Diddley, with whom he sang for a couple of years, Billy Stewart has been called rock 'n' roll's only scat singer and it's true enough. His vocal gyrations are obvious on his biggest hit, a blistering version of Gershwin's "Summertime" that went to number 10 in 1966. The song was a fruitful collaboration with ar-

ranger Billy Davis, who used similar orchestration strategies on hits with Etta James, Fontella Bass, and others. Stewart and two members of his band died in an auto accident in North Carolina.

Dinah Washington, died December 14, 1963, age 39

Rhythm and blues, born Ruth Jones; from Tuscaloosa, Alabama. She was known as "Queen of the Harlem Blues" because her rich, complex sound—embracing elements of jazz, blues, gospel, and pop—was closer to New York's uptown soul than the loud brawl of her home-base Chicago rhythm and blues peers. She scored hits on both charts, pop and rhythm and blues, solo and with Brook Benton. She died from complications of alcohol and weight-reduction pills.

Faces of Death 11:
Organ Failure

Tennessee Ernie Ford, died October 16, 1991, age 72
See Country Corpses.

Stan Getz, died June 6, 1991, age 64
See Blow, Big Man.

Bill Harris, died December 10, 1988, age 63
See Death's Ululating Maw: Vocal Group Deaths.

Eddie Hazel, died December 23, 1992, age 42
See Super Dead.

Howlin' Wolf, died January 10, 1976, age 65
See Tombstone Blues.

Peter Laughner, died June 22, 1977, age 24
See I Wanna Destroy: The Final Death of Rock 'n' Roll.

Clyde McPhatter, died June 13, 1972, age 38
See Twitch and Shout: Rhythm and Blues Deaths.

Memphis Slim, died February 24, 1988, age 72
See Transatlantic Tombstone Blues.

Esther Phillips, died August 7, 1984, age 48
See Twitch and Shout: Rhythm and Blues Deaths.

Johnnie Ray, died February 25, 1990, age 63
See Oozing Crooners.

Chris Wood, died July 12, 1983, age 39
See Blow, Big Man.

15

Imps From Hell

SCREAMIN' JAY HAWKINS, Screamin' Lord Sutch, and Arthur Brown brought madness and cackling flame to rock 'n' roll with broad gestures as demented as they were inspired. All may have been subsequently outmuscled and overshadowed in the early seventies with the coming of Alice Cooper, David Bowie, Genesis, and other major theatrical productions, but that does nothing to obscure their enduring charm. With their calculated presentations of themselves as spawns of the devil, they ludicrously played with the notions of evil and sin for which rock 'n' roll was consistently indicted. None had a morbid bone in his body, but they all sprang like unholy minions out of late-night cable comedies produced in hell, strutting funny toys, weird grimaces, insane laughter, and fire, always fire. They shocked those who would be shocked, and amused the rest. Their moments in the nightclub sun were brief, and then they retired to varying degrees of bitterness, obscurity, and continuing hopes for a comeback.

Of them, Screamin' Jay Hawkins was the first to win attention, in 1955. A former boxer, he came from Cleveland, Ohio, and wrote ludicrous songs about voodoo and liquor, delivering them in a black satin bat-wing cape while waving a skull impaled on a stick — or should I say shtick? He was carried to and from the stage in a flaming coffin (which he had to purchase himself after the National Casket Association, claiming he made fun of the dead, prevented his renting them from local funeral parlors). The wondrous "I Put a Spell on You," recorded in a drunken debauch, should have been a hit, but wasn't; the moaning and groaning throughout was just too much for most radio programmers, even after the really wild stuff at the end was edited out. Nor was anything Hawkins ever recorded a hit, despite — or perhaps because of — the comically menacing image, which he has never been able to shake. Instead, his powerful baritone and blues-shouter stylings were lost, cast aside in favor of a gimmick. But at least it was a *good* gimmick.

Nor has he given up, though he speaks unhappily of the constrictions imposed on him. "I wanna do real singing," he told Nick Tosches in the early eighties. "I'm sick of being a monster." In 1981 he opened for the Rolling Stones in Madison Square Garden, but the Stones required that he do the coffin bit and all the rest. Then he mounted a U.S. tour that relied less on bug-eyed preening, but, with his fast and furious references to fur burgers and sliding down fire hydrants made at venues where he did not feel sufficiently appreciated, he brought new definition to misogynistic lewdness. In 1989 he made a fine appearance in Jim Jarmusch's *Mystery Train* (which charted a series of fictional obsessions with Elvis Presley) and he continues to pursue a recording and performing career, to little avail.

Screamin' Lord Sutch was next up. In Britain in 1958 he formed his band the Savages, a rotating constellation that has included Jeff Beck, Nicky Hopkins, and Jimmy Page. Sutch also was carried to the stage in a coffin, but his was not aflame. He meant to scare teens with a sort of Jack the Ripper thing, but kept it all relatively tame, even camp, wearing a toilet seat for a hat, ha ha. (Satan himself must have blushed.) When Sutch's former mates became stars they lent him a hand with the 1970 album *Lord Sutch and Heavy Friends,* but it never did much and he is now largely a forgotten figure.

Arthur Brown came along in the late sixties to write finis to this whole silly bit of business. But Brown, another Britisher, put a fine exclamation point to it with his group the Crazy World of Arthur Brown and his 1968 number 2 hit "Fire," which opened with a provocative roar: "I am the god of hellfire and I bring you—*fire!*" On his head, in performance, he wore a helmet that was ignited. It was a lovely thing, far better than a toilet seat. Brown hasn't gone away yet. Discovered originally by Pete Townshend, he continued to record albums into the eighties, some of them misfired rock theatrics, others forays into experimental electronics. There is frequently talk of what he may do next and with whom, and some of the names that have come up in connection with his include Robert Fripp, Peter Gabriel, King Sunny Ade, Jack Bruce, and Alan Parsons. He appeared in Ken Russell's *Tommy* (1975) as the priest, and now he lives in Austin, Texas, where he runs a small carpentry and house-painting business with Jimmy Carl Black, formerly of the Mothers of Invention.

Faces of Death 12: Hangings

Badfinger
See Beatles Bugouts.

Ian Curtis, died May 18, 1980, age 23
See I Wanna Destroy: The Final Death of Rock 'n' Roll.

Richard Manuel, died March 4, 1986, age 42
See Sha Na Na, Inc.: The Second Death of Rock 'n' Roll.

Phil Ochs, died April 9, 1976, age 35
See Just Us Dead Folk.

16

Bustin' Glass and the Pompadour: James Dean's Enduring Moment of Death

J AMES DEAN was a method actor who made three movies in the mid-fifties. In *East of Eden* and *Rebel Without a Cause* his smoldering style, à la Marlon Brando, gave definition to the teen angst that was about to overtake popular culture. The characters he played were troubled and inarticulate, as much as anything the result of filmmakers' pretentious preoccupations at the time with heavy psychoanalytic undercurrents. But they were nonetheless raw and powerful characters who tapped an uncharted part of the American psyche, thanks largely to Dean's ability to convey them convincingly.

In many ways James Dean gave rock 'n' roll its look: the sneer, the animal poise, the brooding sensuality, the soulful mumble, even the pompadour, for crying out loud, all found their original popular expression in him. If only he could have sung like Elvis Presley . . . (in your dreams—Dean went for cool West Coast jazz). Elvis, one of Dean's greatest fans, spent much of his early movie career begging for parts like Dean's and even talked seriously about starring in a biographical picture about Dean. When he rented Memphis movie theaters for his all-night film fests, a Dean movie was often on the bill.

Comparing the two, it's clear how much Presley was in Dean's debt. His sound was all his own and it was a great and revelatory thing, but it was Dean who put the fine point on his looks and style, making an impact that went far beyond Elvis. It stood as a viable choice of style for teen males well into the sixties, eventually becoming the clichéd "greaser" look and the model for one of Britain's youth movements, the rockers. Most of the males in 1961's *West Side Story* (whose ties to rock 'n' roll are in spirit rather than in music, God knows) were James Dean knock-offs. In the late fifties, when Eddie Cochran seemed a candidate for making the jump to movies, it was mostly because he had the same kind of good looks as Dean.

But it is James Dean's death that turned him into a lasting icon—and not just the fact of his death, but its manner: plowing his Porsche into Donald Gene Turnupseed's Ford Tudor at eighty-six miles an hour in Paso Robles, California, on September 30, 1955, at age twenty-four. James Dean's death turned out to be much more lasting than anything he did in his life.

His tragedy took wings of its own a few years after the fact, finding its purest expression in an adolescent obsession with squealing tires and busting glass that began surfacing in the early sixties in a pop subgenre jokingly called "death-rock." The term designates a series of saccharine pop tunes in which death by motorized vehicle provides the focus, and death itself the reason for existence. It started in 1960 with "Teen Angel," by Mark Dinning. In "Teen Angel" the singer's girlfriend is plowed over by a train. It was a sensation at the time, a number 1 hit banned outright in Britain and suppressed in many regions of the United States.

Others quickly followed, in an avalanche only partly cynical. In the 1964 number 8 "Dead Man's Curve" by Jan and Dean, the singer heads too fast into a nasty stretch of road. In the 1960 number 7 "Tell Laura I Love Her" by Ray Peterson, the singer dies in an auto race mishap, trying to raise funds for an engagement ring. In "Don't Worry, Baby," a top thirty hit for the Beach Boys in 1964, an auto race is again the subject—the singer's chick soothes his fears telling him to cool it, but the story remains ominously open-ended. And in the 1964 number 2 "Last Kiss" by J. Frank Wilson and the Cavaliers, the singer's girlfriend dies in his arms after an auto accident, and he swears to be good (so he can see his baby when he leaves this world—presumably he will see James Dean too).

More songs from the period were also about death. In the rockabilly-inflected "Endless Sleep" by Jody Reynolds, which hit number 5 in 1958, nearly two years before "Teen Angel," the singer contemplates taking his own life after the ocean-walk suicide of his girlfriend. In "Laurie (Strange Things Happen)," a top twenty hit for Dickey Lee in 1965, the singer meets a nice girl who turns out to have died a year earlier, to the day; he later finds the sweater he lent her lying on her grave. In Lee's first and biggest hit, the 1962 number 6 "Patches" (not to be confused with the later hit by Clarence Carter), the singer cannot have the hand of the one he loves because of social inequalities, so he drowns himself in the river that divides their town. These songs are not about violent auto accidents, but are obviously inspired by the taste for death in songs.

Most of these songs were pure pop, studio concoctions fronted by tender warblers and sweetened with strings and turgid backing vocals. The one song most clearly and darkly connected to James Dean's demise, "Leader of the Pack" by the Shangri-La's, was written by popmeisters Jeff Barry and

Ellie Greenwich. But it was hardened into something quick and real by the flinty, choked-up singing of Mary Weiss (crying for fear of the microphone) along with the gothic production of Shadow Morton featuring, among other things, a real live motorcycle. In the song the singer watches her boyfriend—a wayward delinquent, of whom her parents do not approve (the Shangri-La's career-long bread and butter theme)—die when his motorcycle spins out into a truck.

The song went to number 1 in 1964, its overwrought melodrama inspiring the parody "Leader of the Laundromat" by the Detergents. But it was virtually the end of the unconscious pop fixation with James Dean's speed-fueled auto death. The assassination of John Kennedy a year earlier significantly altered the popular conception of sudden, romantic death, replacing climactic extinguishment with haunting conspiracy as the prevailing feature of pop death.

Faces of Death 13:
On the Highways and Byways

Auto Accidents

Chris Bell, died December 27, 1978, age 27
See I Wanna Destroy: The Final Death of Rock 'n' Roll.

Jesse Belvin, died February 6, 1960, age 26
See Death's Ululating Maw: Vocal Group Deaths.

Marc Bolan, died September 16, 1977, age 30
See I Wanna Destroy: The Final Death of Rock 'n' Roll.

D. Boon, died December 23, 1985, age 27
See I Wanna Destroy: The Final Death of Rock 'n' Roll.

Harry Chapin, died July 16, 1981, age 38
See Death Lite.

Eddie Cochran, died April 17, 1960, age 21
See The Day the Music Died: The First Death of Rock 'n' Roll.

James Dean, died September 30, 1955, age 24
See Bustin' Glass and the Pompadour:
James Dean's Enduring Moment of Death.

Johnny Kidd, died October 7, 1966, age 26
See Sha Na Na, Inc.: The Second Death of Rock 'n' Roll.

Jay B. Perkins, died 1958
See Little Elvis Deaths.

David Prater, died April 9, 1988, age 50
See Souls.

Razzle, died December 8, 1984
See Munching the Corpse: The Utter Assurance of Death's Future.

Bessie Smith, died September 26, 1937, age 43
See Tombstone Blues.

Billy Stewart, died January 17, 1970
See Oozing Crooners.

Motorcycle Accidents

Allman Brothers Band
See Sha Na Na, Inc.: The Second Death of Rock 'n' Roll.

Richard Farina, died April 30, 1966, age 29
See Just Us Dead Folk.

17

Pop Anxiety: "Sally, Go 'Round the Roses"

PERHAPS THE first unfathomable mystery in rock 'n' roll was Elvis Presley's "Blue Moon," recorded in 1954 at Memphis's Sun studios, with Sam Phillips producing, and Scotty Moore and Bill Black providing support on guitar and bass. Its dripping-water clip-clop rhythm, its heavy echo on Presley's keening delivery, and its utter hush remain as strangely affecting as lifting one's head to the night sky and seeing UFOs: a confluence of imagination and technology at once transcendent, powerful, and elusive. As vinyl, memory etched as permanent artifact, it is ultimately more dependent on production than performance. Its strangeness has long invited interpretations related to death and the afterlife and other mysteries of the universe.

But it was never a hit of any kind, though it showed up here and there often enough: thrown onto Presley's first album along with other unreleased Sun material; then released as the A-side of a no-hit single in September 1956, a casual afterthought for RCA, busy by then spewing out Elvis product in every direction; it also appeared on an EP that year; and, twenty years later, on the essential *Sun Sessions* album. All who have heard it remember it. Many think it a little weird.

Such is not the case with the Jaynetts' "Sally, Go 'Round the Roses." That was a genuine hit, reaching number 2 for two weeks as school was getting underway and the leaves were turning in 1963. Unlike Presley's "Blue Moon," lost in an oceanic catalog, it was the only significant success for the Jaynetts. And it is not weird—at least not until you hear it often and listen to it closely, as anyone with a radio tuned to the pop stations would have been forced to do that fall. Perhaps most important, it does not come with the unmistakable if implicit assurance, present in practically everything recorded by Presley (even his lonesomest songs) that all is right with the world—a power in Presley's music that is itself one of the great mysteries of rock 'n' roll. No, there is something infinitely more disturbing about the Jaynetts song.

Many collaborated to create it. The Jaynetts themselves were an ever-shifting group of Bronx gals. The song was written by Zell Sanders, who aided and abetted such New York artists as Baby Washington and the Harptones with her independent J&S label. It was produced by Abner Spector (no relation, on this plane, to Phil). Sanders's daughter Johnnie Louise Richardson (of Johnnie and Joe, she died in 1988 of a stroke) was a member of the Jaynetts touring group and involved peripherally in the recording. In interviews she recalled the sessions as gruelling, many long days lasting over a week. Some estimate that the production cost reached nearly $60,000, an astonishing figure for a single at the time.

Spector derived its mushy, ineffable sound by laying down the basic rhythm track on piano and dubbing mono-to-mono, building it one piece at a time with another piano track, then an organ line, and then the bass guitar, all played by arranger Artie Butler. Then drums were added, and then vocals—Richardson guessed twenty singers all told are used on the final mix. Last, echo was overlaid. Generation loss and studio improvising had created a lush, eerie sound that can never be replicated.

But even that is not the real point. The maddening, inescapable question is: What is this song about? Why are these ghostly people singing it? What do they mean by it?

On the face of it, "Sally, Go 'Round the Roses" seems to be a simple enough story, delivered with a sing-song melody and an easy bouncing rhythm, about a girl who has discovered her lover is untrue and now grieves. But the point of view, like much in this song, remains stubbornly unclear; the chorus of singers is decidedly removed from Sally, only telling her to go 'round the roses ("Roses they can't hurt you"—yeah, right) and not to go downtown ("The saddest thing in the whole wide world/Is to see your baby with another girl"). But then, suddenly, Sally has a secret, which the singers promise the roses won't tell. Could it be the shame of her grief? And what is this business about "Let your hair hang down," which the singers urge on Sally? And then the song fades, clocking in at 3:16.

No questions are ever answered but many interpretations beyond its face value have been advanced. Some claim it is Sally's moment of truth about her own homosexuality. Others see in it a suicide scenario. Some believe it recounts an overwhelming spiritual experience of some kind, perhaps one that drives her mad. The achievement of this song is that the ambiguity of its point of view along with its concrete details allow all these interpretations and more to work. And, by achieving it naturally, without self-consciousness, it set a peculiar standard rarely matched, one that carpetbagged intimations of death and its potent terrors into the daylight of pop music, where it could make the skin of a mass audience crawl. It was the beginning of anxiety in pop music.

The closest anyone has come to it since is the Rolling Stones with "Jumpin' Jack Flash," a number 3 hit in 1968, followed by music of similar if diminishing power and orientation over the next three years. (The album track "Street Fightin' Man" stands as the only match of that hit; together they are the group's two stunningly enduring great moments.) In the Stones' case they uncovered the joy and liberation at the heart of evil, rather than the Jaynetts' troubled conscience in innocence. But both songs remain equally mysteriously and forever disturbing.

If the Stones seem nothing but self-consciousness and manipulation, consider the gulf they breached in five months between "She's a Rainbow" and "Jumpin' Jack Flash." The first is effete and calculated, as is much that preceded it, but the latter certainly is not. Film documentaries and interviews attest that the Stones were as shocked as anyone by this turn of events, as does their subsequent inability to live up to it, coupled with their perfect willingness to exploit it. The Jaynetts, at least, had the grace to bow out, leaving behind only furrowed brows with thin sheens of sweat.

18

Last Laughs: Novelty Artists

MOST NOVELTY artists are hardly rock 'n' roll, but their continuing presence on the charts and over broadcast media—AM-radio, FM-radio, and MTV alike—has brought them into close proximity with rock 'n' roll and they are now indelibly associated with it in many ways. It was not just Buddy Holly and Ritchie Valens, after all, who died in that spectacular plane crash in 1959. The Big Bopper went down too. And the link continues even today; it is a mark of distinction, a signal that one has arrived, to be parodied by Weird Al Yankovic. The people listed below, whose work variously elicits groans and guffaws, are all dead now. Don't laugh. It's not funny.

Jim Backus, died July 3, 1989, age 76
Actor; from Cleveland. He was the voice of Mr. Magoo on the cartoon of the same name, and he played Thurston Howell III on TV's "Gilligan's Island." In 1958 he had a top forty hit (barely—it reached number 40) with "Delicious!," a Mr. Magoo romp. He died of pneumonia.

John Belushi, died March 5, 1982, age 33
Comedian, TV and film actor; from Wheaton, Illinois. Belushi stumbled into musical success covering soul chestnuts with Dan Aykroyd in their Blues Brothers goof, originally intended only as a pre-broadcast audience warmer for TV's "Saturday Night Live." Belushi was Jake Blues and Aykroyd was his brother Elwood; their uniform consisted of fedoras, suits, shades, and briefcases. It was all very eighties; the act was taken to astonishing lengths. First they made a movie (to their credit chockfull of real soul stars, including James Brown and Aretha Franklin) and then, incredibly, they toured, backed by Stax-Volt veterans (also to their credit). Belushi died

of a drug overdose in Los Angeles, quickly becoming one of the most widely mourned stars of the time.

The Big Bopper, died February 3, 1959, age 28
DJ, novelty artist, born Jiles Perry Richardson; from Sabine Pass, Texas. The Big Bopper spent most of his career as a DJ, taking the job straight out of high school. But all the while he was writing novelty and country songs, and in 1958 he finally hit with the number 6 "Chantilly Lace," an instantly unforgettable slab of lascivious teen purity. The tune was actually the B-side of something called "The Purple People Eater Meets the Witch-Doctor," a take-off on earlier novelties from that year. Follow-ups were sparse, largely from lack of time, but included writing Johnny Preston's 1960 number 1 "Running Bear," based on a Dove commercial—that's the Bopper himself, along with country singer George Jones, going "oom-pah-pah-pah" on the chorus. For better or worse, the Big Bopper is probably best remembered now for dying in the same plane crash that killed Buddy Holly and Ritchie Valens, after taking the seat given up for him by Waylon Jennings, who was backing Holly at the time.

Walter Brennan, died September 21, 1974, age 80
Actor; from Swampscott, Massachusetts. America's perennial grandpa, Walter Brennan found his voice—that unmistakable quavering whine—by the time he was forty, primarily winning notice (and in the thirties, three Oscars) as a codger in Hollywood westerns. During his stint as Grandpa on TV's "The Real McCoys," Brennan capitalized on his familiarity to record talk-song singles. The most successful was "Old Rivers," a number 5 tear-jerker in 1962. He died of natural causes after a long and full life, as all grandpas worth their phlegmy coughs should.

Dickie Goodman, died November 6, 1989, age 55
Comedy writer, record company executive; from Hewlett, New York. With Bill Buchanan, Goodman invented the so-called break-in record, which features an interviewer whose questions are answered by bits and pieces from pop songs of the day. They had a number 3 hit in 1956 with "The Flying Saucer (Parts 1 and 2)," but legal wranglings followed and mired down subsequent efforts. Goodman did manage to repeat the formula in the seventies with "Energy Crisis '74" and "Mr. Jaws," the latter a number 4 hit. He committed suicide.

Lorne Greene, died September 11, 1987, age 72
Actor; from Ottawa, Canada. He was most famous for playing Pa on TV's

"Bonanza." In 1964, like Walter Brennan making hay while the sun shone on his TV show (and on the Beatles as well), he had a number 1 talk-song hit with the laughably melodramatic "Ringo." He died of a heart attack.

Jim Henson, died May 16, 1990, age 53
Puppeteer; from Greenville, Mississippi. Henson invented the Muppets in the late fifties for a series of TV commercials and appearances on variety shows of the time, including Ed Sullivan and Perry Como. Then, in 1967, he became involved with the Children's Television Workshop, which launched "Sesame Street" in 1969. Henson's characters—Big Bird, the Cookie Monster, Bert and Ernie, Kermit the Frog, Oscar the Grouch, and more—were a key part of the show's success. In 1970 he scored a top twenty hit with the inane "Rubber Duckie," by Ernie (actually, that's Henson's voice singing), and followed it at the end of the decade with another, "Rainbow Connection," by Kermit the Frog. He died of pneumonia.

"Here Comes the Judge"
Based on shtick from TV's late sixties (and now incredibly dated) "Laugh-In," this song was a hit for two artists who went on to die, as we all must: Shorty Long (see The Motown Morgue) and Pigmeat Markham. Pigmeat, born Dewey Markham, from Durham, North Carolina, was a vaudeville performer before making the switch to TV comedy. He died in 1981, aged seventy-five.

Lord Buckley, died 1960, age 55
Stand-up comedian, born Richard Buckley; from California. Never a musician, Buckley's monologues and bits slung around urban hipster lingo in the service of attacking religion and other middle-class conventions long before Lenny Bruce or even the beatniks. Considered an influence on Bob Dylan, Tom Waits, and others. The circumstances of his death are murky.

David Martin, died August 2, 1987, age 50
Bass player, with Sam the Sham and the Pharoahs; from Dallas. With lead singer and general outré figure Domingo Samudio, who was paying his way through college, Martin formed the timeless Sam the Sham and the Pharoahs, who gave us the raving number 2 "Wooly Bully" in 1965 (which he cowrote with Samudio) and the equally ridiculous and compelling number 2 "Lil' Red Riding Hood" in 1966 (not to mention my own favorite, "Ring Dang Doo"). If the hits were novelties, the band proved itself up to rock 'n' roll of the first rank on their albums. Samudio completed college and now works as a street preacher in Memphis. Martin left the group in

1966 over management conflicts, and opened a television and video repair store in Dallas. He died there of a heart attack.

Hugo Montenegro, died February 6, 1981, age 55
Orchestra leader, composer; from New York. Montenegro was not exactly a novelty artist, but where else does he fit? (I swear he belongs somewhere.) He recorded the music for TV's "The Man From U.N.C.L.E.," but struck his real bonanza when RCA gave him the chore of producing the music from Sergio Leone's so-called spaghetti westerns for album release. All had been scored by Ennio Morricone, an Italian iconoclast. Montenegro followed Morricone's lead, albeit in watered down fashion, and turned out the weird but effectively haunting 1968 number 2 "The Good, the Bad and the Ugly." He died of emphysema.

Nervous Norvus, died 1968, age 56
Truck driver, born Jimmy Drake; from Oakland, California. His "Transfusion," which went to number 8 in 1956, stands as one of the first great death-fixated pop novelties. Unfathomably related, like the later so-called death-rock, to James Dean's demise, its deceptively jaunty surface details a horrific auto accident and the subsequent scene in a hospital emergency room: "Pass the claret to me, Barrett," the gasping narrator jovially declaims. "Slip the juice to me, Bruce." And so forth—Paul Simon shamelessly borrowed the trick for his 1976 "50 Ways to Leave Your Lover." The Nervous One followed it up with something called "Ape Call," and then drifted into the unforgiving mists of obscurity.

David Rose, died August 23, 1990, age 80
Orchestra leader, composer; from London. His biggest hit was the would-be bawdy 1962 number 1 "The Stripper," loved by *Playboy* aficionados everywhere. Other claims to fame for Rose include marriages to both Martha Raye and Judy Garland, and scoring such TV shows as "Bonanza." He died of heart disease.

Jack Ross, died December 16, 1982, age 66
Orchestra leader, trumpet player. His sole hit was "Cinderella," a top twenty hit in 1962—more hipster lingo out of the mold of Lord Buckley, this time working as ironic enhancement and commentary on the glass-slipper-and-ugly-sisters fairy tale.

David Seville, died January 16, 1972, age 52
Songwriter, producer, born Ross Bagdasarian; from Fresno, California.

We have Seville to thank and to loathe for one of the classic, and simplest, novelty gimmicks of the rock 'n' roll era: Alvin and the Chipmunks, that trio of adorable "fun-nee aminals" who basked in the limelight of cartoon TV as well as landing consistently on the pop charts for a few years. Even before the Chipmunks came the technique: playing back voices faster than they were recorded, which was pioneered by Seville on the unforgettable "Witch Doctor," a number 1 hit in 1958 (everybody now: "oo-ee, oo-ah-ah, ting-tang, walla walla bing-bang"). Seville's first foray into concocting number 1 hits had been a collaboration early in that decade with his cousin, literary lion William Saroyan, for Rosemary Clooney's "Come on-a My House." But it's his work as the Chipmunks—Alvin (who constantly misbe-haved and drove "Dave" crazy), Theodore, and Simon, named for execu-tives at Liberty—that catapulted Seville to his greatest successes. "The Chipmunk Song," a Christmas novelty, also went number 1 in 1958, and a few months later the follow-up, "Alvin's Harmonica," peaked at number 3. A series of follow-ups kept the rodents in the public eye until 1961, when CBS premiered "The Alvin Show" on Saturday morning TV; it ran a single full season, then went into reruns for three years. By the mid-sixties, how-ever, Seville was through with the Chipmunks and wanted to be considered a serious songwriter rather than a novelty artist. It never happened. He died of a heart attack.

The Chipmunks survived him. In 1980 an East Coast radio station began playing Blondie's "Call Me" at fast speed, announcing jokingly that it was the Chipmunks. Requests poured in for more. Seville's son, Ross Bagdasar-ian, Jr., along with Junior's wife, Janice Karman, recorded an album, *Chip-munk Punk,* which covered songs by Blondie, the Cars, Tom Petty, the Knack, and more. It was an unqualified smash, outselling most of the mate-rial it covered. Follow-up efforts and a revival of the TV show ensued. Ten years after Seville's death, Alvin and the Chipmunks were more successful than ever.

Allan Sherman, died November 21, 1973, age 48
Comedy writer, TV producer, born Allan Copelon; from Chicago. He scored big with the 1963 number 2 "Hello Muddah, Hello Fadduh! (A Let-ter from Camp)." Jewish humor straight out of *Mad* magazine, it was the kind of thing grade schoolers had a passion for, as was most of the material on his brace of albums (*My Son, the Folk Singer, My Son, the Nut,* etc.). He was also instrumental in creating the game show "I've Got a Secret," which he produced for six years. He died of respiratory failure.

Steve Wahrer, died January 21, 1989, age 47

Drummer, singer, with the Trashmen; from Minnesota. That's Wahrer's breathy basso profundo growl pushing along the Trashmen's biggest, most uncharacteristic, and practically only hit, the 1964 number 4 "Surfin' Bird." Otherwise the band was a perfectly competent surf group. Ironically enough, Wahrer died of throat cancer.

19

Da Doo Ron Death

IMMEDIATELY AFTER rock 'n' roll had been declawed and defanged in the late fifties, an era of mostly bland teen fare (called "high school" by Nik Cohn) was ushered in. Often castigated as one of the low points in rock 'n' roll history, in fact the early sixties produced much of enduring interest, including soul, Bob Dylan, the Beach Boys, and the rise of Motown. Many of the blatantly commercial trends of the time were not so bad either: girl groups came to prominence then, and the twist and other dances spawned discotheques (more on them later). It was also the time of both Phil Spector's and Roy Orbison's greatest work.

Still, there was something a little lifeless and suffocating about it all, as the Beatles' and other British groups' arrivals made clear in 1964. But call it a fallow period, call it the cyclical nature of reality, call it John Kennedy's extended honeymoon, call it what you want. If rock 'n' roll came primarily from the business centers of New York in the early sixties rather than points south, as it had earlier, much of it—particularly from New York's so-called Brill Building songwriters—soared to spectacular heights almost as often as it sunk to insipid depths. The people below, all of whom have died, are also all associated in one way or another with that time.

Patti Barnes, died January 17, 1989
Singer, with the Poni-Tails; from Lyndhurst, Ohio. Barnes, née McCabe, was with the Poni-Tails for their one big moment, the 1958 number 7 "Born Too Late," a sprightly little thing that anticipated one of those unforgettable teen-idol preoccupations soon to follow: sparkling unrequited teen love suffered in high school hallways and classrooms, delivered with nary a hint of feeling. She died of cancer.

Bert Berns, died December 31, 1967, age 38
Songwriter, producer; from New York. He wrote "Cry to Me" by Solomon
Burke, "Hang On, Sloopy" by the McCoys, "Twist and Shout" by the Isley
Brothers (covered by the Beatles), "Here Comes the Night" by Them (with
Van Morrison), and "Piece of My Heart" by Big Brother and the Holding
Company with Janis Joplin. He produced "A Little Bit of Soap" by the Jar-
mels, "Under the Boardwalk" by the Drifters, and "Baby I'm Yours" by Bar-
bara Lewis. These are only cursory highlights. As a talent scout he was
pretty good too, turning up Lulu, Van Morrison, and Neil Diamond. He
died of a heart attack.

Shirley Brickley, died October 13, 1977, age 32
Lead singer, with the Orlons; from Philadelphia. One of the great overlooked girl groups, the Orlons scored big with the 1962 number 2 "The
Wah Watusi," inaugurating yet another in a seemingly endless series of
dance crazes of the time, no one particularly distinct from any other except
in the subtlest nuances of gesture—but isn't that always the way? Their
other hits include the 1962 number 4 "Don't Hang Up" and the 1963 number 3 "South Street." The British Invasion chilled them in 1964, as it did
so many, though eventually they resurfaced on the oldies circuit. Brickley
was shot to death, but details are scanty beyond that.

Dee Clark, died December 7, 1990, age 52
Singer, born Delectus Clark; from Blytheville, Arkansas. He lobbed a number of hits into the lower reaches of the top forty in the late fifties and early
sixties. His biggest was the sleek, classy 1961 number 2 "Raindrops," after
which he dropped from view. But as a generation we can never forget
"There must be a cloud in my head/Tears keep falling from my eye-eye."
He died of a heart attack.

The Drifters
The Drifters were among the longest lived and most successful of all black
vocal groups in rock 'n' roll, but their story is one of continual personnel
changes—a long and complex story with more than a few odd and ironic
twists. The name survived the departure of the original group's founder and
leader, Clyde McPhatter. Then in the late fifties, manager George Treadwell disbanded what remained of the existing group and hired the Five
Crowns (with lead singer Ben E. King), which he renamed the Drifters to
fulfill contractual obligations to the Apollo Theatre. The Drifters "shifted
gears" at that point from a deft rhythm and blues-steeped vocal group to

an uptown soul ensemble, necessarily because they were a different group but also in large measure due to the contributions of production/songwriting auteurs Jerry Leiber and Mike Stoller. The Drifters' hits over the years included a series of rhythm and blues chart-toppers in the mid-fifties ("Money Honey," "Honey Love," and more), the 1959 number 2 "There Goes My Baby," the 1960 number 1 "Save the Last Dance for Me," and the 1963 number 5 "Up on the Roof." Their deaths include Clyde McPhatter, who died in 1972, aged thirty-eight (see Twitch and Shout: Rhythm and Blues Deaths); Rudy Lewis, who died in 1964, aged twenty-seven (he died on the day of the recording session for "Under the Boardwalk," which, as a result, bears the stamp of a tremendous, ineffable sadness); and manager George Treadwell, who died in 1967.

Leroy Fann, died 1973
Bass singer, with Ruby and the Romantics; from Akron, Ohio. He sang in the quartet originally called the Supremes, who eventually came to back lead singer Ruby Nash. Their producer didn't like the name and changed it. As Ruby and the Romantics, their biggest hit was the smooth 1963 number 1 "Our Day Will Come." They also released "Hey There Lonely Boy" that year, which Eddie Holman took to number 2 in 1970 after switching the gender. Fann was killed, though little else is known of his death.

Marge and Mary Ann Ganser
Singers, twin sisters, with the Shangri-La's; from Queens. The twins, who contributed to the 1964 number 1 definitive death-rock epic "Leader of the Pack," as well as the equally impressive 1964 number 5 "Remember (Walkin' in the Sand)" and my own favorite, the 1965 number 6 "I Can Never Go Home Anymore," have been variously pronounced dead and alive over the years. The most recent sources say Mary Ann died of encephalitis in 1971, and Marge died of a drug overdose at some unspecified time. Whatever their true fates, they were certainly part of one of the great melodramatic acts of the mid-sixties, trading on an image of bad girls who were as sensitive as they were wild, and providing a vital starting point for such figures as Joan Jett, Lita Ford, and the group from which those two had in turn emerged, the Runaways. The Shangri-La's also stand as one of the last great hurrahs of American pop music before the advent of the British Invasion.

Samuel George, died March 17, 1982, age 39
Lead singer, drummer, with the Capitols; from Detroit. The Capitols' only

hit came in 1966, but it was a number 7 monster, "Cool Jerk," whose quick-step style and celebration of a dance harked back to sounds from an earlier (and by then already more innocent) part of the decade. They never came even close to matching that moment of glory. George was killed in a fight.

Micki Harris, died June 10, 1982, age 42
Singer, with the Shirelles; from Passaic, New Jersey. The Shirelles were perhaps the greatest of all the girl groups in the early sixties, with such hits as the 1961 number 1 "Will You Love Me Tomorrow?," the 1961 number 3 "Dedicated to the One I Love," and the 1963 number 4 "Foolish Little Girl"; the Beatles thought they were pretty good too and covered their 1962 number 8 "Baby It's You." But the Shirelles were off the charts by 1964, victims of the British Invasion, though they did carry on into the early eighties, mostly on the oldies circuit. After a show in Atlanta, Harris suffered a massive heart attack and died.

Joe Henderson, died 1966
Singer; from Como, Mississippi. Henderson, raised in Gary, Indiana (home of the Jacksons), hit big in 1962 with the number 8 "Snap Your Fingers," a Brook Benton soundalike. Subsequent releases have become collectors items, but they did little for Henderson at the time. He died an unknown in a Nashville hotel room under mysterious circumstances, which is about all that's known about it.

Barbara Lee Jones, died May 15, 1992, age 48
Singer, with the Chiffons; from the Bronx. Jones was with the Chiffons, one of the great girl groups, for all their big moments, including the 1963 number 1 "He's So Fine," the 1963 number 5 "One Fine Day," and the 1966 number 10 "Sweet Talkin' Guy"—all of them memorably boss, uptempo numbers with sharp soaring harmonies. Though their last hit came as late as 1966, they were also basically put out of commission by the British Invasion. But unlike those who simply accepted their fate, the Chiffons sought revenge, sadly enough to their everlasting discredit (see Beatles Bugouts, under Ronnie Mack). Jones died of a heart attack.

Dean Martin, Jr., died March 21, 1987, age 35
Bass player, with Dino, Desi and Billy; from Beverly Hills, California. The success, such as it was, of Dino, Desi and Billy stemmed from their parent-star connections. Martin was the son of soddenly effervescent Dino, Sr.; Desi was Desi Arnaz IV, the son of Ricky and Lucy Ricardo; Billy Hinsche

was the son of the real estate agent who had sold both families their homes; and the group was signed to Reprise, Warner Brothers' vanity label at the time for Rat Pack MC Frank Sinatra. But the success of the trio never really even compared with, say, that of Gary Lewis, son of Jerry Lewis. They enjoyed just a couple of top thirty hits in late 1965, "I'm a Fool" and "Not the Lovin' Kind," and then faded away. Hinsche went on to became a part of the Beach Boys troupe, playing guitar with them on tour. Arnaz tried his hand at acting. And Martin, who was once married to Olympic skater Dorothy Hamill, enjoyed some success as a tennis pro. He died when his Air National Guard jet went into a hillside.

Joe Meek, died February 3, 1967

Producer, founded the Tornadoes; from England. Something like the Phil Spector of Britain, Meek worked with such mid- and late-fifties British figures as Lonnie Donegan and Tommy Steele, before acquiring and then retiring into his own personal studio. Though not a playing member of the Tornadoes, he organized and produced the group and gave them their biggest hit, the catchy, twerpy surf instrumental "Telstar," which went to number 1 in 1963. As innovative a producer as he was, though, Meek was soon lost in Britain's beat group shuffle and was unable to equal the kind of success he'd enjoyed earlier. The despondent, introverted producer finally shot himself at the control board of his studio, making it a point to do so on the anniversary of Buddy Holly's death.

Hugo Peretti, died May 1, 1986, age 68

Producer, songwriter, with Luigi Creatore as Hugo and Luigi; from New York. As half of Hugo and Luigi, Peretti scored a top forty hit in 1960 as a recording act. But mostly the duo confined themselves to producing, songwriting, and overseeing activities at Roulette, RCA, Avco, and other labels. Their first big success was with the pop Jimmie Rodgers, whom they launched with the number 1 "Honeycomb" in 1957, followed shortly by the top ten "Kisses Sweeter Than Wine" and "Oh-Oh, I'm Falling in Love Again." They went on to write and produce for Sam Cooke, the Isley Brothers, and the Stylistics, but the funny thing is they never seemed to have a real handle on their artists, typically confining them to formulas rather than helping them realize an often amazing potential. Well, they got them onto the charts anyway. Peretti died of a long-standing illness but details are scanty.

Kyu Sakamoto, died August 12, 1985, age 43

Singer; from Japan. An enormously popular singer in Japan, Sakamoto managed, through a quirky set of industry circumstances in 1963, to get the biggest U.S. top forty hit of any Japanese artist to date, the number 1 "Sukiyaki." The haunting if somewhat brittle song, untranslated, tells the sad story of a failed romance. It was rechristened "Sukiyaki" for an utterly inane reason (namely, because that was the British distributor's favorite Japanese dish). As has been pointed out, it's the equivalent of calling "Moon River" "Beef Stew." Sakamoto died in the crash of a Japan Airlines 747, which also killed 519 others.

The Singing Nun, died March 31, 1985, age 52
Singer, songwriter, nun, born Jeanine Deckers; from Belgium. In her Belgian convent of Fichermont Monastery, she was known as Sister Luc-Gabrielle, and to Europeans she was *"Soeur Sourire"* ("Sister Smile"). But in the United States late in 1963, Jeanine Deckers was the Singing Nun. For four weeks she and her sweet warble rode the top of the pop charts with a number 1 hit single, the insanely catchy "Dominique," a paean that Deckers herself had written to the founder of her Dominican order. For a time she was all the rage, appearing on the Ed Sullivan show and watching as a movie of her life, *The Singing Nun* starring Debbie Reynolds, was produced and released in 1966. The movie fizzled, however, as Deckers's career had also by then. In 1967 she left the church and released a kind of pro-choice song about oral contraceptives, "Glory Be to God for the Golden Pill." Then she became involved with a woman named Annie Pescher, with whom she founded a center for autistic children. When the center failed, and the Belgian government began procedures to recover back taxes on Deckers's song earnings (all of which she'd donated to the church), the two grew despondent. In a suicide pact, they killed themselves with an overdose of sleeping pills.

Ben Spector, died April 20, 1949, age 46
Factory worker, father of Phil Spector; from Russia. For reasons still largely unknown, Ben Spector committed suicide by carbon monoxide poisoning. Aside from all the rich conjecture it raises to account for Phil's peculiar insularity and self-protectiveness, Ben's epitaph provided the title for Phil's first hit, "To Know Him Is to Love Him," a number 1 smash in late 1958, which Phil scored with the Teddy Bears, writing and producing it when he was just seventeen.

Roland Trone, died 1982
"Don" of Don and Juan, with Claude Johnson, both formerly of the Genies;

from Brooklyn. Their 1962 number 7 "What's Your Name" was the be-all and do-all of their career together, despite numerous attempts to recapture the magic. Johnson is now on the oldies circuit with a new "Don."

Dennis Wilson, died December 28, 1983, age 39
See Friends: Charles Manson and Dennis Wilson.

Faces of Death 14:
Fell Down

Sandy Denny, died April 21, 1978, age 31
See Just Us Dead Folk (Fairport Convention).

Donny Hathaway, died January 13, 1979, age 33
See Super Dead.

Kit Lambert, died March 8, 1981, age 45
See Who's Dead.

Nico, died July 18, 1988, age 48
See I Wanna Destroy: The Final Death of Rock 'n' Roll.

Larry Palumbo, died 1959, age 18
See Death's Ululating Maw: Vocal Group Deaths.

Trouble T-Roy, died July 15, 1990, age 22
See Munching the Corpse: The Utter Assurance of Death's Future.

20

The Motown Morgue

EVERYTHING ABOUT the Motown label, particularly in its sixties Detroit heyday, boils down to one enormously ambitious, talented man: Berry Gordy III. He wrote and produced much of the material; hand-picked the artists, producers, and songwriters; and personally oversaw nearly every aspect of the business throughout that period and for many years after. He is the explanation for all the puzzling contradictions of a great label that should have been even greater. His vision and patience gave Marvin Gaye and Stevie Wonder the opportunity and the time they needed to grow and develop, but his shortsightedness prevented Gladys Knight, the Spinners, and others from fully realizing their capabilities until after they had left Motown. He watered down black rhythm and blues into what was derisively called "cocktail soul" to make it palatable to the white masses. But he also put some of the canniest, funkiest sounds on the pop charts, insisting always on the dance beat groove above all else. He operated with a formula, but it was a formula for success.

Unfortunately, part of that formula also called for brutal competition and unscrupulous exploitation. The environment at Motown was killing, and not all those who passed through survived particularly well, not even their greatest stars—Diana Ross and Michael Jackson are hardly ideal models of human behavior. The list below contains some of the names of those who did not survive at all. More than one has been unjustly underrated or forgotten, or, even worse, was never known in the first place. Yet for every unsuccessful singer, there is another who owes a great deal to Berry Gordy, and some of these are listed below as well.

Florence Ballard, died February 22, 1976, age 32
Singer, cofounder the Supremes; from Detroit. The Supremes, formed in the late fifties by high school chums in a Detroit housing project, became

the greatest of all the girl groups and the most successful sixties group after the Beatles. They started more as Florence Ballard's group than Diana Ross's, but Motown decided to put the focus on Ross, leaving Ballard among the most tragic victims of the Motown system. In the beginning, Diana (then Diane) Ross supplied the raw ambition; Ballard, a versatile rhythm and blues singer, supplied the lead voice and the name to replace their old one, the "Primettes"; and Mary Wilson contributed the cheery disposition. They signed with Motown in 1960. Berry Gordy footed the bill for charm school and let them develop over four years. His patience was rewarded, starting in 1964, when the Supremes scored five consecutive pop number 1s. For Ballard, however, the group's period of spectacular success was marked by deepening desperation as Motown maneuvered Ross to the fore. In early 1967, "People," the last song in which she sang lead was dropped from the stage act; and later that year, with "Reflections," the group became Diana Ross and the Supremes. Ballard began missing shows, forcing Ross and Wilson to go on as a duo. In response, Motown quietly lined up a replacement for her in Cindy Birdsong, of Patti LaBelle's Bluebelles, and abruptly made the switch late that year. Ballard had effectively been fired from her own group, but there was little she could do about it. Lengthy, futile court battles followed as Ballard's fortunes declined and, eventually, with an ever-worsening drinking problem, she returned to her childhood neighborhood, supporting herself and her children for a time with AFDC. Periodically her outlook brightened during the course of the seventies, but then her opportunities always dimmed again. She died of a heart attack related to her drinking and drug problems.

Benny Benjamin, died 1969

Drummer; from Detroit. Benjamin originally signed on as a session player with Motown for the money (what there was of it—for years Motown paid well below union scale), and more importantly for the promise of a chance to record jazz for Motown's Jazz Workshop subsidiary. That opportunity never materialized—or if it did, his work was allowed to sink out of sight fast. Nevertheless, like fellow sessioneer James Jamerson, Benjamin didn't skimp his talents on the pop sessions. His furious drive on the Supremes' "My World Is Empty Without You" is only one example of how the musicians, as much as the stars and producers, were responsible for the hits at Motown. (Rewarding habit: pay close attention to the rhythm section on Motown hits.) Like most of Motown's musicians, Benjamin rarely received credit for his work, let alone fair compensation, and finally, discouraged with his continuing obscurity, he began to drink and grow unreliable. Then his health deteriorated. On one of his last sessions, Gladys Knight and the

Pips' "I Heard It Through the Grapevine," he was reduced to brushing the cymbals. He died of problems stemming from his drinking.

Marvin Gaye, died April 1, 1984, age 44

Soul singer, born Gay; from Washington, D.C. Marvin Gaye was one of the most gifted, influential, and affecting recording artists of his generation. The breathtaking scope of his talent encompassed practically the entire history of black pop music from the fifties forward, including gospel, vocal group, pop, soul, disco, and funk stylings, all of which he delivered with a remarkable ease and a flair that overflowed with nuance. Listening to the best of his music from any point in his enormously wide-ranging career remains an utterly thrilling and satisfying experience — yet there is a pervasive sadness attached to all of it, even the most joyful, which betrays in some fashion the enormous difficulties he encountered in life.

He was born the oldest of three to a father ordained a minister in the House of God, a conservative Christian sect that mixes up elements of orthodox Judaism and Pentecostalism, imposes strict codes of conduct, and observes no holidays. From the evidence, it's likely that his father was a repressed homosexual, and certainly he was alcoholic. He beat Marvin daily throughout Marvin's childhood. After he finished high school Marvin began singing with streetcorner groups, joining Harvey and the Moonglows in 1958 after they'd already scored their biggest hits, "Sincerely" and "Ten Commandments of Love." Harvey Fuqua taught Gaye much about singing and performance techniques, and moved him to Chicago. After the Moonglows broke up Gaye followed Fuqua to Detroit. He signed to Motown in 1961, originally as a session drummer. That year he also married Anna Gordy, Berry's sister, and added the "e" to his name, after the fashion of Sam Cooke but also partly because of his lifelong homophobia. (Oddly, Gaye was offered the opportunity to play Cooke in a biographical picture about the soul star in 1964, but turned it down flat. "I got chills thinking about it," he told his own biographer, David Ritz. "There was no way I'd even consider the role. It made me extremely nervous to even think about a soul singer who gets shot to death.")

Gaye was one of those who clearly benefited from Berry Gordy's fairness and patience. Gordy never let Gaye's marriage to his sister, nor his later divorce from her, interfere with their own relationship, even if Gaye did. At first Motown had hopes for Gaye as another Nat King Cole, and gave him continued shots at it, all of which fizzled and most of which deserved to (although finally in the late seventies he did get it right; the evidence is available on boxed sets). He found his feet in 1963 with rave-ups like "Hitch Hike" and "Can I Get a Witness." During the mid-sixties he started recording romantic ballad duets with Mary Wells and Kim Weston, and most effectively with Tammi Terrell (before her career was cut short by a brain tumor). Such hits as the 1967 number 5 "Your Precious Love" and the 1968 number 8 "Ain't Nothing Like the Real Thing" boasted a gorgeous, emotional sound that largely stemmed from Gaye's sensitive interplay with his partners. Then, produced by Norman Whitfield, Gaye turned to a more sullen, harder-edged approach. This period produced the biggest hit of his career, "I Heard It Through the Grapevine," which spent seven weeks at number 1 in 1968.

Then he embarked on the most radical departure from form ever seen at Motown, before or since. Easily Gaye's finest hour, his self-produced *What's Going On* from 1971 had an enormous impact on soul music and was rewarding on an astonishing number of levels. Its overarching sadness captured perfectly the bewildering sense of the time, calling down its concerns one by one: Vietnam, the environment, urban troubles, a general plea for sanity, and more. Overdubbing afforded the rich tapestry of sound that would remain Gaye's hallmark for the rest of his career — it's no pretentious bluster to compare the album to a painting, painstakingly assembled as it was track by track as if applying brushstrokes. The public liked it too: "What's Going On" reached number 2 on the pop chart, "Mercy Mercy Me (The Ecology)" number 4, and "Inner City Blues (Make Me Wanna Holler)" number 9. The next year Gaye hit with the theme from a blaxploitation movie, *Trouble Man,* and then he switched his focus to sexuality-as-spirituality-as-sexuality with 1973's *Let's Get It On,* a significant starting point for Prince nearly ten years later and a big hit for Gaye at the time.

By the mid-seventies, though, Gaye's personal life was in utter disarray from a set of long-standing and profound personal problems with drugs, women, and taxes. He had his last number 1 hit in 1977 with "Got to Give It Up (Pt. 1)," and then the double album *Here, My Dear* in 1978, the quirky, bitter result of his divorce from Anna, marked the beginning of a self-indulgent, self-absorbed period that lasted the rest of his life. He moved to Europe for several years, mostly to try to avoid his tax troubles, and left Motown for Columbia in 1982. Late that year *Midnight Love,* his so-called comeback album, was released, which resulted in the number 3 hit "Sexual Healing." It was an impressive enough effort, but little was resolved or made better in Gaye's life, and the follow-up tour was a disappointment. His last public appearance was at the 1984 NBA All-Star Game, where he delivered an unforgettable national anthem.

Still avoiding his personal problems, he found himself living with his parents again, where the resentments between Marvin and his father ran deep. On the day before Marvin's forty-fifth birthday they quarreled over his father's treatment of his mother. Marvin lashed out, attacking and beating him. His father calmly left the room, went down the hall to his own room, and returned with a gun. He shot Marvin twice in the chest, the second time at point-blank range. Marvin Gaye died instantly.

James Jamerson, died August 2, 1983, age 45

Bass player; from Detroit. Critic Greil Marcus once described a comprehensive Motown anthology as "James Jamerson's greatest hits," and that's no exaggeration. As Motown's primary session bass player through the sixties, Jamerson's churning, pumping, fluid figures in such songs as the Temptations' "My Girl," Marvin Gaye's duet with Tammi Terrell, "Ain't No Mountain High Enough," the Four Tops' "Bernadette," and others, are a large part of what makes them memorable. An indication of the regard in which he was held is that his parts were rarely written out for him; instead Motown producers just gave him the chord sheet, or let him listen to the melody and lyrics. But, as was the Motown standard, he was rarely credited and poorly paid. He had been won over in the first place with the promise of his own recording career as a jazz player, but as the truth of his situation caught up with him, he began to drink, like Benny Benjamin before him. Then, also like Benjamin, it began to affect his ability to play. He spent much of the later part of his career in and out of rehab centers and died finally of a heart attack, in obscurity.

Hubert Johnson, died July 11, 1981

Singer, with the Contours; from Detroit. Johnson was a cousin of Berry Gordy's friend Jackie Wilson, which was the connection that got the group their Motown contract and their only pop hit—the crude but exciting dance-it-up, written by Berry Gordy, "Do You Love Me," which went to number 3 in 1962 and, because it had been featured in the 1987 movie *Dirty Dancing*, to number 11 in 1988. Johnson committed suicide, but little is known beyond that.

Eddie Kendricks, died October 6, 1992, age 52

Singer, with the Temptations, solo; from Union Springs, Alabama. Eddie Kendricks, who had performed with Paul Williams since their days in Birmingham, was involved in the complex series of events that led to the formation of the original Temptations. After the group was formed and the original "five lead vocalists" strategy abandoned, Kendricks shared the lead duties with David Ruffin. His sweet, easy falsetto, heard on such tunes as Smokey Robinson's "The Way You Do the Things You Do" and Norman Whitfield's "Girl (Why You Wanna Make Me Blue)," contrasted well with

Ruffin's gruff timbre. But, with the number 1 "My Girl," Ruffin stepped forward as the group's star and Kendricks was heard from less, even after Ruffin had left and been replaced by the Contours' Dennis Edwards. Kendricks still had his moments, as on the number 1 "I Can't Get Next to You" in 1969 (with Edwards) or the number 1 "Just My Imagination (Running Away With Me)" in early 1971. Later that year Kendricks left the group for a solo career, going on to score big hits in the 1973 number 1 "Keep On Truckin' (Part 1)" and the 1974 number 2 "Boogie Down," both of them early examples of disco. Kendricks made his last visit to the charts in 1985, with David Ruffin and Hall and Oates, with a top twenty medley. He died of lung cancer.

Shorty Long, died June 29, 1969, age 29
Singer; from Birmingham, Alabama. His one moment was the 1968 number 8 "Here Comes the Judge," inspired by TV's "Laugh-In." The song, and especially the shtick, did wonders for the career of Pigmeat Markham, whose own version only went to number 19, but it did less for Long (who was not, by the way, the saxophone player who played with Elvis Presley). Long had inaugurated Motown's Soul subsidiary in the early sixties with "Devil with a Blue Dress," later a hit for Mitch Ryder. He drowned in a boating accident.

David Ruffin, died June 1, 1991, age 50
Singer, with the Temptations, solo; from Meridian, Mississippi. The lanky guy with the funny glasses, David Ruffin was soldered onto the Temptations by Motown from 1964 to 1968. He lent the group, actually an amalgam of several groups, a good deal of their credentials as a soul outfit with his evocatively rough yet perfectly poised gospel-inflected stylings, a profound influence (for better or worse) on Rod Stewart. Though the Temptations were originally intended as a unique "five lead singers" venture, the spotlight soon came to focus on Eddie Kendricks's falsetto and Ruffin's gruff tenor, and then finally on Ruffin, starting with the 1965 number 1 "My Girl." After delivering steady hits for two years, Ruffin began demanding a separate limo on tours and more money, and finally, just as producer Norman Whitfield was steering the group into their psychedelic soul period, he jumped for a solo career, which netted him two top tens over the years and a lot of obscurity as he battled his own demons, went to jail for tax evasion, and died finally of a drug overdose.

Tammi Terrell, died March 16, 1970, age 23
Singer, born Tammy Montgomery; from Philadelphia. Tammi Terrell was

Marvin Gaye's best singing partner in a series of good partnerships; together they scored four top tens in 1967 and 1968. Before that she had been recorded by Luther Dixon, toured with James Brown, and attended the University of Pennsylvania as a pre-med student. She signed to Motown in 1965 and enjoyed some success as a solo performer, but the real hits came with Marvin Gaye, particularly when Ashford and Simpson, then just breaking in, started writing and producing for them (their songs included the 1968 number 8 "Ain't Nothing Like the Real Thing" and the 1968 number 7 "You're All I Need to Get By"). By all accounts, Gaye and Terrell were never involved with each other romantically, but their duets remain uniquely convincing; something was there. They went on the road together in 1967, but before long Terrell collapsed on stage. A brain tumor was diagnosed and protracted treatment ensued, to no avail. Gaye was devastated by her death, while Motown, trying to keep the sales magic alive, switched in Valerie Simpson for Terrell on some of the later recording dates.

Georgeanna Tillman, died January 6, 1980, age 35
Singer, with the Marvelettes; from Inkster, Michigan. The Marvelettes, discovered through a high school talent contest, was the girl group that gave Motown its first number 1 in 1961 with "Please Mr. Postman" (on which Marvin Gaye plays drums). Accept no substitutes. It was also the first of many impressive hits for the group, including the 1962 number 7 "Playboy" and the 1966 number 7 "Don't Mess with Bill" (the latter written and produced by Smokey Robinson). Tillman married Billy Gordon of the Contours, left the Marvelettes in 1965, and rarely recorded or performed after that. She died of lupus.

Earl Van Dyke, died September 18, 1992, age 62
Piano player; from Detroit. Earl Van Dyke signed on with Motown in 1961 as a session musician, eventually becoming the de facto leader of the so-called Funk Brothers, which included Benny Benjamin, James Jamerson, and others. Like them, he came to Motown to further a recording career as a jazz player, and ended up putting in his best efforts as an underpaid, under-credited player on the pop hits. When Motown moved to Los Angeles in 1971, Van Dyke quit, preferring to stay in Detroit, where he made a living teaching music. He died of prostate cancer.

Mary Wells, died July 26, 1992, age 49
Singer; from Detroit. One of the first Motown stars, she was signed in 1961 after walking in to audition a song she wrote for Jackie Wilson. Smokey Robinson wrote and produced a series of inspired hits for her from 1962

to 1964, including the 1962 number 9 "You Beat Me to the Punch," the 1963 number 7 "Two Lovers," and the 1964 number 1 "My Guy." The Beatles loved her and squired her around when they toured England together in 1964. She escaped Motown the following year because she had signed as a minor, but in hindsight she probably should have stayed. Lured away by the promise of film work her career almost immediately floundered. She moved from label to label for years and then finally to the oldies circuit in the seventies, spending the rest of her career trying to recover former heights. She was married for a time to Cecil Womack, by whom she had three children. She died of cancer.

Paul Williams, died August 17, 1973, age 34
Singer, with the Temptations; from Birmingham, Alabama. Williams was happily tangled in the complicated events that led to the original Temptations, providing both the baritone underpinning and the choreography for many of the group's most characteristic stage moves. But drugs and alcohol became significant problems for him in the late sixties. By the time his friend Eddie Kendricks left the group in 1971 for a solo career, Williams was considered a lost cause and quickly removed from the group. But he was not abandoned by Motown like so many others, and was placed on salary as a consultant. Still, money troubles and a failing marriage, along with unchecked drug and alcohol problems, provided continuing stress. He finally committed suicide, shooting himself in the head in a parked car.

Faces of Death 15:
Alcohol-Related

Florence Ballard, died February 22, 1976, age 32
See The Motown Morgue.

John Bonham, died September 25, 1980, age 32
See Drummed Out.

Steve Clark, died January 8, 1991, age 30
See Munching the Corpse: The Utter Assurance of Death's Future.

Mark Dinning, died March 22, 1986, age 52
See Oozing Crooners.

Alan Freed, died January 20, 1965, age 42
See The Day the Music Died: The First Death of Rock 'n' Roll.

Cecil Gant, died February 4, 1951, age 37
See Twitch and Shout: Rhythm and Blues Deaths.

Guitar Slim, died February 7, 1959, age 32
See Necro-Orleans.

James Jamerson, died August 2, 1983, age 45
See The Motown Morgue.

Chris Kenner, died January 25, 1976, age 46
See Necro-Orleans.

Amos Milburn, died January 3, 1980, age 52
See Twitch and Shout: Rhythm and Blues Deaths.

Jim Morrison, died July 3, 1971, age 27
See Jim Morrison's Beautiful Friend.

Jaco Pastorius, died September 22, 1987, age 35
See Sha Na Na, Inc.: The Second Death of Rock 'n' Roll.

Pigpen, died March 8, 1973, age 27
See The Grateful Dead's Long, Strange Spinal Tap Trip.

Gene Vincent, died October 12, 1971, age 36
See The Day the Music Died: The First Death of Rock 'n' Roll.

Keith Whitley, died May 9, 1989, age 33
See Country Corpses.

21

Transatlantic Tombstone Blues

WHILE ELVIS PRESLEY, Chuck Berry, Buddy Holly, and others in the first wave of U.S. rock 'n' roll provided a major inspiration to British figures who would come to dominate rock 'n' roll in the sixties, Britain did not always bring up the rear in pop music developments. In fact their folk boom, called skiffle and launched circa 1956 with Lonnie Donegan, came a couple of years ahead of the U.S. folk boom—although it was inspired in the first place by Woody Guthrie, Leadbelly, the Weavers, and other American figures of the forties and early fifties, who would have found a secure niche stateside had the U.S. House Un-American Activities Committee seen fit to respect its own heritage.

Similarly, the somewhat underground British passion for the blues in the early sixties anticipated, and eventually did much to define, both the U.S. white-blues explosion that was to come and the resulting rock culture, which tended to prize the blues above all other musical forms. Eric Clapton, perhaps the most significant figure in white blues, may or may not have been God, but he was definitely British. So is everyone on the list below (with one exception), who also happen to be dead (with no exceptions).

Graham Bond, died May 8, 1974, age 36

Hammond organ player. Bond was among those stalwarts, with John Mayall, Alexis Korner, and others, whose scouting abilities tended to outstrip their own talents, or at least their own impact. Bond himself was a protegé of Korner. His Graham Bond Organisation, formed in 1963, saw such players passing through as Ginger Baker, Jack Bruce, John McLaughlin, and Dick Heckstall-Smith. His innovations included playing the Hammond through a Leslie speaker, and he was among the first to use a mellotron. But in the late sixties it all began to unravel for him as he developed an obsession with the occult, believing himself to be the son (natural or otherwise) of

Aleister Crowley and forming bands with names like Holy Magick and Magus. Drug problems and financial pressures took their toll as well, and in 1973 he suffered a nervous breakdown and was briefly institutionalized. The following year his body was discovered under the wheels of a subway train. Whether he died accidentally or by suicide (let alone whether the dark forces were involved) is not known.

Cyril Davies, died January 7, 1964, age 31
Singer, harmonica player. Another protegé of Alexis Korner and a disciple of Little Walter's music, Cyril Davies helped Korner turn up musicians for their Blues Incorporated, which they started together in 1961. Many went on to seminal roles in such groups as the Rolling Stones, Cream, Led Zeppelin, and more. Davies left Korner in late 1962 to form his own Cyril Davies All-Stars, started with the remnants of Lord Sutch's Savages, which included Jeff Beck and Nicky Hopkins. Then, after Davies died, the group's vocalist, Long John Baldry, turned the All-Stars into his own back-up band, the Hoochie Coochie Men. Davies died of leukemia.

Brian Jones, died July 3, 1969, age 27
See Gathering Moss with the Rolling Stones.

Alexis Korner, died January 2, 1984, age 55
Singer, guitar player. In many ways the godfather of the whole British blues scene (even John Mayall first played with him), Alexis Korner's background was in jazz and skiffle. With Cyril Davies he formed Blues Incorporated in 1961, an important way-station for such figures as Mick Jagger, Charlie Watts, Brian Jones, Robert Plant, Jack Bruce, Ginger Baker, and others. Korner also played with touring U.S. bluesmen such as Sonny Terry, Memphis Slim, and Muddy Waters. Though he never won much notice in the United States he was famous throughout Europe and spent the later years of his life lecturing extensively on the history of blues and pop music. The circumstances of his death are not known.

Memphis Slim, died February 24, 1988, age 72
Singer, piano player, born Peter Chatman; from Memphis. Until 1962 American bluesman Memphis Slim's career followed a familiar path: teaching himself to play piano as a boy, as a young man moving to Chicago during the Depression, and winning notice in the U.S. folk boom of the late fifties. He worked with Big Bill Broonzy and Willie Dixon, and wrote the standard "Every Day (I Have the Blues)." Then, in 1962, he toured Europe, to the usual fanfare that greets the best American music there, and elected

to stay in France. It made a world of sense, and in retrospect it is a little surprising more bluesmen did not follow his lead. Memphis Slim may have lived out the last twenty-six years of his life an expatriate, but he also lived it as a respected star in his chosen land. He died of kidney failure.

Keith Relf, died May 14, 1976, age 33

Singer, cofounded the Yardbirds. Relf was the vocalist for the life of the Yardbirds, whose reputation for instability largely derived from its parade of impressive lead guitar players: Eric Clapton, Jeff Beck, and Jimmy Page. The group stands as a crucial link between British blues and the later British psychedelia and progressive rock (and, some even argue, wrongly, the still later heavy metal). They had such pop hits as the number 6 "For Your Love" and the number 9 "Heart Full of Soul," both from 1965, and "I'm a Man," "Shapes of Things," and "Over Under Sideways Down," all of which reached the pop top twenty in the mid-sixties. Relf adapted well to everything, delivering it all with a cutting if brittle warble. After the Yardbirds' break-up in 1968, he went on to Renaissance, Armageddon, and Illusion — all of them art-damaged, ultra-heavy, or both. He died when he electrocuted himself accidentally while practicing.

Ian Stewart, died December 12, 1985, age 47

Keyboardist, with the Rolling Stones. With Brian Jones, Mick Jagger, and Keith Richards, Ian Stewart founded the Rolling Stones in the early sixties. But when Andrew Loog Oldham took over their management in 1963, he was dismissed. Oldham did not believe Stewart suited the image that he wanted to promote of the Stones as slim, snarling animals. Stewart obligingly stepped aside, though he remained associated with the group for the rest of his life as a roadie and frequent session musician. On the side he had a group called Rocket 88, for which Charlie Watts drummed. He died of a heart attack.

22

Beatles Bugouts

THE BEATLES remain a phenomenon of the sixties. They are stuck there, forever mired in their time. Much has been wrongly credited to them: inaugurating the integral concept of the rock group, single-handedly reviving rock 'n' roll, inciting a generation to cultural revolution, creating unheard of unity in Western civilization, and more. None of it was true. What they did offer (along with others in the British Invasion) was an utter lack of complicity in American life and, by extension, American tragedy. Emerging in the United States in the traumatic aftermath of the John Kennedy assassination, the Beatles seemed all good spirits and boyish innocence. Events of 1964 (see particularly the March and April pop charts, when at one point 13 percent of the Hot 100 belonged to the Beatles, at another point the entire top five) showed what a powerful attraction they were for a culture traumatized by an unthinkable event.

But the Beatles were not as innocent as they seemed, at least not in the way they'd been taken, nor did they remain so removed from U.S. life. By the time John had made his odd inflammatory statements about the Beatles and Jesus in 1966, they were a firmly entrenched part of American life. Thus it made all the sense in the world when John, in particular, fought to live in the United States in the seventies (just as it also made a kind of sense for the U.S. government to harass and persecute him). Throughout the sixties all the Beatles' actions—drugs, TM, thinly conceptual work, internal strife—seemed to prefigure and even direct the ongoing moral crisis in the United States, which served to make them more popular. But in retrospect it was all illusion; the Beatles were always only unconscious reflections, never messiahs.

Hailed as "bigger than Elvis," an incontrovertible fact at the time, they have diminished remarkably over the years. They were on hand for the conception of rock culture, which gestated several years before being born at the Monterey Pop Festival in 1967. But it's clear now that Dylan and the British blues players had vastly more to do with that than the Beatles. They contributed the weakest "major" album in all of rock 'n' roll, *Sgt. Pepper's Lonely Hearts Club Band,* and were in fact neatly supplanted the following year by the Rolling Stones (finally: they'd been chasing the Beatles for five years). The Stones' *Beggars Banquet* marked the beginning of a pop hegemony that lasted until 1972 with music that was fresh, complex, dangerous, thrilling, and still emerging from the familiar country and blues sources — music that has remained far more influential and vital than nearly anything in the Beatles' canon.

But give the Beatles their due. In their time they were wonderful fun; perhaps you had to be alive and aware then to know. They marched in the vanguard of an enormously affecting explosion of pop sensibility. Their early work (taking Buddy Holly and Chuck Berry as its starting point) finished the work begun by fifties rock 'n' roll, altering forever our concepts of pop music. Such mid-sixties albums as *Rubber Soul* and *Revolver* stand up to the very finest work from a fertile period, including significant contributions from Dylan, the Beach Boys, and Phil Spector, and they supersede everything the British Invasion had to offer before 1968. Even the later Beatles albums and hits boast undeniable charms, though their conceits and insulations now mostly only date them.

Below is a list of figures connected to them who are now dead. Some owe debts to the Beatles; others may invoice the Beatles in heaven.

Badfinger

Seventies pop group; from Liverpool. Badfinger was something of a Beatles soundalike, and as such were a tonic to those who mourned the passing of the Fab Four. Their Liverpool ties had originally brought the band to the Beatles' attention through Paul's father, and then Paul, George, and Ringo took it from there — signing them to Apple, producing them, and in many ways staying close to guide them along. But Badfinger was its own band too; their Beatles-like sound was natural enough for them and rarely seemed artificial or strained — no easy thing, as subsequent failed efforts have shown. Members changed continually, but focused on Pete Ham, Tom Evans, Joey Molland, and Mike Gibbins (Tony Kaye from Yes passed through in the late seventies). Ham and Evans had the pop knack and did most of the writing. Their hits included the 1970 number 7 "Come and Get It" (produced by Paul, from the film *The Magic Christian* with Ringo), the number 8 "No Matter What" from the same year, "Day After Day" (produced by George), which went to number 4 in 1972, and, later that year, the top twenty "Baby Blue," which was produced by Todd Rundgren.

Ham and Evans also wrote the 1972 number 1 "Without You" for Nilsson. Then, in the mid-seventies, they suddenly swooned, losing their pop Midas touch in the chaos of Apple's final days. They left for Warner Bros. in 1974, but as complex management problems set in and bad blood with Apple continued, things only got worse. Despondent over events and prone to depression, Ham hanged himself in 1975, at age twenty-seven, effectively breaking up the group. They re-formed in 1978, but it turned out to be the same story all over again, except this time, despondent over events and prone to depression, it was Tom Evans who hanged himself, in 1983, at age thirty-six. End of band. Subsequently they have won a rabid cult following, and their albums are now highly prized, particularly 1970's *Magic Christian Music* and *No Dice,* and 1971's *Straight Up,* even while Joey Molland has slowly carved out a career for himself as an interesting pop performer.

Brian Epstein, died August 27, 1967, age 32

Manager, record store owner; from Liverpool. Brian Epstein may have bungled their management, missed their point, and been motivated only by a sexual interest in John, but he did discover the Beatles. When he told anyone who would listen in 1962 that his new group was going to be bigger than Elvis, he was closer to the truth than even he imagined—far closer. But no one could have predicted the dimensions of the psychic explosion at hand. Epstein dressed them up in cute matching suits, sent them to the barber for cute matching haircuts, and the world took care of the rest. It was estimated at one point that 75 percent of the world knew who the Beatles were (and that is fame, brother—at the time, that would have been 3,000,000,000 people).

Yet with all that marketing clout—and please excuse the crass point of view, but we are talking here about a business manager—Epstein let one obvious opportunity after another slip away. Whether it was a good thing or a bad thing must be for others to judge, but none of those Beatles lunchboxes, wigs, dolls, food, games, not even the television cartoon series, netted the Beatles much of anything. Even their own work was lost: most Beatles songs are owned by other interests now, and to this day Paul is working to get them back. Epstein as manager could not cope with any of it and ultimately lost control of all of it. The strain was too much for him. But it was a monumental task never before asked of anyone, and the tantalizing question remains: What would Colonel Tom Parker have done? Answer: We're all probably better off not knowing. Epstein died alone in London, while the Beatles were in India with the Maharishi Mahesh Yogi studying TM. His death resulted from an overdose of sleeping pills, later ruled accidental.

Mal Evans, died January 4, 1976, age 40
Bodyguard; from Liverpool. Mal Evans was brought on as the road manager for the Beatles in 1963 and, after they retired from touring, stayed with them as a general assistant (read: schlepped equipment at studio dates). He remained in touch with them sporadically after the break-up. He had serious drinking and drug troubles that steadily worsened. He was finally shot dead in a motel by the Los Angeles police, after resisting arrest in an alleged incident in which he used a gun to threaten a woman.

Dick James, died February 1, 1986, age 65
Music publisher, singer; from England. As a singer, Dick James's career was over by the early fifties, though he was long remembered for singing the theme song for British TV's "Robin Hood." As a music publisher, James was the first to sign the Beatles, setting up Northern Songs for them in the early sixties before their enormous vault to fame. It made him a millionaire. Always willing to take a chance on untried talent, he also worked with Billy J. Kramer, Gerry and the Pacemakers, and Elton John and Bernie Taupin. John and Taupin, however, ended up suing him in a protracted dispute over royalties. He died of a heart attack.

Bert Kaempfert, died June 21, 1980, age 56
Bandleader; from Germany. Kaempfert cowrote one of Frank Sinatra's signature songs, the 1966 number 1 "Strangers in the Night," but more pertinently (and improbably) he was the first to produce the Beatles, in Hamburg early in 1961, shortly after his own number 1 U.S. hit that year, "Wonderland by Night." The session was set up to record Tony Sheridan, a British vocalist also stranded in Hamburg. Kaempfert had signed him to Polydor and arranged the session; Sheridan asked to be backed by the Beatles. That day Sheridan recorded "My Bonnie Lies over the Ocean" and "When the Saints Go Marching In"; the Beatles recorded "Ain't She Sweet" and George's instrumental jab at British hit-makers the Shadows, "Cry for a Shadow." Kaempfert, unimpressed with their name or their material, renamed them the Beat Brothers for the release.

John Lennon, died December 8, 1980, age 40
Singer, songwriter, cofounded the Beatles; from Liverpool. The murder of John Lennon, who in so many ways represented the heart and soul not just of the Beatles but of all sixties rock 'n' roll, was perhaps the most emotion-

ally felt of all rock deaths. Certainly there was an equal outpouring of emotion for Elvis Presley, and perhaps as much in some quarters for Buddy Holly, Jimi Hendrix, and Janis Joplin. But John Lennon's death stunned more than any of them. He was just emerging from a long period of silence, with a vigor as surprising as it was refreshing, and he seemed in command of his powers as never before, at a time when rock 'n' roll and the world desperately needed his voice. It was the time immediately following the first landslide election of Ronald Reagan, a discouraging prospect to so many who had embraced all that Lennon seemed to stand for and believe in. If the two events were unrelated, and clearly they were, they are indelibly linked on an emotional level. Not only had Ronald Reagan been elected president, with all his cold, brutal values coming to ascendance—but the one rock star who seemed the warmest and most human (much of that merely public image, as it turned out) was summarily slain a month later. Asked about Lennon's death within days of its happening, Ronald Reagan cupped a hand to an ear and then shrugged and grinned, saying something affably inaudible to the crowd of reporters. He obviously didn't care.

But don't get mixed up about John Lennon. His true genius, which he practiced all his life, was to make people love him. As a human being, he was seriously troubled, the result of a lifetime of festering pain. Separated from his parents as an infant (his father went off to sea and his mother on to the next relationship and an early death), he was raised by his aunt, Mimi Smith, in a middle-class setting. He had a behavior problem all through school, but early on found something like salvation, or at least balm, in U.S. rock 'n' roll. He formed his first band at age sixteen. Paul McCartney attended a performance in 1957 and shortly afterward became a member. McCartney's musical skills impressed Lennon—and Lennon's savvy impressed McCartney. Soon they had agreed that everything written by either would from that point on be credited to "Lennon-McCartney," a promise they kept for nearly fifteen years. George Harrison eventually joined and, later, Pete Best, who was replaced on the brink of the group's breakthrough by Ringo Starr.

Known variously as the Quarry Men, Johnny and the Moondogs, and the Silver Beatles, they finally settled on the name the Beatles, after the Crickets, whom they idolized, with Lennon misspelling it to make a pun on "beat group." In 1960, a four-month stint in Hamburg, Germany, playing some eight hours a night, helped them get their impressive performing act together and provided the physical endurance training they needed to survive Beatlemania when it hit. The last pieces to fall in place were a manager and a record deal, both of which had happened by mid-1962. Lennon, who had been deeply involved with Cynthia Powell since 1957, married her in 1962 when she became pregnant with Julian. The Beatles' enormous success, which followed almost immediately, was beyond belief. As mere mortals, we can only try to imagine what it was like to be a Beatle between 1964 and 1970. Lennon on touring: "Oh, it was a room and a car and a car and a room and a room and a car." Fast-forward to Lennon in a 1966 interview with British journalist Maureen Cleave: "Christianity will go. It will vanish and shrink. I needn't argue that; I'm right and I will be proved right. We're more popular than Jesus now." He was to pay dearly for those remarks, which raised a stink some six months later in the United States and earned him and the group lasting enmity from many.

The Beatles retired from the road shortly after that, at the end of 1966 — in hindsight that was the beginning of the end. In November of 1966 Lennon met Yoko Ono at a gallery opening; almost immediately they hit it off, and she started to pursue him. But Lennon was not available yet. He was still married, and busy making his contributions to the vastly celebrated *Sgt. Pepper.* In reality it was an album all too sorely wanting in concept and containing more filler than the two previous outings (*Revolver* and *Rubber Soul*) combined. But still it has somehow insinuated itself as a lasting hippie totem and a permanent symbol of the times. The Beatles then embarked on a very sad and a very silly time, with LSD adventures at home, TM adventures in India, the death of Brian Epstein (with whom Lennon did or did not have sex on a vacation in Spain in 1963 — Lennon was always exceptionally touchy on the subject), the dissolution of Lennon's marriage, and the formation of Apple. Meanwhile, as the moral center of the United States dissolved the Beatles had somehow become an integral part of that dissolution, every step of the way. No one knew quite how or why or what it all meant, but few denied it. The *White Album* seemed to capture the sense of 1968. *Abbey Road* seemed to capture the sense of 1969. *Let It Be* seemed to capture the sense of 1970. It didn't matter when any of them were recorded. How did they do that?

And then, finally, the group broke up. Lennon, switching his psychic allegiance and expectations from Paul McCartney to Yoko Ono, was ultimately traumatized by it, as his public statements and behavior at the time made clear. But the impact of this difficult time on him resulted in some of his most fascinating and enduring work: 1970's *John Lennon/Plastic Ono Band* and 1971's *Imagine,* both of them startling testaments to scathing self-disclosure.

Somehow, when Lennon opened up and exposed all his running sores, everyone's first impulse was to respond with love. There lay his true genius, the evidence of which really became obvious after his death. Those gut-wrenching albums set the tone for Lennon in the seventies, a decade that was not good to him despite the stories that claimed otherwise. He spent the first half fighting the U.S. Immigration Department for his green card, drinking heavily, and yawping for peace. (We almost have to assume that Lennon, an unusually violent man in his personal life, was driven by his overwhelming need for the "of mind" type despite his focus on war; he doubtless understood the interconnectedness at some level, or so we may hope.) He spent the second half of the decade in seclusion after the birth of his son Sean. Reports conflict on his activities then, some claiming that he baked approximately as many loaves of bread as Jesus distributed with the fishes in the miracle described in the Bible, others reporting a series of ugly psychotic episodes. The ("just gimme some") truth is no doubt somewhere in between, and we will likely never know it. Yoko, at any rate, was in charge of their financial affairs, and Lennon was mostly on sabbatical from life.

Then a sudden creative fit in 1980 resulted in the material for *Double Fantasy*. The album came together extraordinarily quickly and was released in November. Still in a creative frenzy, the couple were already at work on their next project when, coming home late from a session, Lennon was hailed by Mark David Chapman, a fan to whom he'd given an autograph earlier that day. He turned and Chapman shot him five times with a .38 revolver. Lennon was rushed to the hospital but pronounced dead on arrival from a massive loss of blood. Chapman later claimed it was Lennon's remarks in 1966 on Jesus that drove him to his act, but more likely he was just a schnook in search of fame. He found it.

Julia Lennon, died July 15, 1958, age 44

John's mother; from Liverpool. Julia married John's father, Freddy Lennon, when she was twenty-four and gave birth to John, her only child by Freddy, when she was twenty-six. By the time John was born, Freddy, a ship's steward, was spending most of his time at sea. When he was six months old Julia sent John to be raised by her sister Mimi and Mimi's husband George. Though Julia and Freddy were never divorced, Julia moved in with a man named John Dykins shortly after John went to live with Mimi and lived with him for the rest of her life. Dykins and Julia had two children together. Julia also had a fourth child by another man, a Norwegian ship's captain. As a child, John saw little of Julia, but they renewed contact in his early teens. He found her exciting and fun compared to his authoritarian Aunt Mimi, and Julia encouraged John to play the guitar. Years later John wrote one of his most beautiful songs, the spare, lilting "Julia," and even later one of his most harrowing, "Mother," for her. Their bonding did not last long. Just a month before Elvis Presley's mother died, Julia was run over by a car as she was leaving Mimi's after a visit, and died instantly. John was seventeen.

Ronnie Mack, died 1963
Songwriter, producer; from New York. Ronnie Mack was a free-lance songwriter and producer in New York who began working with the Chiffons in 1960. The association bore no real fruit until 1962, when Mack wrote "He's So Fine." It was recorded, but the finished product had to be shopped around to some thirteen labels until finally Laurie snatched it early in 1963. Then, within a few months, it went to number 1 for four weeks. But shortly after that Mack collapsed in the street and was hospitalized with Hodgkin's disease. The gold record for "He's So Fine" had to be presented to him at his bedside, and he never left the hospital alive. Nearly ten years after his death, the estate of Mack took George Harrison to court, charging plagiarism of "He's So Fine" for "My Sweet Lord." They won a partial victory. To mark the occasion the Chiffons, by that time struggling on the oldies circuit, recorded their own version of "My Sweet Lord." It flopped. Who said there's no such thing as justice in this world?

Mary McCartney, died October 31, 1956, age 47
Paul's mother; from Liverpool. Though Mary McCartney's death was not as lastingly traumatic to Paul as John's mother's was to him (or Presley's mother's was to Elvis), Paul wrote "Let It Be" in her memory during the midst of the Beatles' break-up in 1969 — one painful loss clearly resurrecting memories of another. She died of breast cancer when Paul was fourteen.

"Paul McCartney," died circa 1966
In 1969 the rumor that Paul McCartney had died three years earlier raged around the world, coinciding with increasingly widespread suspicion of a conspiracy behind the assassination of John Kennedy, and once again demonstrating the unfathomable connection between the Beatles and Kennedy's death. It was also the first appearance of the conspiratorial tone in relation to a rock death, one that would surface again the following year with the actual deaths of Jimi Hendrix, Janis Joplin, and, in 1971, Jim Morrison. Like most things connected with the Beatles, however, the "Paul Is Dead" commotion was more fun; it involved only conspiracy, not death. Evidently originating with a Michigan underground newspaper, the motives and real point of view of the newspaper remain murky. Maybe they were stoned. But they set forth "evidence" of Paul's demise in an auto acci-

dent ("he blew his mind out in a car") and his subsequent replacement by an imposter (the action taken by Brian Epstein to protect the Beatles' financial interests, of course), derived from liberally interpreted details of Beatles albums artwork and songs.

On the front cover of *Sgt. Pepper,* a hand appears over Paul's head, a symbol of death in India; in the inside gatefold, Paul is wearing a black armband emblazoned "OPD," a Canadian acronym for "Officially Pronounced Dead"; on the back Paul's back is turned to the camera and the words "Without You," from the lyrics to "Within You Without You," crawl from his head. It was said that the title of *Magical Mystery Tour,* which appears in stars on the album cover, would, when held upside down to a mirror, reveal a phone number that could be dialed for details of Paul's death, though somehow no one ever actually seemed to be able to get through. In the song "Glass Onion" John sings, "And here's another clue for you all/The Walrus was Paul" (some cultures consider a walrus a symbol of death). The cover of *Abbey Road* was a complex tableau: Paul is barefoot, like a corpse, and out of step with the others; John is in white like a preacher, Ringo in black like a pallbearer, George in denim like a gravedigger. A license plate on a nearby Volkswagen reads "28 IF," which means Paul would have been twenty-eight years old had he been alive. These are just the high points; dozens of other "clues" emerged. Paul patiently continued to deny the fact of his death, and within six months the rumors were forgotten, leaving many wondering how they had ever got caught up in it in the first place.

Jimmy McCulloch, died September 27, 1979, age 26

Guitar player; from Scotland. McCulloch moved widely in British rock circles. He came from a musical family with a Cowsills-type act that opened for the Who in the mid-sixties; later, Pete Townshend included him in Thunderclap Newman. McCulloch joined Stone the Crows in 1972 for their last album, *'Ontinuous Performance,* after Les Harvey's spectacular electrocution death (see Guitar Heroes). Then he played with John Mayall's Bluesbreakers for a short time before Paul McCartney asked him to join Wings in 1974. McCulloch stayed with Wings for three years, and was on hand for their enormous mid-seventies tour. He left to join the re-formed Small Faces late in 1977 and appeared on their last album, *78 In the Shade.* The details of his death are scanty.

Murray the K, died February 21, 1982, age 60

DJ, born Murray Kaufman. Murray the K emerged as the successor to Alan

Freed's jabbering wild-style DJ throne in late-fifties New York, adding the since much-copied technique of a barrage of sound effects (squealing auto brakes, sneezes, cavalry bugle charges, etc.). But he's probably best remembered now for jumping on the Beatles bandwagon when they first arrived in the United States in 1964, appointing himself the "fifth Beatle," a term with varying connotations that was later applied to George Martin, Yoko Ono, and others. Murray the K also made an appearance in the Beatles' second movie, *Help!*. He died of cancer.

John Rostill, died November 26, 1973, age 31
Bass player, with the Shadows; from England. Though the Shadows never had a U.S. hit, they were something like the Ventures of the United Kingdom and spent much of their career as the backing group for Cliff Richard. One of the first songs ever recorded by the Beatles, George Harrison's "Cry for a Shadow," was a deliberate hoot at the group. Rostill, who replaced Brian "Liquorice" Locking in 1964, was at least the third bass player for them since their formation in the late fifties. Rostill was associated with the Shadows for most of the rest of his life, but also put in time performing with Olivia Newton-John and Tom Jones. He was killed by accidental electrocution while practicing in his home studio.

Rory Storm, died September 27, 1972
Singer, born Alan Caldwell, with Rory Storm and the Hurricanes; from Liverpool. Rory Storm was an athletic, energetic performer, given to pumping up the crowd during his time with the Hurricanes by clambering all over the stage equipment. They were a big hit in England, especially in Liverpool, but it never translated to the United States. In 1962 Storm's popular drummer, Ringo Starr, was lured to the Beatles, and it was all downhill from there. Their moment had passed them by. Ten years later, shortly after the death of his father, Storm and his mother died in what appeared to be a double suicide, from an overdose of sleeping pills.

Stuart Sutcliffe, died April 10, 1962, age 21
Bass player, painter; from Liverpool. Sutcliffe, a promising art student, befriended John Lennon in 1957 and, despite a complete lack of musical experience, played bass for a short time with the Beatles, then known as the Silver Beatles. It was Sutcliffe who originally gave the group its name, based on the Crickets, and he played with them during their first, four-month stint in Hamburg, Germany, in 1960. Paul never liked him. When the group returned to England, Sutcliffe, beginning to suffer serious headaches, quit the group and stayed in Germany to pursue his painting. Little more than

a year later, with their fortunes rising, the Beatles returned to Hamburg for a lengthy engagement at the Star-Club. Sutcliffe was looking forward to seeing them again, but died the day before they arrived, of "cerebral paralysis due to bleeding into the right ventricle of the brain" — his brain was expanding, literally growing too large for his skull.

Face of Death 16:
Deaths Accompanied By
Public Outpourings of Emotion

Johnny Ace, died December 24, 1954, age 25
See The Ghost of Johnny Ace.

Duane Allman, died October 29, 1971, age 24
See Sha Na Na, Inc.: The Second Death of Rock 'n' Roll.

John Belushi, died March 5, 1982, age 33
See Last Laughs: Novelty Artists.

Sam Cooke, died December 11, 1964, age 29
See Souls.

James Dean, died September 30, 1955, age 24
See Bustin' Glass and the Pompadour:
James Dean's Enduring Moment of Death.

Marvin Gaye, died April 1, 1984, age 44
See The Motown Morgue.

Jimi Hendrix, died September 18, 1970, age 27
See Guitar Heroes.

Buddy Holly, died February 3, 1959, age 22
See The Day the Music Died: The First Death of Rock 'n' Roll.

Meredith Hunter, died December 6, 1969
See Gathering Moss with the Rolling Stones.

Brian Jones, died July 3, 1969, age 27
See Gathering Moss with the Rolling Stones.

Janis Joplin, died October 4, 1970, age 27
See Sha Na Na, Inc.: The Second Death of Rock 'n' Roll.

John Lennon, died December 8, 1980, age 40
See Beatles Bugouts.

Bob Marley, died May 11, 1981, age 36
See Death inna Babylon.

Roy Orbison, died December 6, 1988, age 52
See The Day the Music Died: The First Death of Rock 'n' Roll.

Elvis Presley, died August 16, 1977, age 42
See The Big Elvis.

Ritchie Valens, died February 3, 1959, age 17
See The Day the Music Died: The First Death of Rock 'n' Roll.

23

Gathering Moss with the Rolling Stones

THERE WAS a time when the Rolling Stones seemed to be the epitome of rock stars who had consorted with Satan. In the United States they had long been at pains to pose as the "dark side" of the Beatles' bright pop vision. Their original manager Andrew Loog Oldham saw to that, eliminating their keyboard player Ian Stewart because he didn't look raffishily youthful enough, and cultivating a bad-boy image in marked opposition to Brian Epstein's presentation of the Beatles. Presenting themselves in relation to the Beatles was not really so surprising, given the stakes that success in the U.S. marketplace offered—even if they did present themselves as the Beatles' opposite. The Animals tried the same thing and succeeded to some extent, while Herman's Hermits went the other way, cleaning up what Epstein had been unable to with the Beatles, and winning a sizable share of the British Invasions's chart domination with pop music as cuddly and adorable as their smiling mugs. As it turned out, no one, not even the Beatles, had the vision or the staying power of the Rolling Stones.

When the Stones began to write their own material in the mid-sixties, they continually, with great calculation, evoked brutal points of view that no one else wanted to adopt in their music. "Time Is on My Side," "Heart of Stone," "(I Can't Get No) Satisfaction," "Get Off My Cloud," "19th Nervous Breakdown," "Mother's Little Helper," "Have You Seen Your Mother, Baby, Standing in the Shadow?"—all were bitter pills indeed, delivered with a sneering facade behind which there seemed to be only further layers of contempt. The Rolling Stones obviously didn't mean anyone any good. They may have reserved their most acrimonious resentments for middle-class convention, with which by then a whole generation could identify, but the articulation of those resentments was never for the benefit of you or me.

There was something decidedly voyeuristic and forbidden about the whole Rolling Stones thing, just as there was something a little distasteful and off-putting. If it was easy to champion the Beatles, who were witty and charming, it was harder to get behind the Stones, who were sullen and selfish, and seemed dangerous—somehow you knew they could hurt you if you let them. But the result was that they were utterly irresistible. The Beatles' *Rubber Soul,* with its fully realized "Norwegian Wood," "Think for Yourself," "Girl," even the somewhat questionable "Run for Your Life," may have been appropriate for any social occasion. But the Rolling Stones' parallel *Aftermath,* with its equally realized "Paint It Black," "Lady Jane," and utterly questionable "Under My Thumb" and "Stupid Girl," was not. The album was best suited for listening to alone in your room late at night, because it unleashed feelings of which you were afraid, or ashamed. That's what made it great.

Shortly after that, with the Rollings Stones' release of *Their Satanic Majesties Request,* their response to the Beatles' *Sgt. Pepper's Lonely Hearts Club Band,* the Satanic posturing began in earnest. What before had been only darkly hinted at was now developed in plain public view of all. But, truth be told, *Satanic Majesties* was a ludicrous and unbelievable album. It still seems a very silly and stupid move on the Stones' part—it was no *Sgt. Pepper* by any stretch, and not even a worthwhile departure. Even worse, except for one or two outstanding tracks (notably "2,000 Light Years from Home") it was by far their weakest album to date.

But if nothing else, *Satanic Majesties* did put forward the idea of a link between the Rolling Stones and Lucifer. That was fortuitous, because what happened next was at once very simple and yet very hard to explain: with the release of the album *Beggars Banquet* and the single "Jumpin' Jack Flash" in 1968, the Rolling Stones became the greatest rock 'n' roll band in the world. It was to prove a preeminence they would sustain, with a kind of grace and overweening effortlessness, for five years. Suddenly, somehow, the Rolling Stones had left everyone far behind, spitting up their dust, even the Beatles, whom the Stones had haplessly trailed for five years.

They did it on the strength of music that was deeply connected to blues and country forms (unbeknownst to many rock fans, who largely despised country music). Yet it was music that had been radically transformed into rock 'n' roll. It was fresh and exciting and different. The best of it—"Jumpin' Jack Flash," "Brown Sugar," and especially "Street Fighting Man," their single greatest song ever—reached back to dark, terrifying shards of American life and history, places it seemed impossible for any British kid in his twenties to reach. Using their force in the service of a deceptive indifference and contempt, they almost casually lobbed it forth, but with an unmistakable passion as surprising as it was ferocious. The recent documentary of their career, *25 X 5,* which otherwise dwells far too much on the band's tiresome later activities, sets the suddenness of this arrival into stark relief. One day they were sullen fake Beatles, complying with Ed Sullivan's demands to clean up "Let's Spend the Night Together"—and the next, with "Jumpin' Jack Flash," they had become something else entirely, something godlike.

In the midst of this astonishing transformation, the question arose continually: How did they get this far, this fast? Well, you know the answer that started to circulate. And why not? The apocryphal ties to Beelzebub had been further underlined on *Beggars Banquet* in the much celebrated if generally overrated "Sympathy for the Devil," which features a happy-skippy rhythm track over which Jagger struts and preens insufferably (though Richards does finally come through with the prize, making it at least a worthwhile listen in its context). The Satan connection made a kind of sense, offering some kind of explanation, however weird, for the years of bitterness and contempt, and then the sudden prominence. And the Stones, or more specifically Mick Jagger and Keith Richards, never ones to miss a marketing trick, didn't do much to discourage the chatter. (See also Nicholas Roeg's disturbing *Performance*, which stars Jagger and postulates an effete, almost convincing sort of devil-worshipping rock star; released in 1970, it was filmed in 1968.)

But, make no mistake, they paid for it. The Devil will have his due every time; ask Robert Johnson or Jerry Lee Lewis if you don't believe me. At their peak the Rolling Stones paid the stiffest price of all—sudden, withering, humiliating powerlessness and death. The first casualty, of course, was Brian Jones, the founder of the band, who died on July 3, 1969, at the age of twenty-seven. Like Mick Jagger, Jones loved the idea of fame every bit as much as he loved American blues (for his part, Keith Richards probably loved the music more than either of them, and was simply willing enough to shoot for the fame too). They met when all three were scuffling around London playing blues in the early sixties. When the band was finally set in 1963, with Charlie Watts and Bill Wyman as the rhythm section and Oldham managing, they had their first United Kingdom hit with a cover of Chuck Berry's "Come On." Their second was "I Wanna Be Your Man," written by John Lennon and Paul McCartney. Therein lay the key to their initial vault to fame.

Once on top, in the mid-sixties, Jagger and Richards began to maintain their position, under the direction of manager Oldham, by working out their songwriting chops, which developed to a degree surprising to many observers. Jones, who still had the potential for something like George Harrison status, earned his keep and helped get them through the time by lending texture, atmosphere, and hooks to their songs with such widely varying instruments as the dulcimer, sitar, marimbas, bells, and more. But though he was musically adventurous and all that, he was increasingly irrelevant, devolving gradually into a kind of precious aesthete, eclectic but largely ineffective. Jagger and Richards needed him less and less. Drug problems and interpersonal difficulties (Anita Pallenberg had been his girlfriend first) only made his position more intractable. Jones was in such poor shape by 1967 that he barely contributed to *Beggars Banquet,* and within a year of its release he had departed, citing musical differences. A month later he was found dead, drowned in his swimming pool, with levels of alcohol and barbiturates in his system high enough that the coroner ruled it "death by misadventure." At a Hyde Park concert two days later to debut Jones's replacement, Mick Taylor, Jagger read an excerpt from Shelley and released a thousand butterflies.

But romantic poetry and butterflies in quantity were not enough for the Devil, and five months later he took his next piece of flesh at the Altamont Speedway in California, just as the band was nervously attempting to kick-start "Under My Thumb." The death of Meredith Hunter, at the hands of Hell's Angel Alan David Passaro (in what was later ruled a "justifiable homicide"), stands as perhaps the most terrifying instance of any single rock 'n' roll death, fan or otherwise. Three others died that day, but Hunter's death, captured on film for the Maysles brothers' documentary *Gimme Shelter,* resonates more than any other.

The Stones, on their first U.S. tour since their success at Woodstock three years before, had been baited into giving a free concert by journalists who complained they were exploiting their opening acts, B.B. King and Ike and Tina Turner, by paying them too little, and their audience by charging them too much (ticket prices for the tour were the highest ever for any rock act at the time). The whole idea was clearly a mistake, but not wanting to lose their credibility with the Woodstock generation the Stones elected to give the free concert, in the Bay Area. It gradually ballooned into an all-day event that included Santana, the Jefferson Airplane, the Flying Burrito Brothers, and Crosby, Stills, Nash and Young, with the Stones set to headline.

The Real Big Mistake, however, lay in using the Hell's Angels to provide security, a mistake further complicated by paying them in cases of beer. Altamont turned out, of course, to be the same nightmare of disorganization that Woodstock had been, but this one was not held together by peace, love, and understanding. The Angels reportedly spent the day hassling everybody in sight, jumping and beating people at will, including members of the bands. For the most part their strategy worked—people were fearful and behaved. But when they started knocking Hunter around as he was trying to get close to the stage, he became angry and pulled a gun. Within minutes he was disarmed and dead, the victim of knife wounds to the back.

The Rolling Stones survived—not without scars, but they did survive and they survived well. They accomplished it by a simple expedient: getting shut of the Devil, taking themselves as far from him as fast as they could. *25 X 5* also documents that fact, showing how after 1969 they pulled their hands from the fire ("Sympathy for the Devil" was dropped from their set list for more than ten years) and shaped an act more broadly cartoonish—"It's only rock 'n' roll but we like it," indeed. At the end of the documentary, with Keith Richards showing clear regrets they had ever toyed with Satan, the Rolling Stones of the late eighties solemnly offer unbelievable bromides about the enduring importance of family in a man's life. Their music suffered after they parted company with the Devil. Over the years it has swooned into doldrums, only occasionally brightened, by 1978's *Some Girls,* 1981's "Start Me Up," and a few other largely isolated points. Yes, their music suffered all right—but they are alive to tell the tale.

24

Who's Dead

WHAT, AFTER all this time, are we to make of the Who? Forget, first, everything you've heard about mods and rockers and the climate of British pop music subcultures in the early sixties. It explains nothing about their enormous success in the United States. Look instead to the best documentary on the Who, 1979's *The Kids Are Alright* (named after an early song), which gets right to it—at bottom the Who were kids and little more, a raffish, misbehaved bunch of boys acting out every hormone impulse that ever twitched a muscle of theirs, without a thought in their head except what might give them a laugh. The Who stands as a triumph of blind testosterone. If they provided a model of liberation for boys (and girls) everywhere, that never made them geniuses. They barely even had a clue what they were about themselves, Pete Townshend's highly quotable profundities notwithstanding.

But it did prevent them from becoming pompous buffoons—once again, Townshend's statements notwithstanding. Perhaps the Who came as close to the ideal of Elvis Presley as any rock band of their era, with an innocent yet total embrace of rock 'n' roll as salvation and way of life. If that ideal contains the seeds of its own betrayal, and it does, it only makes the act of embracing it all the more striking, noble, and ludicrous. The most profound line the Who ever uttered turned out to be the most obvious lie: "Hope I d-die before I g-get old." Its accomplishment is that it's perfectly understandable, as a sentiment *and* as a lie.

Don't get mixed up on this. The Who were something very special. Unlike the Beatles, they simply could not be prevailed upon to behave. But, unlike the Rolling Stones, they never had any truck with Satan and his work. They were just four wild cases: singer Roger Daltrey a ruffian, bass player John Entwistle a gifted player with a demented outlook, guitar player and chief songwriter Pete Townshend a violent brooder, and drummer Keith Moon in a class by himself. Breaking in as one of the most elemental thrash-it-ups ever, in all of rock 'n' roll, they had a right good time sticking their post-teen frustrations into the world's face, pioneering the gesture of destroying their instruments as the climax to their stage act. And if that gesture ultimately became a cliché and an act genuinely deserving of condemnation from the politically correct—well, still, wasn't it a glorious moment when Pete Townshend beat Abbie Hoffman off that Woodstock stage with his guitar? *That's* the kind of peace, love, and understanding to which most of us can relate.

When—even as early as the late sixties—the Who began to feel the compromising effects of creeping old age (some would call it maturity), and then when they felt death's sting, it hit them hard, and it obviously hurt. But you really can't have it both ways. Either you get old, or you die. There is some choice in that equation but age, as the Who were to discover, only makes the ponderous weight and oppressive responsibility of the choice just that much more evident. Over the years, their ability and their inability to address exactly that point—either you get old, or you die—has served as the yardstick of their continuing viability, and lack of viability.

The first sign of trouble was "Young Man Blues," which became a part of their live set in the late sixties and was slotted as the opening track of their revelatory 1970 album *Live at Leeds*. By all rights the Who probably should have been dead by then already. But they weren't, and this cover of an old Mose Allison tune carped loudly about not getting theirs because the older generation was standing in the way. At the same time, however, the song belonged to a tradition, which implicitly acknowledges the validity of the older generation and the systems of tutoring and mentoring that provide continuity and meaning in the world. Even more telling, Townshend by then was tramping around after a geezer, Meher Baba, and hanging on his every word.

The decline toward old age never slows for a second, as they were discovering, and with 1971's *Who's Next* they were clearly groping to come to terms with it. The cover art showed them zipping up after taking leaks on a monolithic symbol of the establishment, but the opening track, "Baba O'Riley," absurdly castigates their followers as a "teenage wasteland." With all of them all too rapidly approaching age thirty, their vision was growing increasingly fuzzy, even as hard-won experience was lending their music a remarkable authority and impact. That was the paradox. While the group spent much of the seventies running in place—attempting, alternately, to overcome or to escape the stigma of their 1969 "rock opera" *Tommy*—their music nevertheless remained a dependable ballast at a time when rock 'n' roll was splintering apart everywhere. Among other things, that meant they were in a position to take a refreshingly gracious view of punk-rock when it came along, though they had to know it meant them no good.

And then came the deaths. The first—Keith Moon, on September 7, 1978, at age thirty-one—was the most traumatic. Moon had long represented the irrepressible spirit of the Who, but it was finally that irrepressible spirit that killed him, and the surviving three knew it. One of the greatest of all rock 'n' roll drummers, it was Moon who brought a good deal of the legendary manic element to the band. Notorious for destroying things off-stage as well as on, particularly hotel accommodations and expensive cars, Moon kicked every single wild element of the band up a notch or two, bringing an unmistakable glee to the proceedings. A lifelong lover of surf music, particularly the Beach Boys and Jan and Dean, he moved to California in the early seventies and hung out with Nilsson and Ringo Starr, drinking and carousing. But it all finally caught up with him and he died, typically enough, from an overdose of Heminevrin, a prescription drug used to control alcoholism.

That was the end of the Who, though they have yet to admit it. They replaced him with former Small Faces drummer Kenney Jones, adding session keyboardist John "Rabbit" Bundrick while they were at it. They took their act to the road, not without misgivings, but they had a new album (*Who Are You,* Moon's last) and two movies (*The Kids Are Alright* and *Quadrophenia*) to promote. And, paradoxically perhaps, they were more popular than ever— *Who Are You* had joined their earlier efforts of that decade as a staple of FM-radio, and their shows were selling out within hours.

And that is how, a little more than a year after the death of Moon, the Who found themselves looking death squarely in the face again. This time it was the horrific deaths by trampling of a group of anonymous fans. Their names don't matter nearly as much as their number: eleven—eleven people died, and the Who unknowingly played a rock 'n' roll show for their killers. Talk about teenage wasteland. It happened in the U.S. heartland, in Cincinnati, on December 3, 1979. The 18,000 tickets for that show had been sold as festival seating, a first-come first-served system, and had sold out the day they were put on sale. Hours before the show's scheduled 8:00 P.M. start, fans had begun to gather outside the doors of the Cincinnati Riverfront Coliseum. At 7:00 P.M., the doors still were not open and the crowd was growing impatient and restless. Finally—some speculate because the crowd heard a soundcheck and thought it was the show starting—a glass door was shattered and fans poured through, vying for the precious front-row seats, surging in a powerful mass and trampling whatever got in their way. That included eleven fans who fell to the floor and never got up again. Eight others were injured in the melee. Fearful of a riot, officials let the show go on as scheduled. Band members were not informed of the deaths until after the show.

The incident slowed them significantly but even that didn't stop them. They toured in 1982, claiming it was their last ever and a farewell to their fans. But 1989 saw them doing it all over again. They were no longer singing "Young Man Blues," in short, and by then it was all too evident they were in it only for the money. They felt they needed it and they could get it, and that was justification enough. And it's likely enough they will do it again, if the market projections are right.

Over the years, Daltrey has attempted a career as an actor and also released a number of solo albums. Entwistle released some solo albums too but has mostly kept to himself. Townshend, who lost a good deal of his hearing from tintinnitus, a condition brought on by years of deafening concerts, also released solo albums (some of them very good) and has pursued a variety of literary ambitions. Most recently, in 1992, he was at work on a stage production of *Tommy,* which premiered in San Diego to mixed reviews and eventually appeared on Broadway in 1993. The Who ended a long time ago, clearly enough, but the question remains: What, after all this time, are we to make of them?

One other Who death worth mentioning is Kit Lambert, their second and most effective manager in the sixties. Lambert discovered the group in 1964, when they still called themselves the High Numbers. At the time Lambert was a filmmaker looking for a rock group to appear in a film on which he was working. Along with his partner, Chris Stamp, he took over the management of the group from Pete Meaden. He changed their name to the Who, directing and encouraging their combative, disruptive image —the onstage destruction of instruments, the seemingly unwarranted arrogance in interviews. With 1966's *Happy Jack,* he became involved in producing the music, eliciting Townshend's grandiose tendencies toward "rock opera." Lambert was, in part anyway, behind the lengthy "A Quick One" on that album, and "Rael" on the next, 1967's *The Who Sell Out.* His crowning glory, perhaps, was Townshend's still interesting *Tommy* (the album by the Who, that is, and only the album by the Who).

By the early seventies, however, Lambert's influence was on the wane, and by 1974 he was out. He spent the rest of his life in retirement with an ever-worsening drug problem. In 1976, a ward of the court because of his bizarre behavior while living in Italy (where he called himself Baron Lambert), Lambert returned home to live with his mother. There, five years later, he took a fall down a flight of stairs and fractured his skull. Three days later he died. He was forty-five.

25

Souls

S OUL MUSIC was the natural evolution of black pop music after rhythm
and blues — and it happened, in the mid-fifties, just as white pop music
was absorbing rhythm and blues and transmuting it into rock 'n' roll. Soul,
even more than rhythm and blues, relied on gospel forms and for the most
part focused, like crooning, on a single powerful singer who just shut his
or her eyes and wailed mightily. Its most important figures were James
Brown, Ray Charles, Sam Cooke, and, later, Aretha Franklin, all of whom
reached their peaks at a time when white kids were eagerly absorbing much
that was happening in black pop music. Thus, parallel to rock 'n' roll yet
distinct from it, it's not easy to pigeonhole soul; the more's the pity.

Emotionally it's a more mature musical form than either rock 'n' roll or
rhythm and blues, relying on adult concerns and feelings. It's not surprising
that white rock 'n' roll fans who encountered soul music through blues or
singer/songwriter music, or other antecedents to rock, were the most ready
to embrace it. In its way, soul has a decidedly collegiate flavor. But because
of its deep roots in gospel music — in effect it *is* gospel music, albeit
secularized — it is also a more profoundly felt, almost spiritual music.

Soul music led to other forms of music that remained distinct from rock
'n' roll. Sly Stone began to borrow from it to work out the parameters of
street-oriented funk. Later it was pushed further from rock 'n' roll, in one
direction by George Clinton in the seventies, and, still later, in another
direction, by eighties rappers. Marvin Gaye, meanwhile, heralded a self-
absorbed and studio-bound style intensely connected to soul (and much
else), which resurfaced later in the iconoclastic, insular work of Prince and
Michael Jackson.

None of that is rock 'n' roll — it is music increasingly drifting from the
blues and in touch only nominally, if at all, with country. (See Ray Charles's

1962 *Modern Sounds in Country and Western Music* for how bizarrely effective a black treatment of country can sound; but for God's sake don't go to it expecting to hear country music.) On the other hand, if rock 'n' roll is something more than simply two discrete musical forms colliding, if it is in fact the place where key cultural forces of American life can meet and work out their differences, in pain, celebration, and triumph, then soul music, produced and played by blacks and whites together, was the apotheosis of rock 'n' roll in the mid-sixties. And all that it spawned, from funk to disco to rap, is perhaps more transcendentally rock 'n' roll than anything else, including (or perhaps especially) rock culture and punk-rock.

Soul music, as such, also ended in painful death—the end of the so-called golden age of soul is commonly dated from the assassination of Martin Luther King, Jr., on April 4, 1968, after which some of its most important figures encountered significant difficulties. Producer Jerry Wexler, for example, a white man from New York who worked at Atlantic with Aretha Franklin among many others, was hung in effigy at the 1968 convention of the National Association of Radio and Television Announcers in Atlanta. Yet for all that, the music made by those on the list below and many more besides lives on today with all its vitality undiminished, raising the pertinent point, for this section anyway (and, increasingly, for subsequent sections as well): What does it really matter anyway what you call it if it's damn fine music? Everyone on the list below is dead, and they also, for the most part, made damn fine music.

The Bar-Kays, December 10, 1967

From Memphis. Along with Booker T. and the MG's, the Bar-Kays were an important element in the Stax-Volt mix, serving as the session and touring band for many of the label's acts. They had their own hit in 1967 with the number 17 "Soul Finger" (complete with party effects), then went out on tour with Otis Redding, who was capitalizing on his astonishing appearance at the 1967 Monterey Pop Festival and just beginning to break through to a white audience. Four of the six members of the band were killed in the same plane accident that killed Redding: keyboardist Ronnie Caldwell, aged nineteen; drummer Carl Cunningham, aged eighteen; saxman Phalon Jones, aged eighteen; and guitar player Jimmy King, aged eighteen. Only trumpet player Ben Cauley and bass player James Alexander survived, Alexander because he was not on the plane. The two prevailed, however, forming a new Bar-Kays a year later, playing with Isaac Hayes on some of his best work, including "Theme from Shaft," and in 1976 scoring a top thirty hit with the disco "Shake Your Rump to the Funk."

Sam Cooke, died December 11, 1964, age 29

Singer; from Chicago. With his pure tenor and uncanny, intuitive ability to fit gospel techniques (sudden soaring vocal swoops, sensual meditations on a single phrase, and the dynamics of call and response) into a pop song format, Sam Cooke along with Ray Charles and James Brown invented soul singing as we know it. But where Charles and Brown were generally feverish and emotional, Cooke was always cool and poised. If producers Hugo and Luigi locked him into a supper-club sound, and if RCA restricted him to teen fare, still he managed to overcome it all and brought something beautiful and unmistakable into the world. His influence is enormous; Marvin Gaye and Al Green, particularly, owe him significant debts. In addition, his acceptance as a genuine hero for the times ran deep. Despite the sordid circumstances of his death, his funeral services attracted nearly two hundred thousand people in Los Angeles and Chicago and his powerful posthumous hit, "A Change Is Gonna Come," signaled a new era in black America.

It was not by accident that Cooke delivered gospel to pop. He first broke in as a teenager in 1951 with the Soul Stirrers, eventually becoming their lead vocalist. Even as a gospel singer he was an innovator; where others sang hard and raspy to emphasize their passion, Cooke remained a model of control, letting his powerful voice dart across melodies and through phrasings almost like a blues guitar. His timbre boasted a sophisticated air of world-weariness that would later bring depth to even the silliest pop tunes he was forced to record. And he always boasted an innate rapport with audiences (Cooke was long underrated as a live performer, partly because he deliberately stiffened up for white audiences). But Cooke always wanted more than just to be a gospel star. In 1956, he released "Lovable," his first essay at pop, under the name Dale Cook (his last name really had no "e"; the addition of one was an affectation later borrowed by Marvin Gaye, and dallied with by Dionne Warwick). No one was fooled, least of all Cooke's label head Art Rupe, of Specialty, who fired him from the Stirrers. But the mistake was Rupe's: in 1957, with Keen, Cooke released the biggest single of his career, the gorgeous number 1 "You Send Me." Then, moving to RCA in 1960, he released a steady stream of top twenty hits, including "Chain Gang," "Twistin' the Night Away," and others. Clearly hitting his peak, Cooke began consolidating his gains with careful business ventures: his own record label, Sar/Derby, music publishing, and singer management. Signings to his label included the Valentinos with Bobby Womack, Lou Rawls (with whom Cooke sang on one of his best songs, "Bring It on Home to Me"), Johnnie Taylor, Mel Carter, and Billy Preston. It's really not too outlandish to say that Cooke could have become one of the most influential black entrepreneurs of the decade, rivalling even Motown's Berry Gordy.

But violence and sudden death haunted his life. Late in 1958 he and Lou Rawls were injured in an auto crack-up, Rawls critically. The next year, his first wife was killed in another auto accident. In 1963, Cooke's youngest child, Vincent, drowned in his swimming pool. And then, in Los Angeles, on the night of December 10, 1964, Cooke (remarried by then to high school sweetheart Barbara Campbell) met a young woman named Elisa Boyer at a small party. According to testimony at the inquest convened to investigate the incident — testimony that has been disputed by Cooke's last manager, Alan Klein — Cooke took Boyer against her will to a motel and registered them as "Mr. and Mrs. Cooke." Boyer testified that she asked to be taken home while still at the registration desk, but that Cooke forced her to the room, where, she said, he "began to rip my clothes off." When Cooke went into the bathroom, Boyer escaped, taking his clothes with her, and went to a phone booth to call the police. Dressed only in a sports coat and shoes, Cooke went after her. Believing she had returned to the office of the motel's manager, fifty-five-year-old Bertha Franklin, Cooke pounded on the door, demanding entry. He finally broke down the door and attacked Franklin, whereupon she drew her .22 caliber pistol and shot him three times. Cooke, wounded, charged Franklin again. She picked up a stick and clubbed him. By the time police finally arrived, he was dead.

Lee Dorsey, died December 1, 1986, age 61
See Necro-Orleans.

Marvin Gaye, died April 1, 1984, age 44
See The Motown Morgue.

Joe Hinton, died August 13, 1968, age 39
Singer, with the Chosen Gospel Singers, the Spirits of Memphis, solo. After putting in some futile time, commercially speaking, on Don Robey's Houston-based Duke and Peacock labels, the largely obscure Joe Hinton scored a number 13 hit in 1964 with an impressive version of Willie Nelson's "Funny (How Time Slips Away)." Then, like time and the song, the singer himself slipped away, four years later, in Boston, of "natural causes."

O'Kelly Isley, died March 31, 1986, age 48
See Twitch and Shout: Rhythm and Blues Deaths.

Al Jackson, died October 1, 1975, age 39
See Drummed Out.

King Curtis, died August 13, 1971, age 37
See Blow, Big Man.

David Prater, died April 9, 1988, age 50
Singer, with Samuel Moore, of Sam and Dave; from Ocilla, Georgia. Both Sam and Dave grew up singing in church (Moore in Miami, Prater in Georgia) and had embarked on solo careers before meeting and teaming up in 1958. After kicking around together for several years they signed to Stax in 1965, with whom they scored three major hits: the 1966 number 21 "Hold On! I'm a Comin' " (suppressed in some regions for its supposed sexual connotations, which may explain its relatively poor chart showing), the 1967 number 2 "Soul Man," and the 1968 number 9 "I Thank You." But the union became a rocky one, marked by continual fights after Prater shot his wife in 1968 and escaped the consequences due to obscure legal circumstances. Moore says he lost all respect for Prater at that point, but Moore himself was on his way to becoming a heroin addict by then. Their career was revived in the early eighties due to the attention won by the Blues Brothers, but the animosities ran too deep and they couldn't keep it together. They split up for good in 1982. Prater found a new Sam (Daniels), while Moore recorded a bizarre "Soul Man" duet in 1986 with Lou Reed. Prater died in an auto accident.

Otis Redding, died December 10, 1967, age 26
Singer, songwriter; from Macon, Georgia. One of the great soul singers of his generation, uniquely capable of delivering the music to a white audience, Otis Redding started out idolizing Little Richard (who also hailed from Macon, as did the Allman Brothers). Much of Redding's earliest work is completely in the Little Richard style—wild, screeching frenzies of rhythm and vocal attack. But in fact Redding had something uniquely his own to offer, as he eventually proved.

He broke in singing occasionally with the Macon-based Johnny Jenkins and the Pinetoppers; legend has it that by day Redding served as Jenkins's chauffeur. It was true, at least, one day in late 1962 when Jenkins asked for a ride to Memphis to audition for the fledgling Stax. There, after Jenkins and the Pinetoppers had done their stuff, some recording time still remained and Redding was put on the mike. The first tune he tried was "Hey, Hey, Hey," in the Little Richard vein—not impressed, Stax president Jim Stewart told him the world was better off with just one Little Richard. So Redding ran through a ballad, "These Arms of Mine." Stewart was still not entirely convinced, according to reports, but he released it as a single anyway and it went to number 20 on the rhythm and blues chart early the next year. Redding was effectively launched. He quickly proved himself not just as a capable songwriter, but as a potential goldmine, working with Jerry Butler to come up with the top thirty "I've Been Loving You Too Long" in 1965; with Booker T. and the MG's guitar player Steve Cropper for "Mr. Pitiful" and what turned out to be his biggest hit, the uncharacteristically sweet, posthumous 1968 number 1 "(Sittin' on) The Dock of the Bay"; and, on his own, working out "My Lover's Prayer" and the classic "Respect," number 1 in 1967 for Aretha Franklin.

In performance, Redding's rough-hewn baritone rode a tight, furious rock band (sometimes the MG's, sometimes the Bar-Kays, sometimes a combination of them or others). For much of his career in the mid-sixties his success and recognition was largely confined to the rhythm and blues (i.e., black) audience, though that changed somewhat when he reluctantly covered the Rolling Stones' "Satisfaction"—he was not happy to be imitating white imitators, but the ploy worked, winning him increased airplay on white pop stations. His career took its biggest step forward in 1967 following his appearance at the Monterey Pop Festival with a memorable, show-stopping set. White rock fans were clearly ready for him in a big way. But Redding never lived to see his efforts bear their greatest fruit. Written as a gesture of thanks to everyone at Monterey, "Dock of the Bay" was not even released until after his death. In icy flying conditions, his plane went into Wisconsin's Lake Monona, killing him and four members of the Bar-Kays. Redding was already a giant and still on the rise, and he was only twenty-six.

David Ruffin, died June 1, 1991, age 50
See The Motown Morgue.

Joe Tex, died August 12, 1981, age 49
Singer, born Joseph Arrington, Jr.; from Rogers, Texas. After doggedly paying his dues for some ten years, Tex hooked up with Buddy Killen's Nashville-based Dial label in 1964 for a series of hits that included the 1965 number 5 "Hold What You've Got" and the 1967 number 10 "Skinny Legs and All," which together captured his two basic approaches: either dispensing advice in turgid morality tales or yukking it up at the expense of the gals. Shortly after his last hit, the 1977 number 12 disco "Ain't Gonna Bump No More (With No Big Fat Woman)," Tex became a Muslim minister and took to calling himself Joseph Hazziez. He died of a heart attack.

Jackie Wilson, died January 20, 1984, age 49

Singer; from Detroit. Jackie Wilson was one of the liveliest and most charismatic performers of his generation, rivaling even James Brown. He was discovered at a talent show by Johnny Otis in 1951 (along with Hank Ballard and Little Willie John—it must have been some show!), and joined Billy Ward and the Dominoes after Clyde McPhatter had trained him and left the group in 1953. Wilson went solo in 1956, hitting first with Berry Gordy's "Reet Petite," then scoring with the 1959 number 7 "Lonely Teardrops" (also by Gordy) and many others, including the 1963 number 5 "Baby Workout" and the 1967 number 6 "(Your Love Keeps Lifting Me) Higher and Higher." The big band arrangements, particularly on the earlier tunes, often sound corny now, perhaps reflecting the influence of his idol Al Jolson—but Wilson's athletic, dynamic vocals cut through the pomp and bluster every time. He was legendary as a live performer, dependably whipping crowds into slavering frenzies.

In 1961, on the day after Valentine's Day, a female fan broke into his New York apartment demanding attention and threatening to shoot herself if she didn't get it. Wilson took a bullet trying to disarm her and had to be hospitalized; he recovered and the hits kept coming. But, a decade later, even as his shows remained exciting, he was increasingly viewed as an anachronism, and by the mid-seventies had been relegated to the oldies circuit. On September 25, 1975, playing a Dick Clark revue at the Latin Casino in Cherry Hill, New Jersey, he suffered a massive heart attack and stroke on stage—reportedly just as he was delivering the line, from "Lonely Teardrops," "My heart is crying, crying." (Top that, anyone.) Wilson then fell into a coma from which he never emerged. For over eight years he lay in a nursing home bed until he finally died, having never regained consciousness.

Faces of Death 17:
Famous Dates in Rock 'n' Roll Death

February 3

The Big Bopper, died February 3, 1959, age 28
See Last Laughs: Novelty Artists.

Buddy Holly, died February 3, 1959, age 22
See The Day the Music Died: The First Death of Rock 'n' Roll.

Joe Meek, died February 3, 1967
See Da Doo Ron Death.

Ritchie Valens, died February 3, 1959, age 17
See The Day the Music Died: The First Death of Rock 'n' Roll.

July 3

Jim Backus, died July 3, 1989, age 76
See Last Laughs: Novelty Artists.

Brian Jones, died July 3, 1969, age 27
See Gathering Moss with the Rolling Stones.

Jim Morrison, died July 3, 1971, age 27
See Jim Morrison's Beautiful Friend.

August 16

Robert Johnson, died August 16, 1938, age 27
See Hellhound on His Trail.

Elvis Presley, died August 16, 1977, age 42
See The Big Elvis.

Babe Ruth, died August 16, 1948, age 53

November 22

Janet Ertel, died November 22, 1988
See Oozing Crooners.

John Kennedy, died November 22, 1963, age 46

Ted Taylor, died November 22, 1987
See Death's Ululating Maw: Vocal Group Deaths.

December 8

Gregg Allman, born December 8, 1947
See Sha Na Na, Inc.: The Second Death of Rock 'n' Roll.

Hollywood Fats, died December 8, 1986, age 32
See I Wanna Destroy: The Final Death of Rock 'n' Roll.

John Lennon, died December 8, 1980, age 40
See Beatles Bugouts.

Jim Morrison, born December 8, 1944
See Jim Morrison's Beautiful Friend.

Herbert "Tubo" Rhoad, died December 8, 1988, age 44
See Death's Ululating Maw: Vocal Group Deaths.

Marty Robbins, died December 8, 1982, age 57
See Country Corpses.

26

Paramilitary Pop

OVER THE years rock 'n' roll for the most part has remained politically neutral. Every now and then, as in the late sixties, it has drifted toward a kind of watered-down leftist stance, originating in oversimplified middle American thinking and wantonly applied to such complex matters as world peace and prosperity. Rock 'n' roll's most effective political stance, argued by example, has always been for anarchic liberation and the embracing of the ecstatic life. In short, rock 'n' roll, despite its business-as-usual commercialism, has always tended toward transcendent politics.

For a brief period starting in 1965, however, just as Lyndon Johnson was escalating the Vietnam War, a hawkish, right-wing strain of pop music rippled across the pop charts. Among the first was Barry McGuire's "Eve of Destruction," which catapulted to number 1 in the summer of 1965. Written by P.F. Sloan (with Steve Barri) heavily influenced by Bob Dylan, "Eve of Destruction" details the troubles of the day: the burgeoning civil rights movements, the Vietnam War, the intractable conflicts in the Middle East, and the incongruities of an expensive space program.

The version of "Eve of Destruction" that reached the radio and the charts and the hearts and minds of Americans was the rough mix that Sloan and McGuire slapped together in the studio late one night, from which the finished production was to be built. But it caught on almost immediately after a radio station got a hold of the tape and began playing it. Its raw power, even more than its overt message, spoke to something in the air. Despite its liberal agenda, the *sound* of this remarkable protest song was something else entirely — it was militant, plain and simple, an initial volley in the confrontations that escalated in the aftermath of the assassination of John Kennedy. And even more: revelling in its anger, "Eve of Destruction" seems just plain eager for a glorious, apocalyptic end to the world.

It is, however, ultimately reined in by its own inhibited and unconvincing self-righteousness, politely declining to drive the final nail home (even just an insane cackle might have done it). It never quite delivers on its promise, and ends up subtly undermining itself. It was not surprising that McGuire disappeared completely with the song (how could he possibly have followed it up?), nor that he became a born-again Christian a few years later. In a way, "Eve of Destruction" anticipated the ferociousness of punk-rock, but it was clearly a product of its time—a time when, after years of significant problems being repressed, the two sides of any issue could only be polarized, seeking confrontation as an end in itself, preferable to resolution: black and white, old and young, hawk and dove, and, later, men and women.

Enter Staff Sergeant Barry Sadler's "The Ballad of the Green Berets." The impact of this talky doggerel should not be underrated. It spent five consecutive weeks at number 1 in 1966, which is no small accomplishment. Consider for a moment some of the significant chart math associated with it, which gives an indication of just how seriously its sentiments, now thought of as camp, were taken at the time. (Then again—who knows?— perhaps it was the government buying all those singles with tax dollars to encourage support for U.S. involvement in Vietnam.) In the all-time "Hot 100" of the period from 1955 to 1991, as compiled by Joel Whitburn, it ranks number 91—ahead of the Beatles' "Can't Buy Me Love" and the Bee Gees' "Stayin' Alive." It is ranked the number 21 single of the sixties, ahead of "Sugar, Sugar" by the Archies and "(Sittin' on) The Dock of the Bay" by Otis Redding. And it is ranked the number 1 single of 1966, ahead of "The Sounds of Silence" by Simon and Garfunkel, "These Boots Are Made for Walkin' " by Nancy Sinatra, "When a Man Loves a Woman" by Percy Sledge, "96 Tears" by ? and the Mysterians, and "Good Vibrations" by the Beach Boys.

Sadler's plodding number, girded by a martial snare and muted horns and inflected by surprisingly gentle country touches, sang the praises of the U.S. Army Special Forces, otherwise known then as the Green Berets. It was later revealed that the Green Berets operated illegally throughout the Vietnam War (along with everyone else involved in it, including the North Vietnamese, the Cambodians, and the Laotians). The Green Berets were, in fact, carrying out military operations in Vietnam as early as the fifties. Sadler's number, coming at a time when serious debate over the appropriate aims and goals of U.S. involvement in Vietnam was beginning to be heard, no doubt played its part in urging people to just shut up and go along with official U.S. policy, which depended at the time on a lot of Cold War mumbo-jumbo about communism.

Sadler never even came close to repeating his success—the similarly minded "The 'A' Team," which reached number 28, also in 1966, marked his only return to the top forty. But his life nevertheless provides an interesting set of twists and turns. He was the son of a plumber and a waitress who spent their lives as itinerant gamblers, traveling from place to place looking for action, and he really was a Green Berets sergeant, who served in Vietnam until he suffered a leg injury and was discharged in the mid-sixties. In 1978 he killed songwriter Lee Emerson Bellamy in Nashville in a fight over a woman; no charges were ever filed against him. In 1981 he was in trouble again after assaulting a former business partner, but the charges were dropped. Said Sadler, "I'm a Green Berets. If I'd shot him, he'd be dead." Case closed. In 1988, in a decidedly fishy incident, a burglar broke into his Guatemala home (what was Staff Sergeant Barry Sadler doing with a Guatemala home?) and shot him in the head, which resulted in brain damage. He died of a heart attack in 1989, aged forty-nine. (Six weeks later U.S. forces entered Panama.)

Other examples of paramilitary pop during that time include Senator Everett McKinley Dirksen's "Gallant Men," which reached number 29 in 1967. The song itself merely extolled the virtues of soldiers and soldiering in tiresome fashion, but perhaps its greatest impact came from inspiring producer Chip Taylor's "Wild Thing." Under Taylor's guidance the Troggs classic was delivered, complete with ocarina, as by "Senator Everett" on one side and, what turned out to be the actual hit, "Senator Bobby" (Kennedy) on the other. Then there was Victor Lundberg's smug, disturbing "An Open Letter to My Teenage Son," a number 10 hit also in 1967. Reportedly one of the fastest selling spoken-word records ever, it urged youngsters to cut their hair and shut up, or face their parents' rejection. With fatherly love like that who needed military brutalities?

In 1971 came one last spoken-word hit (most of these right-wingers seemed notoriously unable to carry a tune), this one from something called C Company featuring Terry Nelson. The "Battle Hymn of Lt. Calley" defended Calley as a soldier doing his duty and peaked at number 37. Calley, of course, was the United States Army officer court-martialed that year for the 1968 massacre of 347 civilians at My Lai, in Vietnam; one of the most atrocious events of the war—or, more likely, one of the most atrocious events whose details became known.

Then there was Neil Young's angry rap at the U.S. government, "Ohio," a top twenty hit in 1970. Recorded by Crosby, Stills, Nash and Young within days of the massacre at Kent State University of four unarmed students by inexperienced National Guardsmen, "Ohio" was a strident, hectoring indictment of both the incident and the Nixon administration, whose recent military action—the invasion of Cambodia by U.S. forces—had given rise to the campus demonstration in the first place. Like "Eve of Destruction," "Ohio" came on as a call for peace and justice, but was driven by a dark, violent impulse toward confrontation and forceful action.

Of course, other songs may also be counted as paramilitary pop of a kind. Such songs as the Shirelles' "Soldier Boy," a number 1 hit in 1962 over three years before the U.S. escalation of involvement in Vietnam, and Bo Donaldson and the Heywoods' "Billy, Don't Be a Hero," a number 1 hit in 1974 (nominally it was about the Civil War, but consider its attitude and its release date). But they are not quite in the same league as "Eve of Destruction" and the others.

Faces of Death 18: Heroin

Tommy Bolin, died December 4, 1976, age 25
See Guitar Heroes.

Tim Buckley, died June 29, 1975, age 28
See Just Us Dead Folk.

Brian Cole, died August 2, 1972, age 28
See Death Lite.

Darby Crash, died December 7, 1980, age 22
See I Wanna Destroy: The Final Death of Rock 'n' Roll.

Tim Hardin, died December 29, 1980, age 39
See Just Us Dead Folk.

James Honeyman-Scott, died June 16, 1982, age 25
See Stop Your Sobbing.

Janis Joplin, died October 4, 1970, age 27
See Sha Na Na, Inc.: The Second Death of Rock 'n' Roll.

Frankie Lymon, died February 28, 1968, age 26
See Death's Ululating Maw: Vocal Group Deaths.

Stefanie Sargent, died June 28, 1992, age 24
See Munching the Corpse: The Utter Assurance of Death's Future.

Will Shatter, died December 9, 1987, age 31
See I Wanna Destroy: The Final Death of Rock 'n' Roll.

Hillel Slovak, died June 27, 1988, age 25
See Munching the Corpse: The Utter Assurance of Death's Future.

Vinnie Taylor, died April 17, 1974
See Sha Na Na, Inc.: The Second Death of Rock 'n' Roll.

Johnny Thunders, died April 23, 1991, age 38
See I Wanna Destroy: The Final Death of Rock 'n' Roll
(The New York Dolls).

Sid Vicious, died February 2, 1979, age 21
See I Wanna Destroy: The Final Death of Rock 'n' Roll.

Danny Whitten, died November 18, 1972, age 29
See Sha Na Na, Inc.: The Second Death of Rock 'n' Roll.

Andrew Wood, died March 19, 1990, age 24
See Munching the Corpse: The Utter Assurance of Death's Future.

27

The Death Wish as Ethic: Lou Reed

PERHAPS NO one in rock 'n' roll has ever taken more misplaced flak from detractors than Lou Reed and the Velvet Underground—on the other hand, perhaps no one has ever won such an endless stream of uncritical praise from followers (well, maybe Elvis). Such are the difficulties associated with making the call on a person whose most influential band's most famous calling card seems to be that old joke about them which I will now repeat in the hope that no one will ever have to hear it again: Though perhaps fewer than 50,000 people bought the Velvet Underground's albums when they first came out, every one of them went on to form a band.

The most commonly heard complaint about Lou Reed and the Velvet Underground seems to be based chiefly on casual listenings of "Heroin," "Venus in Furs," and perhaps "Sister Ray"—it was, namely, the charge that they glorified violence, death, and depravity. I have seen people shudder at the line "despite all the amputations" in "Rock & Roll," as if it were something out of de Sade (when in fact it has more to do with Murray the K and soft-drink commercials). The alienation factor might have been a brilliant public relations coup—in fear and loathing there is power, after all, as the subsequent ballooning of their reputation after their career was officially over demonstrated—but the Velvet Underground just wanted to be rock stars like everyone else at the time. In the end, it was evidence of how far off course the wrong image can seem to push people, because the fact is that few in rock 'n' roll have ever been as stringently moralistic, as puritanical, as Lou Reed.

Periodically, throughout Reed's solo career, generous exceptions have been made for him by those who despise him. You could almost hear them yelping in surprise: "Hey, this guy's funny!" (1972's *Transformer*). "Hey, this guy's sensitive!" (1976's *Coney Island Baby*). "Hey, this guy's got some insight!" (1982's *The Blue Mask*). "Hey, this guy really cares!" (1989's *New*

York). They admired the pop sizzle of 1984's *New Sensations* and the adrenaline nerve of 1978's *Street Hassle* and the bludgeoning pathos of 1973's *Berlin.* But the attitude remained that the best of Lou Reed's work was little more than surprise strayings from his normal ground of hedonism and decadence.

Actually, Reed's most powerful work (the bulk of it anyway) was already prefigured in the Velvet Underground — and what has been seen as his glamorous wastrel exercises are actually the exceptions (the homosexual pose of the seventies, a stage act circa 1974 that involved a broadly played drug-injection scenario, and 1975's *Metal Machine Music,* a two-record set of horrible screeches and drones presented with a completely straight face). The facts are clear. You don't reach the age of fifty and produce a sizable body of work by living a dissipated life.

So here's where things get weird. Take apart the work of Lou Reed while with the Velvet Underground, and his similarity to Ernest Hemingway, of all people, begins to emerge. Both show a preference for dry, clipped, unadorned delivery — exaggerated in Hemingway by his rule of no adjectives, in Reed by his infatuation with binaural stereo. Both maintained enormous egos and managed superhuman reputations in their personal lives, under the cover of others labeling them geniuses. But most importantly, for both Reed and Hemingway the death wish has never been a mere cowardly longing for oblivion, but rather an ethical impulse to a necessary test of spiritual fitness.

For both men, facing the risk of death — even more, the choice of death — is the most profoundly moral act of which we are capable. If Hemingway found it in challenging primitive rural nature in all its forms, in fishing and hunting and bullfighting, Reed found it in challenging primitive urban nature in all its forms, moving through the rhythmic, pulsating big-city landscape to score drugs, make sexual connections, and have a few laughs. Trust me on this one — in the right circumstances, landing a cab can offer the same thrill of poise, timing, and survival as landing a marlin.

Hemingway and Reed have both sought to observe people in extreme circumstances, thinking that was how to see them at their best. But neither confined himself to mere observation. Both participated in the life they observed. (This is perhaps the neatest explanation for Reed's substance-abuse problems, which lasted many years and are otherwise not our concern. Hemingway's alcoholism, by the same token, lasted all his life.) That desire to be at once involved and detached, to risk everything for the sake of art and simply because it is the right thing to do, is exactly what lends Reed's canon its gritty authenticity — *and* its great beating heart, a heart as severe as it is tender.

Let's forget, for now, Reed's gorgeous romantic streak, which has surfaced all through his career, from the first song on the first Velvet Underground album ("Sunday Morning") to his most recent work, 1992's *Magic and Loss* and the 1990 collaboration with John Cale, the Andy Warhol tribute *Songs for Drella*. His most notorious songs, "Heroin" and "Venus in Furs," glorify nothing that does not deserve to be glorified. Wiping out psychic pain, no matter how briefly, stands as an astonishingly wonderful thing in its own right. But in the ways described in these songs this momentary escape from pain is ultimately false too; Reed knows that and never looks away from it, never pretends otherwise. These are not songs about having fun, but songs about sin—and the very idea of sin arises from a profoundly moral view, not a decadent one.

"Heroin" describes a person consciously facing an enormous choice. "I have made a big decision," Reed's junkie croaks early on, "I'm gonna try to nullify my life." That's hardly glorification—most of us can understand the impulse toward annihilation, but only a few of us figure heroin is an acceptable way to respond to it. That is the strength and power of this song. If "Heroin" manages to convey all the seductive appeals of oblivion, it never comes close to recommending it as a course of action. In the end the junkie's choice is disturbing, not least because we have been artfully and carefully presented a way in which to connect with it, but also because the choice to reject life so clearly meets with Reed's disapproval.

Similarly, "Venus in Furs" explicitly rejects the notion of sexual deviance in a barter-and-exchange setting as anything close to liberating. Its main character, Severin, is clearly a schnook, for whom Reed, the singer, has nothing but unconcealed scorn. Even the "whiplash girl-child" is more a pathetic figure than anything, not really a sexual object at all to anyone but Severin, and ultimately just another victim of a sordid system that benefits no one, offering only fleeting balm to those who embrace their demons rather than face them. No one in this song, least of all the bitingly sarcastic Reed, has much fun.

Ellen Willis, in her essay on Reed and the Velvet Underground in the anthology *Stranded,* cuts to the quick. "Life may be a brutal struggle, sin inevitable, innocence elusive and transient, grace a gift, not a reward," she writes. "[N]evertheless we are responsible for who and what we become. Reed does not attempt to resolve this familiar spiritual paradox, nor does he regard it as unfair. His basic religious assumption (like Baudelaire's) is that like it or not we inhabit a moral universe, that we have free will, that we must choose between good and evil, and that our choices matter absolutely; if we are rarely strong enough to make the right choices, if we can never count on the moments of illumination that make them possible, still it is spiritual death to give up the effort."

Lou Reed has never stumped for spiritual death—his work and his life have continually demonstrated that. But, as with Hemingway's bullfighter, time and again he seems to need to face down—in dramatic fashion—the death wish, that alluring, painful longing to see everything end. He has managed it too, often enough, and conveyed it so effectively in his work that it speaks powerfully to that same impulse in everyone. If I were a betting man, I might wager that Reed will not arrive at Hemingway's pathetic end.

28

The Death Wish as Fetish: Leonard Cohen

L EONARD COHEN, a native of Canada like some of the very best American rock 'n' roll figures, including Joni Mitchell, Neil Young, and most
of the Band, first came to prominence in the late fifties as a poet and literary
figure, writing and publishing novels and collections of poetry. It shows,
both in the deliberate manner with which his lyrics draw scenarios and in
his flat, monotonous presentation of them. He made the shift to music
partly as a commercial move (we all have to make a living, and anyone can
tell you poetry is no way to do it), but there was more to it than that. Inspired by the fusion that beat-generation writers were attempting between
literature and bop and post-bop jazz, Cohen himself took a turn at it.

Nothing much came of that. But nearly ten years later, with rock 'n' roll
and folk-rock and rock having come to ascendance, he took another stab
at it. This time it was in the funereal hush of gentle acoustic guitars and
careful studio inflections, and this time it worked—to an astonishing degree. The best and most focused of it is still found on his first album, 1968's
Songs of Leonard Cohen, which contains all the disquieting seeds of his
greatest insight: the acceptance and exploration of the deeply forged links
between sex and death and religion.

What exactly provokes the curiously inert quality of Cohen's work is
hard to say, just as it is hard to say what drives him forward into life. In
his songs passion seems a lie, sentimentality an embarrassment, suicide a
bother—and messy. Life occurs in a gloomy twilight, marked by random
copulation in which, nonetheless, some sense of the eternal may be
glimpsed, in fleeting flashes of beauty. Yet Cohen will also swear that even
beauty itself is finally a lie, leaving only memory. And that memory is always a lie, perhaps the most deceitful of all.

For Leonard Cohen, the death wish—that enduring desire, conscious and
unconscious, to put an end to the frustrating senselessness that life mostly

offers us—is far more than a useful affectation, though it is that too, of course. But more poignantly, in his best work (especially "Suzanne" and "Famous Blue Raincoat") Cohen focuses on how that painful longing rears suddenly at those times, in sex and religious ceremony, when we seem the most ready to embrace life on its terms. The need to be connected coupled with the knowledge of finality are ultimately so linked for Cohen that he comes to appreciate the tension between them almost for itself, turning the death wish into a kind of totem or fetish, which seems to leave him suspended between his choices.

Cohen's primary motivation finally seems to come from the connection he sees between women and the unyielding forces of nature. Nature is marked by death, but in many ways sex is as close as we can get to nature. In retrospect, that first album's back cover captures his concerns and attitude in a single, inspired image—a vivid, almost cartoonish, depiction of a nude woman, chained and engulfed in flames, raising her hands in supplication, though her face remains a stoic mask of faith. It looks like the Madonna, but what would she be doing there? Perhaps it is Joan of Arc. Perhaps it is Eve, cast into hell for betraying mankind.

More likely it is just another one of the anonymous (albeit frequently named) women who populate Cohen's songs of eternal weariness, of struggle without redemption—women uniformly knocked awry by unspecified factors in the world. Call it the horror of life. But they are nonetheless women who stand as irresistible objects of desire to Cohen; he has nothing to give them, but happily takes what they offer, in the brutally cold yet somehow tender negotiation of live-and-let-live that marks all his work. Few actually die in Cohen's songs—that would cause too much unseemly drama—but no one is ever particularly alive either.

Even so, his granite facade does present something like a program for living, a timely if calculated and shell-shocked design for dealing with the horrors of Vietnam and the political assassinations and riots of the time. But something has always been missing from his work (is it really as simple as warmth?), which makes it all the more fascinating and even, somehow, touching. He is like a religious zealot minus the innocence, like Job after the wager, like Abraham traumatized at the peak of the knife's arc. And it is not even so exalted—it is a feeling most of us know.

Interestingly, as Cohen drifted from his cold flatness and into more structured and melodic songs over the course of his career, with country and even pop inflections showing up in the late seventies and eighties (one album was produced by Phil Spector), his original style was increasingly appropriated by Lou Reed. Always something of a monotone himself, Reed began to use it, like Cohen, as a strategy for underlining his morbid themes, starting as early as 1976's *Coney Island Baby* and 1978's *Street Hassle* (it's particularly obvious in the title song from the latter album, which largely anticipated the best of Reed's work a decade later). Unlike Cohen, however, Reed has always reserved a measure of hope and faith for life.

Did I say no one dies in a Leonard Cohen song? I take that back. "Chelsea Hotel No. 2" is about Janis Joplin: "I remember you well in the Chelsea Hotel / you were talking so brave and so sweet / giving me head on the unmade bed / while the limousines wait in the street," he starts. "I don't mean to suggest that I loved you the best / I can't keep track of each fallen robin / I remember you well in the Chelsea Hotel / that's all I don't think of you that often," he concludes. Somebody light a candle.

29

The Death Wish as Gesture: Iggy Pop's Small Still Voice

O NE TIME through his very best album, 1977's *Lust for Life,* should be enough to convince even the most hardened that there is not an awful lot of longing for death within the soul of Iggy Pop. The title itself betrays little irony, as the joyfully grinning mug of Ypsilanti, Michigan, native James Osterberg on the cover only underscores. And the sheer exuberance of such numbers as "Success," which finally disintegrates under the weight of its own utterly infectious joy, brings it all home to roost. But then the very next song, "Turn Blue," which he opens by addressing Jesus himself ("Jesus?" he peeps into the silence at a sudden break, "This is Iggy," and then mewls, "You might as well come with me for the ride"), stands as a complex, powerful, confused number that plays like a suicide note improvised on the spot, right there in the studio before God, musicians, and technicians. Those two tracks together pose the central problem of Iggy Pop.

From the beginning, Iggy Pop's work has been marked by a protracted struggle to justify joy in the face of despair—even as far back as 1969, when he first emerged from Detroit with the Stooges calling himself Iggy Stooge (a name more appropriate to his place in history, if doubtless harder on him personally). In his first recorded statement, following a ferocious heralding by a fuzztoned wah-wah guitar, he cries, "Well, all right!" and continues, "Well, it's 1969, OK/War across the U.S.A./ Well, it's another year for me and you/Another year with nothin' to do." He's having plenty of fun with these radically flat declarations, at once antiestablishment and antihippie—you can hear it in his voice.

But they're tearing him up too, or something is. You can hear that in his voice too. Back then he acted out his inner conflicts and turmoil in performance, as a maniac on the stage covering himself with peanut butter and broken shards of glass, thrashing about furiously and cutting himself open, throwing himself into his audiences and continually baiting them to further excesses of abuse. That vein of self-destructiveness (which, simply as a matter of growing up, he dispensed with in the mid-seventies) later earned him frequent notice as a godfather of punk-rock, but all too few punks recognized the pain that self-destructiveness caused him, and how deeply it ran. It was the punks who were confused. They saw the violence he directed toward himself and assumed the joy they heard came from that. Not so — at heart, he has always been a giddy optimist embracing life.

Iggy Pop stands as the link between the blind groping toward apocalyptic resolution as expressed by Jim Morrison, whom he idolized, and the teen angst that continues into adult life (question: does it ever go away?) realized perfectly in the early commercial exercises of Alice Cooper. But Iggy Pop's closest spiritual brother in all of rock 'n' roll is Jonathan Richman. Like him, Iggy loves life and music and people and performing, and always has. Unlike Richman, however, Iggy is not willing to look away from the horrors that continually undercut affirmation. He understands that the seeds of both joy and despair exist within each other, that both are forever linked, and that neither one is possible without the other. After all, affirmation of life can be empty, a mere gesture — such as the promises offered by hippies seeking to make a better world by wishing for it (that generation's subsequent actions in the eighties may have provided a far truer measure of their priorities).

But if affirmation as an empty gesture horrifies him, he finds the death wish as a gesture even more repugnant. Iggy Pop, struggling throughout his career to balance and acknowledge this conflict, has suffered emotional and mental problems that have seen him institutionalized. But he has always clung to the belief that life can be good and it doesn't have to be bad. Early on, the result of his own biology as much as anything, he stumbled onto the perfect metaphor for his dilemma: sex — as balm, as salvation, and most importantly as the single most meaningful act of existential courage (forget Camus's identification of that with suicide). If it is affirmation that Iggy Pop lusts for, he is happy to find it in lust itself.

Thus, if sex is a preoccupation that recurs constantly through Iggy Pop's canon, it is not often marked by lechery or guilt. At worst, as in the early years, it is somewhat damaged by what we may as well call low self-esteem, as in "I Wanna Be Your Dog" and "Dirt" — which nonetheless make a point. More often it is an unaffected expression of health itself, refreshing in its straightforward and unpretentious vigor. Compare his "Girls," from 1979's *New Values* ("Some have beautiful shapes," he sings, "I wanna live to be ninety-eight"), with the Rolling Stones' "Some Girls" of the year before, which mocks lechery and sexual guilt by replicating it, in perfectly creepy fashion, finally evincing only a disturbing anger and contempt toward women. Iggy's song, by contrast, has only affection at its heart.

It is this credible attitude toward sex that makes *Lust for Life,* and especially "Turn Blue," the overwhelming tour de force it is. It's commonly argued that by providing some kind of steadying effect on the wild fluctuations of Iggy Pop's life David Bowie has brought out the best in him. But actually the reverse is true, as this album clearly shows. All through it, on songs like "Some Weird Sin" and "Sixteen," Bowie's music rises to the occasion of Iggy's lyrics (or perhaps only the potential of his lyrics—much here sounds, and reads on the lyric sheet, as though it were improvised in the studio), providing musical settings that function almost like the snake in the Garden of Eden, sleazy pieces of charged atmosphere that continually challenge Iggy to surrender to temptation and debasement.

But Iggy never bites, and on "Turn Blue," in fact, completely turns the tables. It is the one song on the album whose lyrics are not printed on the cover, leaving us to make do with what we hear and think we hear. Bowie's rough-hewn choir opens it with a single word: "Nazarene." Then Iggy steps in, spying a beautiful black woman in a Cadillac and calling our attention to it, just before he addresses Jesus, who shifts in and out of the song as the focus of Iggy's monologue. It is never clear exactly what is happening, or "where" the song is "taking place" (and for the most part the racial references remain obtusely inert). But it seems likely the singer, who keeps repeating "I shot myself down" and "I shot myself up," has just committed suicide, or at least died accidentally. Clearly this song is about death—clearly Iggy is dealing with final matters of the soul. And what he wants, all that he wants, is to be loved for himself, for the pain he suffers from others "stepping on our hearts" to be understood: "You got nobody left but me," he cries from the depths at one point. "Well, accept me, don't reject me/Don't forget me."

That, and little more, is all that anyone wants: acceptance and affirmation, which particularly nowadays comes rarely and at high cost—and, as Iggy Pop knows well and argues by example in his music, it can only be achieved in life, never in death. Death comes to all of us, he'll concede, but it's not worth glorifying. He never has and he likely never will.

30

Friends: Charles Manson and Dennis Wilson

THE BEST that anyone can tell, there was nothing in this world that Charles Manson wanted more than to be a singer/songwriter pop star. Long before he had ever assembled his dreadful "Family" and lodged them on the Spahn Movie Ranch in the Simi Valley, near Los Angeles, he had spent a good deal of time knocking around Calfornia like a minstrel, playing the guitar and writing songs. Not as much time, perhaps, as he'd devoted to stealing cars, forging checks, burglarizing homes, and pimping—he had spent more than half his life in prison, after all. But, the best that anyone can tell, that hadn't changed his ambitions. When Manson met twenty-three-year-old Dennis Wilson of the Beach Boys in 1968 he had hopes that this was going to be the break he needed to set up in show business.

They met through a peculiar set of circumstances, which nonetheless were typical for all involved. One day in the late spring of 1968 Wilson picked up a couple of hitchhikers—Ella Jo Bailey, who called herself Yellerstone, and Patricia Krenwinkel, who called herself Marnie Reeves. He didn't know it at the time, but they were members of Manson's Family. He talked himself up to them as a Beach Boy and eventually took them to his rented home on Sunset Boulevard to show them his gold records. As he'd hoped, he ended up having sex with them (later he found the experience had given him gonorrhea). When he returned home again late that night after a studio session, Manson and the Family were there waiting for him, hanging around smoking pot, drinking, and rummaging through his refrigerator for food.

They stayed for most of the rest of that summer, in what came to be called Manson's "Sunset Boulevard period." At first Wilson was perfectly happy with the arrangement. Orgies were a daily routine, and in many ways he and Manson saw eye to eye on things. More likely, Wilson was an easy victim for Manson's overpowering personality. They lived the late-sixties California youth culture life to the hilt that summer, with plentiful sex and psychedelic drugs. Wilson footed the bill, but it was no hardship on him financially.

Manson, however, was nursing his own agenda—he saw Wilson as his key to becoming a pop star. At the time, the Beach Boys were beginning their long decline, following the *Smile* fiasco and the change in the cultural climate in the late sixties. But the momentum from their successes still lent them credibility with Capitol, who'd helped them set up their own label, Brother. Wilson, impressed with Manson's songs, worked to get them recorded. He introduced Manson around to the Beach Boys and others at Brother, and finally booked time for him in his brother Brian's new studio in Brian's home.

With engineer Stephen Despar, Manson laid down some half dozen tracks that summer, intended as demos. Reports on their quality vary, but most indicate they were passingly fair, anyway. Manson and Dennis had hopes that producer Terry Melcher (Doris Day's son, who had engineered the early success of the Byrds and then Paul Revere and the Raiders) would step in to polish them and help pitch Manson to a label. Some eight months later, however, in the spring of 1969, Melcher auditioned him and turned him down.

By that time relations between Wilson and Manson had soured. Toward the end of the previous summer, Manson's presence in his home had become increasingly disturbing to Wilson and his friends. Manson's psychotic side periodically surfaced—at one point, when Wilson was not there, Manson had threatened to rape his girlfriend of the time, Croxey Adams, at knifepoint (Adams had made a point of maintaining her distance from Manson and his Family all summer). Wilson, who was afraid of Manson and didn't want to confront him, finally escaped him by simply moving out of the rented home, leaving the eviction honors to his landlord.

But Manson never let Wilson get out of touch for long, and continued to pressure him to help with his music. As a result, Wilson eventually talked the Beach Boys into recording one of Manson's songs. The group changed the chorus hook for Manson's "Cease to Exist" to "cease to resist," and re-titled the song "Never Learn Not to Love." The changes enraged Manson, but the song does appear on the Beach Boys' 1969 album *20/20*, and was also the B-side of the album's first single, "Bluebirds over the Mountain," which reached number 61—likely the highest charting to date for a mass murderer.

But this was the end rather than the beginning of Manson's career as a singer/songwriter. Manson knew it, and somehow came to hold Terry

Melcher responsible for his relatively dismal showing. As Manson began to plot his revenge, he became deeply obsessed with the Beatles' just-released White Album, which he believed was delivering him veiled messages, including a strategy for psychological terror called "Helter Skelter."

And that is how one of the most infamous crimes of the era occurred. Manson knew that Melcher had moved from his rented home on Cielo Drive early in 1969, but as part of a campaign of terror directed against him Manson and his Family entered the house in the early evening of August 9, 1969, and viciously slaughtered everyone present: Sharon Tate, who was two weeks short of bearing a child by her husband Roman Polanski, Jay Sebring, Abigail Folger, and Wojtek Frykowski.

For Manson, it was his crowning moment of glory. He was arrested a few months later and a widely publicized trial followed. He was finally a pop star. For the victims' families and friends, it was a senseless tragedy. For Melcher, it was the beginning of a protracted period of traumatic anxiety. And for Dennis Wilson, it was just another sad chapter in a confused life, perhaps the most telling.

Of the three Wilson brothers, Dennis was the middle child, separated by two years from both Brian and Carl. He was designated the troublemaker in the family, a title he also held within the group. He never finished high school, having been expelled for fighting, but the Beach Boys provided a haven of sorts for him, and a source of income. He was the group's only surfer. At their first recording session it was Dennis who suggested surfing as their ticket to success, to the annoyance of everyone else in the group. But he was right, and the subsequent dividends proved as enormous as they were memorable, with an impressive string of hits between 1963 and 1966, including the number 1 "I Get Around" in 1964, the number 1 "Help Me, Rhonda" in 1965, and the number 1 "Good Vibrations" in 1966. Their 1966 album *Pet Sounds* still stands as one of the greatest of all rock 'n' roll albums.

But the legendary problems of the superficially sunshine-and-brightness Wilson family ran deep (it seems likely from the evidence that Murry, their father, was sadistically abusive). Dennis was a profoundly troubled person, every bit as troubled as his more fabled brother Brian. Married five times— twice, consecutively, to Karen Lamm, and last to Mike Love's illegitimate daughter Shawn, some twenty years his junior—the addictions of Dennis were prodigious and wide-ranging, and included cocaine, heroin, alcohol, and, above all others, sex (his partners likely numbered well into four figures).

Of his involvement with Manson, Dennis Wilson, declining comment, had this to say in 1976: "I don't talk about Manson. I think he's a sick fuck.

I think of Roman and those wonderful people who had a beautiful family and they fucking had their tits cut off. I want to benefit from that?" But Manson's intrusion on Wilson's life was altogether too eerily appropriate in many ways. All his life those who knew Wilson begged him to seek treatment for his problems, but he never did, and finally, on December 28, 1983, drunk, he drowned while swimming in the ocean in conditions that were far too cold for it. He was thirty-nine.

31

Sha Na Na, Inc.:
The Second Death of Rock 'n' Roll

BY 1970 there no longer seemed to be such a thing as rock 'n' roll. The term itself had become an embarrassment, painfully reminiscent of naive teen years of yore. In the mid-sixties, after the British Invasion and Bob Dylan took root, drug use and opposition to the Vietnam War mounted and began to create a new kind of urban bohemian—namely, the hippie. The music that had started out combining the powerful blues feel and energy with the structures and attitudes of country music began to be more comfortably called simply "rock." After the Monterey Pop Festival in 1967, that trend locked in and quickly took on a life of its own. That summer, the "Summer of Love," it became a kind of totem as the first two "important" "rock" albums emerged and roosted atop the album charts all summer: the Beatles' *Sgt. Pepper's Lonely Hearts Club Band* and the Doors' self-titled album debut.

Already rock was something different than rock 'n' roll. It came in albums from stores, not singles on the radio, and it hewed far closer to the blues, repudiating its connection to country music, which was openly detested by most rock fans (estimable country artists such as Merle Haggard, meanwhile, were only too happy to return the favor in such baiting classics as "Okie from Muskogee"). Britain's Cream, the first rock supergroup, was perhaps the best example of the new rock. Composed of "super-members" from other groups, hence the name, they jammed long and sultry, if a little self-consciously, on the basic blues riffs they'd learned from the classic recordings of U.S. blues players, scoring on the radio only as some kind of concession to their record company. They themselves were above that. The new avenue proved a great boon to many deserving blues artists, such as B.B. King, Muddy Waters, Howlin' Wolf, Lightnin' Hopkins, and John Lee Hooker, who found a whole new audience of a size they never could have imagined before. But in the long run rock 'n' roll in this extended form never seemed so lifeless and prone to formula.

Even so, it was popular at the time, popular enough to define the era. In the late sixties a whole new cast of players with strange new names stepped in, some from England, still cruising on the credibility won by the groups of the British Invasion, others from San Francisco's Haight-Ashbury neighborhood, just transformed into a bohemian conclave with a worldwide profile. The new players were united by their allegiance to the blues, by a received political consciousness out of singer/songwriter music ("folk-rock," by Dylan, the Byrds, Simon and Garfunkel, and others in the mid-sixties was the beginning of the change from "rock 'n' roll" to "rock"), and, above all else, by self-indulgence: Big Brother and the Holding Company with Janis Joplin, Cream, the Grateful Dead, the Jefferson Airplane, the Jimi Hendrix Experience, the Electric Flag, Canned Heat, Buffalo Springfield, Country Joe and the Fish, Quicksilver Messenger Service, the Incredible String Band, Ten Years After, Moby Grape, and countless more.

Most of them played at Monterey and also, its opposite bookend of the era, at the Woodstock festival in 1969. It's clear now that in many ways the two events marked the beginning and end of rock and rock culture, though rock continued to be felt as easily the most pervasive of all the jumbled mess of pop music choices for another ten years. But the era definitely came to some kind of screeching halt with the second round of spectacular rock 'n' roll deaths: the separate demises of Brian Jones, Jimi Hendrix, Janis Joplin, and Jim Morrison, which made the same enormous, traumatic impact in the early seventies as the payola scandal and the various troubles of Chuck Berry, Jerry Lee Lewis, Little Richard, and the death of Buddy Holly had made in the late fifties.

But the deaths of Jones, Hendrix, Joplin, and Morrison, the Mount Rushmore of rock culture, had a slightly different twist. The figures from the first wave of rock 'n' roll had been seen as complicit in their fates. By choosing rock 'n' roll, by choosing to embrace a celebratory (not to mention celebrity) life, and showing a willingness to step outside the confining "norms of society," they had declared themselves willing to pay the price, even death, for their career choice. It was that simple, and it was part of what lent their gesture so much power. (Jerry Lee Lewis, as usual, is something of the square peg here, his contours fitting a little more closely with the later punks, who happily and openly affirmed death and destruction because it represented an end to the pain of a deceitful existence. But that is not the only impulse driving him, and Jerry Lee Lewis must finally be counted a case unto himself.)

The sixties figures were seen as having dared death and yet remaining, somehow, undeserving of it. This attitude is seen best in perhaps the greatest symbolic event of the period, the break-up of the Beatles. Like divorce, it was death and it wasn't; as it was the best choice in a scenario that didn't allow many options. Thus the Beatles were not held responsible for their own demise (but, in the best tradition of divorce, sides were taken, mostly between Lennon and McCartney).

Equally, during this time, the rock stars who died were seen as innocent casualties in an unjust war. It was as if these people, despite the evidence, didn't participate in their own deaths in any way whatever. As with John Kennedy, whose assassination started people thinking this way, the so-called counterculture deaths were popularly perceived as the result of conspiracies and outside forces. Which is not to say these things don't happen. Still, from the best evidence the Beatles chose to dissolve the group on the basis of irreconcilable differences, and as for Hendrix, Joplin, Morrison, et al., each died by his or her own hand, albeit accidentally, from drug-related causes.

But since it was an era rife with the idea of conspiracy, absurd questions began to be raised about the dead: Did Mick Jagger and Keith Richards (in some versions, in league with Satan) want Brian Jones out of the way permanently and forever? Did President Nixon and the CIA want to eliminate the threat of youth revolution by systematically eliminating their most popular and outrageous heroes? (It is clear something like that was involved in the case of John Lennon's protracted attempts to seek permanent residency in the United States. It was no coincidence that not until Watergate had ended, and a new era begun, was his status finally settled.) It is plain unlikely any of these sixties figures died for political reasons (or, in the case of Morrison, that he didn't actually die). They were victims of their own longings for fame and their naiveté about how the world works, a common symptom even today among people who came of age in the sixties, when everything seemed possible just by wanting it.

That era was marked by the quiet decline of independent record labels and the resumption of power by the major companies. Among the independent labels, all the big players in rock 'n' roll were going under: Chess went belly up at that time, Atlantic and Elektra came under larger corporate umbrellas (eventually controlled by Warner Bros.), Motown increasingly copied the practices of the majors, and Sun was long since out of it.

Finally and yet somehow suddenly, nearly two decades after Columbia's A&R chief Mitch Miller had sniffed at rock 'n' roll as a passing fad, the majors had figured out how to adapt to it. The fundamental power of the original music was simply denied, derided, and lost in the haze of the compromised pop music of the early sixties. And then along came rock, the perfect substitute: marketable and amenable to packaging on albums, which could be retailed for over five times as much as rock 'n' roll's product, singles, and had the potential for far better profit margins. And the new acts could be managed, easily enough, once they'd caught the scent of money. After Monterey, most of the significant rock artists came under contract to major labels, with big fat deals about which they were not about to squawk.

Among them were the Mount Rushmores. In 1966 Allen Klein negotiated for the Rolling Stones with Decca and won them the best recording deal ever at the time. The Doors' spectacular success guaranteed them rank and privilege at Elektra. And shortly after the Monterey festival, Warner Bros. and Columbia, respectively, snagged Hendrix and Joplin. Then came the pressures for product, for which none of these anti-professionals were particularly equipped. Professionalism was never supposed to be the point, so they thought; all four had been inspired in the first place by Elvis Presley's implicit call to liberation and the anarchic freedom promised and delivered in that heady first wave of rock 'n' roll.

But suddenly, especially for Brian Jones, as Jagger and Richards found their corporate feet, it seemed to be professionalism that mattered above all else. Similarly, Hendrix's astonishing guitar playing and deceptively casual songcraft were not considered enough—managers, promoters, and audiences wanted a showman. Joplin, on the other hand, a consummate performer capable of dependably working crowds into a frenzy, could never get the recorded product to measure up, and was consequently hounded to improve it. Morrison, for his part, responded to the pressures by growing ever more recalcitrant and impossible.

They were victims, all right, but not of a web of government moles. No, they were victims of a commercial star system. On the face of it it was a system as egalitarian and utopian as anyone could hope for—after all, if scruffy hippies and youngsters in their twenties can make it big, anyone can, right?—but in fact it represented the utter co-optation of the most dearly held values of the rock culture, which, as the cliché rightly has it, were stolen from a whole generation by big business interests and sold back at a tidy profit. (Todd Rundgren, in 1975: "I thought we were supposed to be free/But we all got sold.")

At the time, many had an inarticulated feeling for what was happening, but it was hard to see through the murk of a seeming youth revolution and a simultaneous political swing to the right by the U.S. electorate. It was hard to see anything at the time. Absolutely everything seemed to be changing at such thrillingly reckless events as the 1968 Chicago Democratic Convention or the Tet offensive, earlier that year, in Vietnam, or at the time of the Kennedy and King assassinations. But people who loved the music knew something was wrong, even if they couldn't say what it was. *Rolling Stone* and *Creem* critics carped endlessly about "sell-outs" and "hype," even as they hopped planes to elaborate junkets.

And pretty soon the death knell for rock 'n' roll began to be heard again, although, interestingly enough, it was sounded somewhat more cautiously this time, as if a lesson had been learned by the alarmist pronunciamentos of the late fifties. Even more interesting, this caution continued apace until, when in the late seventies rock 'n' roll really did die, virtually no one took note of it. But in 1970 people were willing to step forward and call attention to what was happening. "A cycle is coming to an end," Jon Landau wrote in *Rolling Stone* late in 1970. "The process of creating stars has become a routine and a formula as dry as an equation. . . . [A]midst the economic tightening in the industry, and the changing character of the audience, something new is forming. Whether or not it will lead to something basically different than the music of the last six years cannot be discerned as of yet, but the change is now."

One group who underwent their rite of passage at Woodstock — in fact were an enormous hit there — represent all that was wrong with rock 'n' roll and rock during this period, and much that has stayed wrong: Sha Na Na. Their TV show, let alone their records, do not survive them well, exposing a crappy group with minimal musical or cultural sense. But it was never their TV show, let alone their records, that put them over. It was the attitude behind the act, lumping all fifties rock 'n' roll styles — rockabilly, vocal group, New Orleans rhythm and blues, Chicago rhythm and blues, and more — into a mushy, daffy, mugging, empty shtick. Their claims on credibility stemmed from the presence of saxman Lennie Baker, who had played with Danny and the Juniors, but it was clear from the beginning they had no feeling for the music or what it stood for or could be. To them, and to the rock audience who lapped it up at Woodstock, it represented at once everything they loathed and loved about life in the fifties — naive, sheltered, unknowing, silly (in retrospect qualities now more usefully ascribed to rock).

No one could have performed a more important service in the co-optation of the music. Sha Na Na introduced a new generation, and a significant one, to nostalgia, the self-deceiving survival mechanism of a culture that can never forget its past because it so resolutely refuses to admit it has one. "Look," it says, "how silly we once were, ha ha. How far we have come since then." And there you have Sha Na Na, and the kernel of all nostalgia fixations that have raged way out of control since that time. Today's reflexive nostalgia for the seventies, the time when nostalgia got underway in earnest, only underlines its severity.

Rock 'n' roll, however, was not dead yet. It was on its deathbed, resting comfortably, through much of the seventies, but it was not dead. As the decade produced a series of hyphen-rock spin-offs (jazz-rock, country-rock, glitter-rock, punk-rock, you-name-it-rock), the best of it picked up pieces of the original music that had been discarded during the sixties, finding new ways to make it come alive again. Perhaps the truest work in the linear continuum from the fifties came out of the glam-rock scenes in London and New York, which ultimately served as the aesthetic precursors to punk-rock and the final demise of rock 'n' roll. Such figures as David Bowie, Lou Reed, and Marc Bolan, emerging from folk-rock origins emphasizing structure, introduced complex layers of meaning and gesture even as they reintroduced song architecture, while others, such as the New York Dolls, the Ramones, and again Lou Reed, laid in the fifties' implied anarchic liberation across the noisy charging attack of rock, picking up where mid-sixties garage bands, aping the British Invasion groups, had left off.

Retired to a nursing home as it was during the seventies, rock 'n' roll was mainly relegated to watching as young turks stepped in to create forms related to but utterly different from it. The process was identical to that of rock 'n' roll emerging from blues, country, and rhythm and blues. The origins of metal as we understand it today came not with Blue Cheer or Led Zeppelin or, God knows, Alice Cooper. It came with Ozzy Osbourne's Black Sabbath, whose first album was released in 1970 (Osbourne himself, of course, being quite familiar with Blue Cheer and Led Zeppelin and, God knows, Alice Cooper). Sly Stone, meanwhile, in his brief moment of glory represented the bridge between the soul annex of rock 'n' roll and the funk that came along to replace it, which was also a departure from rock 'n' roll, particularly in its most commercial form, disco. After rock 'n' roll cashed in its chips at the end of the decade, its place taken by punk-rock, these were to stand as the three major strains of pop music into the nineties: heavy metal, rap born of funk, and postpunk rock.

Wasted

Allman Brothers Band
White blues-rock band; from Macon, Georgia. Along with the inferior but similarly oriented Lynyrd Skynyrd, the Allman Brothers were the great doomed rock band of the seventies. They provided consistently great moments, usually live, through impressive chops coupled with a surprising knack for beautiful tunes. Their southern-fried sound, perhaps the decade's most characteristic after disco, eventually devolved into the sorry exercises

of Black Oak Arkansas, Molly Hatchet, and others, but the Allmans always had something special about them with their perfect fusion of infectious, uptempo blues and a Grateful Dead-like penchant for long, rambling jams. Like the Dead, their two drummers provided a complex texture to the foundation; unlike the Dead, they could hold attention. Of the brothers, slide guitar player Duane, a seasoned session player, was the elder of singer/keyboardist Gregg, by a year. Duane died in a motorcycle crack-up in 1971, just months after the release of their breakthrough, and best, album, *Live at Fillmore East,* aged twenty-four. The group did not attempt to replace him but did carry on, Duane's interplay with guitar player Dickey Betts sorely missed. Little more than a year later, bass player Berry Oakley died in another motorcycle crack-up, three blocks from the site of Duane's; he was also twenty-four. The coincidence of place, along with the seemingly relentless attrition, gave them their image as a doomed band. Separate scandals in the mid-seventies involving Gregg's short-lived marriage to Cher, and then the drug trial of their manager, Scooter Herring, in which Gregg testified against Herring, also contributed to the legend. But in the long run nothing stopped them, and the road stretches on still for the Allman Brothers Band, though not, truth be told, without suppressed yawns.

Mike Bloomfield, died February 15, 1981, age 36
See Guitar Heroes.

John Bonham, died September 25, 1980, age 32
See Drummed Out.

Paul Butterfield, died May 4, 1987, age 44
Harmonica player, founded the Paul Butterfield Blues Band; from Chicago. A key figure in the U.S. white blues revival of the mid- sixties, Butterfield's band included Mike Bloomfield, Elvin Bishop, and the rhythm section from a Howlin' Wolf band. His first album was good basic blues, solid if not sensational, but from then on all his work tended to be marred by experiments: horns, jazz structures, East Indian inflections, etc. But he never stopped trying. In 1981 he contracted peritonitis, which required two operations and a lengthy recovery, after which he returned to recording and performing again. He released his last album in 1986, and then "natural causes" caught up with him, though what was natural about dying at his age has never been properly explained.

Tommy Caldwell, died April 28, 1980, age 29
Bass player, with the Marshall Tucker Band; from Spartenburg, South

Carolina. Caldwell played bass with the Marshall Tucker Band, seventies FM-radio regulars specializing in white Southern boogie. Like his brother Toy, the group's lead guitar player, Tommy had played in groups since the mid-sixties. Formed in 1971, the band scored a couple of top forty entries, but mainly they earned their bread and butter as an AOR act, going platinum with 1975's *Searchin' for a Rainbow* and 1977's *Carolina Dreams*. Along with country-fusion act Sea Level, they played at Jimmy Carter's inauguration in 1977. Tommy Caldwell died from injuries suffered in an auto accident.

Canned Heat
White blues band; from Los Angeles. The core of Canned Heat was formed in the mid-sixties by two guys with big record collections: Bob "The Bear" Hite and Al "Blind Owl" Wilson. Hite was overweight and Wilson extremely nearsighted, hence the nicknames. Both played harmonica and sang—Hite in a raspy shout, Wilson in a cool, eerie falsetto. Wilson also played guitar. Together with Wilson and alone (after Wilson's death) Hite maintained the band through continual personnel changes, ringing up a number of good albums and even some radio hits ("On the Road Again" in 1968 and "Going Up the Country" in 1969, both top twenty). In the seventies they recorded with both John Lee Hooker and Little Richard. Wilson died in 1970 of a drug overdose, aged twenty-seven; Hite suffered a heart attack in 1981, aged thirty-six. And that was the end of the band.

Gene Clark, died May 24, 1991, age 46
Singer, guitar player, with the Byrds; from Tipton, Missouri. In the early days of the Byrds, Clark vied with Roger (née Jim) McGuinn for leadership of the group. Clark wrote much of the material that appeared on their albums, and frequently fought with McGuinn over the direction of the group. He finally left them in 1966 to escape the conflict, and spent the rest of his life pursuing an obscure solo career that nonetheless boasted its critical partisans. His death was chalked up to natural causes, though he had a history of substance-abuse problems.

Miles Davis, died September 28, 1991, age 65
Jazz trumpet player; from Alton, Illinois. Miles Davis was a jazz giant whose career spanned bop and fusion. For much of that time he made an enormous impact on everything he touched or even came near, including fusion, which he was instrumental in inventing. His influence on rock began to be felt with the amplified sounds of 1968's *Miles in the Sky* and 1969's *In a Silent Way*. But he broke the game wide open with 1970's *Bitches Brew*,

an astonishing stew of electronic sounds spread across four LP sides, featuring contributions from saxophone player Wayne Shorter, bass clarinet player Bernie Maupin, guitar player John McLaughlin, keyboardists Chick Corea and Josef Zawinul, and many more. That project alone spawned Weather Report, the Mahavishnu Orchestra, and Return to Forever, and influenced such British underground players as the Soft Machine, Robert Fripp, and others. But Davis was not through yet; over the next five years he advanced ever further into the netherest regions of sultry funk, recording great yawps of burbling, driving atmosphere that were uniformly disturbing and seductive: 1971's *Jack Johnson* and *Live/Evil*, 1972's *On the Corner*, 1974's *Big Fun*, and more. An auto crack-up in 1972 broke both his legs, slowing him considerably, and in 1976, still recovering, he retired from music. He was never a gracious entertainer, rarely playing encores, but his standing as a giant is unquestioned among rock and jazz fans alike. In the eighties he emerged again as a recording artist, with occasional performances, but he stayed well back of the cutting edge. Why shouldn't he? His work was done. He had taken rock and jazz beyond their artificial boundaries and aimed them squarely into the future. We have not even caught up yet to his early-seventies work—it is *still* ahead of its time. He died in Santa Monica of pneumonia, respiratory failure, and a stroke.

Mama Cass Elliot, died July 29, 1974, age 32
See Just Us Dead Folk.

Brian Epstein, died August 27, 1967, age 32
See Beatles Bugouts.

Tom Fogerty, died September 6, 1990, age 48
Guitar player, with Creedence Clearwater Revival; from El Cerrito, California. Tom, the older brother of guiding force John, was relegated to what he saw as the second fiddle role of rhythm guitar player with Creedence, one of the few great rock 'n' roll bands in the rock era. In early 1971 he left them to pursue a solo career, which effectively ended the troubled Creedence, though they carried on for another year or two as a trio. Tom went on to work with such players as Merl Saunders and Jerry Garcia, but nothing much ever came of his projects. In 1980 Creedence re-formed to play at his second wedding. Five years later, John made a resounding return to public notice, but little was ever heard from Tom again. He died of respiratory failure.

Marvin Gaye, died April 1, 1984, age 44
See The Motown Morgue.

Lowell George, died June 29, 1979, age 34
Guitar player, cofounded Little Feat; from Arlington, Virginia. Growing up in southern California, he played with the Standells ("Dirty Water"), the Seeds ("Pushin' Too Hard"), and Frank Zappa's Mothers of Invention, before forming Little Feat with another ex-Mother, Roy Estrada. But the group's heady mix of boogie, gospel, funk, rhythm and blues, and more, basically remained a career-long secret in the United States, despite an unending series of critical hosannas and their continuing ability to fill halls and even arenas across the country. Just as George was going solo, he died of a heart attack, which later turned out to have been drug-related.

Bill Graham, died October 25, 1991, age 60
Promoter, born Wolfgang Grajonca; from Berlin. Born of Russian parents in East Berlin, Bill Graham gravitated to the United States through a series of European orphanages, followed by a stint in Korea and any number of odd jobs as he put himself through college. In his early thirties, he became one of the great entrepreneurs of rock. In 1965 he began booking concerts in San Francisco, eventually turning an abandoned skating rink into the Fillmore West, one of the legendary sixties venues. In 1967 he turned a former New York moviehouse into the Fillmore East, and between them they hosted virtually all the greats of the era. After he closed them in 1971 (saying the counterculture had become too commercialized) he went on to promote tours and organize festivals, including the Watkins Glen Summer Jam in 1973, the biggest of its kind ever. In his time Graham worked with Bob Dylan, the Band, the Rolling Stones, Crosby, Stills, Nash and Young, and many more, and had a hand in putting together 1985's Live Aid. He died in a helicopter accident, which, like chips off the old flinty block, his sons are holding Pacific Gas and Electric Co. responsible for, in a lawsuit they have filed.

Albert Grossman, died January 25, 1986, age 59
Manager. Never as hard-nosed as Colonel Tom Parker, as fortuitous as Brian Epstein, as slimy as Andrew Loog Oldham, or as visionary as Malcolm McLaren, Albert Grossman nonetheless had enough of all those qualities to almost single-handedly launch folk-rock and, indirectly, its darling child, rock (b. Monterey, 1967). His clients included Janis Joplin, and the Band, as well as such singer/songwriter luminaries as Bob Dylan, Joan Baez, Peter, Paul and Mary, Gordon Lightfoot, and others. He helped start

the Newport Folk Festival, for many years one of the most significant venues for upcoming singer/songwriters and rediscovered blues musicians alike. It was also the place where Dylan was booed for appearing with a rock band in 1965. Grossman kept the label Bearsville going through the seventies, which among other things kept Todd Rundgren going through the seventies. Grossman died of a heart attack, mid-flight en route to a conference in Cannes.

John Hammond, Sr., died July 10, 1987, age 76
Producer, record company executive; from New York. Hammond was perhaps the most important musical talent scout of this century. His discoveries include Robert Johnson, Billie Holiday, Charlie Christian, Bob Dylan, Aretha Franklin, and Bruce Springsteen. He came from a wealthy family, which allowed him the leisure to pursue his interest in music during the Depression, when he began his long association with Columbia. He produced Bessie Smith's last sessions and Billie Holiday's first in 1933, and then went on to champion Benny Goodman and Count Basie. In 1936 he was the first to record Lester Young solo. During the late thirties he mounted his "Spirituals to Swing" concerts at Carnegie Hall—he tried to book Robert Johnson but was too late (Johnson had already died), so he settled for Big Bill Broonzy. Others on the bill included Joe Turner and Sonny Terry. In the early forties he maneuvered guitar player Charlie Christian into Benny Goodman's sextet. During that time he also became an officer of the NAACP. (It's ridiculous trying to keep up with this guy.) After a hiatus from Columbia he returned in the fifties and signed, among others, Pete Seeger, George Benson, Leonard Cohen, Dylan, Franklin, and Springsteen. (Eventually Aretha Franklin left Columbia for Atlantic to get the right kind of production support.) Dylan was initially called "Hammond's folly" and Springsteen suffered for years under inappropriate promotion (with which Hammond was not involved), but both came through eventually, proving themselves beyond a shadow of a doubt and helping nail down Hammond's richly deserved larger-than-life status.

Jimi Hendrix, died September 18, 1970, age 27
See Guitar Heroes.

Brian Jones, died July 3, 1969, age 27
See Gathering Moss with the Rolling Stones.

Janis Joplin, died October 4, 1970, age 27
Singer; from Port Arthur, Texas. Janis Joplin died within weeks of Jimi

Hendrix, which, along with a similar trajectory in their careers, has indelibly linked them as the great sixties casualties, symbols of the end of an era. It's true enough, to some extent — the inside-out parallels are certainly there: Hendrix was a black man headed for color-blind outer space, Joplin was a white woman headed deep into the painful heart of the blues. But if Hendrix's death seems tragic now, Joplin's seems merely inevitable. Her pain was so enormous it's hard to imagine what she could have done, or where she could have gone. Even as a bohemian, perhaps especially as a bohemian, she always longed for the middle-class comforts that reflected her background: simple acceptance, conventional values, bedrock security, love. But they always eluded her, and she continually jeopardized her opportunities for them by extremes of behavior. The source of her daunting pain remains a mystery. What did she want? What did she need?

She ran away from home at seventeen and spent years singing in clubs in Austin and Houston, finally arriving in California in 1965, where she eked out an existence drawing unemployment and going in and out of college. Drugs burned her there, and she returned to Texas in 1966 for a marriage that never happened. Plans to join the 13th Floor Elevators were overturned when San Francisco scene-maker Chet Helms went to Texas to get her for Big Brother and the Holding Company. Shortly after that they were booked to play the Monterey Pop Festival, and things began to happen fast then and in big ways. Albert Grossman signed on to manage her and secured a deal with Columbia in 1967. *Cheap Thrills* was released in 1968; the album went to number 1, and spawned the hit "Piece of My Heart," which went to number 12 that year. Joplin's big screech, an open wound clearly in need of first aid, had found some kind of home in mass adulation — though it was hardly the best home for her, all things considered. Fame alone could never be enough to satisfy her. Turmoil and increasingly heavy drinking ensued; she dumped the band and recorded a solo album in 1969, but by then she was into heroin. Her next outing was her best, and her last: *Pearl,* with the haunting posthumous number 1 hit written by Kris Kristofferson, "Me and Bobby McGee." The album evinced increasing self-assurance, stylistic range, and poise, but it no longer mattered. After years of chemical abuse her body finally gave out late one night in a room at Hollywood's Landmark Hotel, from a heroin overdose, ruled accidental.

Johnny Kidd, died October 7, 1966, age 26
Singer, born Frederick Heath; from England. Here was a man way ahead of his time. Starting in 1959 Johnny Kidd appeared with his band, the Pirates, in black leather and eyepatch; and they played *loud.* As a threesome, Johnny Kidd and the Pirates charted a path for heavy metal, power

trios, and glam-rock, as if it had all been rolled together and tossed into a timeshift. Perhaps it was. Perhaps time travel is in our future. But if Kidd's music was loved even at the time, and it was, no one had a clue what to do about it. In 1960 the band scored a number 1 U.K. hit with "Shakin' All Over," which Kidd cowrote—rockabilly so hard it was practically fossilized. Beyond that, however, there was practically nothing. The Guess Who covered it and took it to the top thirty in the United States in 1965, and the Who put a version of it on their 1970 LP *Live at Leeds*. In the eighties Motorhead and Girlschool teamed to cover another Kidd number, "Please Don't Touch." By the time of most of this activity, however, Kidd was dead and mostly forgotten, having died in an auto accident.

John Lennon, died December 8, 1980, age 40
See Beatles Bugouts.

Phil Lynott, died January 4, 1986, age 34
Bass player, songwriter, founded Thin Lizzy; from Ireland. As a black man from Ireland, Lynott had many sources to draw on, and draw on them he did, rocking hard in the mid-seventies with a sound that mixed up blues and boogie with metal, and had something else quite intangible to recommend it as well. But only the 1976 album *Jailbreak,* along with its number 12 hit "The Boys Are Back in Town," ever gained significant notice. Lynott stands as one of the great overlooked bridges between rock and postpunk, along with Chrissie Hynde and Garland Jeffreys, as he adapted well to the coming of punk-rock, playing with Rat Scabies of the Damned, Midge Ure of Ultravox and the Rich Kids, and others in the crowd. But like so many he was not immune to the attractions of drugs. An overdose put him into a coma for the last week of his life, and pneumonia and a heart attack finally killed him.

Lynyrd Skynyrd, October 20, 1977
White boogie-rock band; from Florida. Lynyrd Skynyrd was named for its founding members' high school gym teacher who hated party-hard longhairs. At first the group was famous for its three-guitar frontline, its sassy response to Neil Young's "Southern Man"—"Sweet Home Alabama," a number 8 hit in 1974—and its tribute to Duane Allman, "Free Bird," which ultimately ranked second only to Led Zeppelin's "Stairway to Heaven" as the most tiresome FM-radio staple of the decade. Then, following an airplane crash in 1977 that killed two members (singer Ronnie Van Zant and guitar player Steve Gaines) and one of their back-up singers (Gaines's sister Cassie), they became known for the monumental, legendary dimensions of

their curse. The cheap ironies surrounding the accident seemed endless. The tour was called "Tour of the Survivors." It was in support of an album, *Street Survivors,* whose original cover (pulled by MCA after the accident) showed the band engulfed in flames. The album featured a song called "That Smell," about death. The legend continued into the next decade as surviving guitar player Allen Collins, who formed the short-lived Rossing-ton-Collins Band with other Lynyrd Skynyrd survivors after the accident, became wheelchair-bound from a 1986 alcohol-related auto accident, and then died of pneumonia in 1990. In 1987 Lynyrd Skynyrd re-formed, with Ronnie's brother Johnny Van Zant taking his place and the frontline reduced to two guitars. So far there is nothing to report.

Richard Manuel, died March 4, 1986, age 42
Piano player, founding member of the Band; from Canada. Manuel was a member of the Band from their earliest days backing Ronnie Hawkins in the early sixties. Toward the end of that decade the quintet emerged as major rock heavyweights after extensive woodshedding with and without Bob Dylan, on Dylan's *Basement Tapes* and their own *Music from Big Pink* and *The Band.* Manuel contributed "Tears of Rage" and much more to the essentially democratic, almost benignly anarchic group whose deep roots in U.S. music and culture belied their (mostly) Canadian backgrounds. It was powerful, revelatory music that transcended rock even as it contained all the seeds of rock 'n' roll. But it never caught on commercially, and as their fortunes waned and their music lost its focus they formally hung it up in 1976. Martin Scorsese documented the moment in the film *The Last Waltz.* In early 1986 the group re-formed, minus guitar player Robbie Robertson, with the idea of touring again. But Manuel, plagued over the years by depression and drug problems, chose that moment to hang himself.

Bob Marley, died May 11, 1981, age 36
See Death Inna Babylon.

Steve Marriott, died April 20, 1991, age 44
Singer, guitar player, cofounded the Small Faces, Humble Pie; from England. Steve Marriott earned impressive mod credentials with a series of U.K. hits with the Small Faces in the mid-sixties, and also cowrote the group's only song that also charted in the U.S., the 1968 number 16 psychedelic classic "Itchycoo Park." Then, in search of heavy credibility, he formed Humble Pie with Peter Frampton, which worked fine, musically, until Frampton was driven away and boogie became the focus—at which point commercial success erupted, only to disappear almost as quickly.

Marriott then spent the rest of his life chasing past glories and, alternately, playing pub-rock. He died in a house fire.

Freddie Mercury, died November 24, 1991, age 45
Singer, born Frederick Bulsara, with Queen; from Zanzibar. At the time of this writing Freddie Mercury stands as the latest example of how death is a very fine career move indeed. The re-released "Bohemian Rhapsody," along with much of the Queen catalog—due in part to the former's fortuitous appearance in the film *Wayne's World*—returned to impressive chart heights in 1992 and, from the sidelines, critics have feverishly begun to rewrite history. But let's not get carried away. Any way you look at it, Queen was not that good. A hyphen group if ever there was one, they emerged from the periphery of glam-rock, by way of an arch take on art-rock, striking gold in 1976 with the number 9 "Bohemian Rhapsody." It was something of a surprise at the time for such a long, weird song. It did even better in 1992, reaching number 2, emphasizing the fact that it's not just long and weird but also good. They followed it, back in the seventies, with catchy tunes in the service of poor albums: 1978's "We Are the Champions" b/w "We Will Rock You," which both found their way into the hearts of sports enthusiasts, and 1980's "Crazy Little Thing Called Love" and "Another One Bites the Dust," which both reached number 1 as listenable-enough fake new wave. Then there was a Lennon tribute with David Bowie, sporadically diminishing hits, solo albums, live albums, and long silence. Mercury died of AIDS, having never really come out of the closet—no doubt for highly defendable commercial reasons.

Keith Moon, died September 7, 1978, age 31
See Drummed Out.

Rushton Moreve, died July 1, 1981, age 33
Bass player, with Steppenwolf; from Los Angeles. Rushton Moreve was the original bass player with Steppenwolf. He departed quickly, before they had even recorded their first album, but he was with them long enough to cowrite "Magic Carpet Ride" with John Kay, the East German emigré who was the leader of the group. The song went to number 3 in 1968 as the follow-up to their number 2 "Born to Be Wild" from earlier in the year. Together they stand as the signature songs of the band, whose shades'n'leather image updated Marlon Brando's *Wild One* look of the fifties and made them spokesmen for outlaw bikers and disaffected youth everywhere. Moreve died in an auto accident.

Jim Morrison, died July 3, 1971, age 27
See Jim Morrison's Beautiful Friend.

Felix Pappalardi, died April 17, 1983, age 44
Producer, bass player, with Mountain; from the Bronx. After playing bass
with Tim Hardin, Felix Pappalardi came to prominence as the producer of
Cream, for whom — along with his wife, Gail Collins, and Eric Clapton — he
wrote "Strange Brew." He also produced the Youngbloods' debut in 1967.
After Cream dissolved late in 1968, Pappalardi joined forces with Leslie
West (née Weinstein) to form Mountain. In 1969 they played Woodstock,
which effectively launched them. Their only hit was the top thirty "Mississippi Queen" in 1970, but it went on to become an FM-radio staple while
their first two albums, 1970's *Mountain Climbing* and 1971's *Nantucket
Sleighride,* both went gold. After that, however, it was downhill, and by
1973 Pappalardi was back in the control booth, though he returned to action now and then with the group over the years. Collins, his wife and songwriting collaborator, shot him to death, but the details of their dispute are
not known.

Gram Parsons, died September 19, 1973, age 26
Singer, songwriter, born Cecil Connor; from Winterhaven, Florida. Parsons is legendary for creating country-rock, though many, even Ricky Nelson, were moving in that direction at the time. Still, Parsons was clearly one
of its finest practitioners, his mid-sixties International Submarine Band
(formed after running away from his Georgia home and enrolling in Har-
vard, then dropping out) among the best of its type. From that he moved
on to the Byrds, in Los Angeles in 1968, providing a good deal of direction
for their still impressive *Sweetheart of the Rodeo.* He quit them after three
months, though, to avoid touring South Africa, and formed the influential
Flying Burrito Brothers, in yet another impressive outing. The Flying Burrito Brothers numbered the Rolling Stones among their fans, which led to
their appearance at Altamont. After a motorcycle accident in 1970 slowed
him some, Parsons went solo, with Emmylou Harris by his side. A couple
of years later he died from drug-related heart failure, alone in a motel room.
In accordance with his wishes, his body (which, in a famous incident, had
to be stolen by friends) was cremated and the ashes scattered at the Joshua
Tree National Monument.

Jaco Pastorius, died September 22, 1987, age 35
Fusion bass player, with Blood, Sweat and Tears, Weather Report, Joni
Mitchell, solo; from Norristown, Pennsylvania. A gifted player with tech-

nique to burn, Pastorius paid his dues in Florida playing one-offs with Motown acts, country bands, and even lounge combos on cruise ships. When he finally drifted into Weather Report in 1976, six years after they'd formed, he helped them find major commercial success with the seventies FM-radio staple "Birdland," from 1977's *Heavy Weather*. He was diagnosed an alcoholic manic-depressive, which was reflected in the extreme ups and downs of his life and career. At the end he was destitute. He died from injuries suffered in a fight trying to force his way into a nightclub.

Pigpen, died March 8, 1973, age 27
See The Grateful Dead's Long, Strange Spinal Tap Trip.

Jeff Porcaro, died August 5, 1992, age 38
See Drummed Out.

Carl Radle, died May 30, 1980
Bass player; from Los Angeles. Carl Radle was a utility player who put in time with Gary Lewis and the Playboys, Delaney and Bonnie, and many others. After playing with Derek and the Dominoes on *Layla* he stayed with Clapton for most of the following decade. Little is known of the details of his death.

Otis Redding, died December 10, 1967, age 26
See Souls.

Keith Relf, died May 14, 1976, age 33
See Transatlantic Tombstone Blues.

Stacy Sutherland, died August 24, 1978, age 32
Guitar player, with the 13th Floor Elevators; from Austin, Texas. Stacy Sutherland was a founding member of Texas's 13th Floor Elevators, considered by many to be the first, and certainly one of the best, psychedelic rock bands. Much of that can be chalked up to singer Roky Erickson's decidedly weird songs along with his utterly chilling, scabrous vocal performances. Sutherland did his bit too, contributing a quick and sure hand on guitar, with suitably breakneck tempos. But it was a short-lived group, washed up by 1969 despite their glory days at the Avalon in San Francisco. Sutherland was shot to death by his wife, though details beyond that are scanty.

Vinnie Taylor, died April 17, 1974

Guitar player, with Sha Na Na. Formed in 1969 by students at Columbia University, Sha Na Na was one of the first and most effective rock 'n' roll revival groups, for better or (more likely) for worse bringing nostalgia to a generation until then unconsciously starving for it. As Charlie Gillett put it, "Good night, America." Taylor replaced one of the group's original guitar players, Chris Donald, in 1970. After he died, of a heroin overdose, he was replaced in turn by Elliott Randall. Though Taylor appeared on many of their albums, he never made it to the TV show, which did not debut until 1977.

Stevie Ray Vaughan, died August 27, 1990, age 35

See Guitar Heroes.

Danny Whitten, died November 18, 1972, age 29

Guitar player, with Crazy Horse. Whitten was the original guitar player for Crazy Horse, Neil Young's perennial backing band and a useful barometer of Young's state of mind for over twenty years now, from "Cinnamon Girl" to *Ragged Glory.* When Young is with them he tends to be focused and potent; when not, he is usually pursuing a tangent that's not working. Whitten's death from a heroin overdose, along with Crosby, Stills, Nash and Young roadie Bruce Berry's the following year, inspired one of Young's very best albums, 1975's stark and chilling *Tonight's the Night,* which stands as one of rock's most honest and telling treatments of death.

Tom Wilson, died September 6, 1978, age 47

Producer. Tom Wilson was one of the great unsung producers of the sixties—partly because he imposed so little of himself on the work, instead conforming to the artist's vision, and partly because he worked with so many who counted for so much, just as they were hitting their greatest strides: Bob Dylan, the Velvet Underground, the Animals, Frank Zappa, Simon and Garfunkel, the Soft Machine, and more. Wilson's first break came in late 1963, when Bob Dylan's manager Albert Grossman insisted John Hammond be taken off the production role on Dylan's third album, *The Times They Are A-Changin'.* Wilson, a member of Columbia's A&R staff, stepped in to take his place. He stayed with Dylan for his next two albums—*Another Side of Bob Dylan* and the breakthrough *Bringing It All Back Home*—until Dylan, in turn, insisted that Wilson be yanked. (Wilson did produce "Like a Rolling Stone" on the next album, *Highway 61 Revisited.*) Perhaps Wilson's most daring move came in 1965 when he took Simon and Garfunkel's placidly lilting "Sounds of Silence" and put a jangling rhythm section behind it, without the knowledge, let alone the consent, of the duo. The move worked. The song went to number 1, helping to launch folk-rock and establishing Simon and Garfunkel for a long career. Wilson also produced the Animals in their psychedelic period ("San Franciscan Nights," "Monterey," "Sky Pilot (Part One)," etc.), the Velvet Underground's first album (the cover credit to Andy Warhol notwithstanding), and *Freak Out* by the Mothers of Invention. He died of a heart attack in Los Angeles.

Max Yasgur, died February 8, 1973, age 53
Dairy farmer; from upstate New York. Max Yasgur's 600-acre farm provided the site for Woodstock after the people who were to put up the original site pulled out at practically the last minute. Yasgur helped to provide food and water to the crowd during the festival, and was outraged when he saw his neighbors selling water. "I never expected the festival to be this big," he said at the time. "But if the generation gap is to be closed, we older people have to do more than we have done." Two years later he sold his farm outright and moved to Florida, where he died of unspecified causes.

Faces of Death 19:
Death at Three Early Ages

27

Chris Bell, died December 27, 1978, age 27
See I Wanna Destroy: The Final Death of Rock 'n' Roll.

D. Boon, died December 23, 1985, age 27
See I Wanna Destroy: The Final Death of Rock 'n' Roll.

Roger Lee Durham, died October, 1973, age 27
See Super Dead.

Pete Ham, died April 23, 1975, age 27
See Beatles Bugouts (Badfinger).

Jimi Hendrix, died September 18, 1970, age 27
See Guitar Heroes.

Robert Johnson, died August 16, 1938, age 27
See Hellhound on His Trail.

Brian Jones, died July 3, 1969, age 27
See Gathering Moss with the Rolling Stones.

Janis Joplin, died October 4, 1970, age 27
See Sha Na Na, Inc.: The Second Death of Rock 'n' Roll.

Jim Morrison, died July 3, 1971, age 27
See Jim Morrison's Beautiful Friend.

Pigpen, died March 8, 1973, age 27
See The Grateful Dead's Long, Strange Spinal Tap Trip.

Al Wilson, died September 3, 1970, age 27
See Sha Na Na, Inc.: The Second Death of Rock 'n' Roll
(Canned Heat).

33

Lester Bangs, died April 30, 1982, age 33
See I Wanna Destroy: The Final Death of Rock 'n' Roll.

John Belushi, died March 5, 1982, age 33
See Last Laughs: Novelty Artists.

Ronnie Goodson, died November 4, 1980, age 33
See Death's Ululating Maw: Vocal Group Deaths.

Donny Hathaway, died January 13, 1979, age 33
See Super Dead.

Johnny Horton, died November 5, 1960, age 33
See Country Corpses.

Blind Lemon Jefferson, died December, 1930, age 33
See Tombstone Blues.

Jesus Christ, died circa A.D. 29, age 33

Rushton Moreve, died July 1, 1981, age 33
See Sha Na Na, Inc.: The Second Death of Rock 'n' Roll.

Keith Relf, died May 14, 1976, age 33
See Transatlantic Tombstone Blues.

Bon Scott, died February 19, 1980, age 33
See Munching the Corpse: The Utter Assurance of Death's Future.

Vinyl LP, R.I.P.

Keith Whitley, died May 9, 1989, age 33
See Country Corpses.

42

Alan Freed, died January 20, 1965, age 42
See The Day the Music Died: The First Death of Rock 'n' Roll.

Micki Harris, died June 10, 1982, age 42
See Da Doo Ron Death.

Eddie Hazel, died December 23, 1992, age 42
See Super Dead.

Jimmy Hodder, died June 15, 1990, age 42
See Drummed Out.

Freddy King, died December 28, 1976, age 42
See Guitar Heroes.

Richard Manuel, died March 4, 1986, age 42
See Sha Na Na, Inc.: The Second Death of Rock 'n' Roll.

Elvis Presley, died August 16, 1977, age 42
See The Big Elvis.

Peter Tosh, died September 11, 1987, age 42
See Death inna Babylon.

32

Jim Morrison's Beautiful Friend

AFTER ELVIS PRESLEY, no dead rock star has remained quite so pervasively alive in quite such a creepy fashion as Jim Morrison. His persona was reanimated in the late seventies, following the publication of a sensational biography and his subsequent embrace by well-intentioned new wave poseurs, and he has not really rested since. He has appeared on the cover of *Rolling Stone* three times since his death, he has appeared on the cover of *Spin,* a magazine that began publication fourteen years after his death, and in 1991 he was the subject of a (hopelessly out of it) movie by Oliver Stone.

Morrison, the oldest son of a navy career man who eventually rose to the rank of admiral, was a behavior problem through much of high school and college, which included UCLA film school. In 1965, on the Venice beach, he recited a poem he'd written, "Moonlight Drive," to keyboardist Ray Manzarek, who thought it, and him, groovy — that was the beginning of the Doors. Guitar player Robby Krieger and drummer John Densmore were recruited. Manzarek supplied bass lines with his left hand on the organ, and all four contributed songs and arrangements. Morrison had read widely in literature and philosophy and experimented extensively with psychedelic drugs, which led to their heavy name, from Aldous Huxley quoting William Blake in *The Doors of Perception.*

The Doors quickly became a controversial if short-lived house band at the Whiskey-a-Go-Go in Los Angeles, with a series of now legendary, hysterically pitched shows that clearly blazed one of the paths to performance art before there was even such a concept. As a group, they stretched their material and pushed it to its anarchic limits, blasting a *loud* cacophony of sound behind Morrison, who brayed incantations and exhortations improvised on the spot. That was when they worked out, segment by segment, the long and weird exercises for which they became known as avatars of the sixties underground and avant-garde. Songs included "The End," "When the Music's Over," and the infamous "Celebration of the Lizard." It was also, likely enough, the time and place to see them.

In 1966, they signed to Elektra and went on, astonishingly, to score hits, number 1 hits: 1967's "Light My Fire" and 1968's "Hello, I Love You," along with a handful of others that landed in the top forty. Their 1967 self-titled debut album was a pure revelation, both commercially and artistically, and spent the "Summer of Love" lodged at number 2 behind the Beatles' *Sgt. Pepper* on the albums chart. The Doors had sacrificed few of their aesthetic priorities to win that success—though "Light My Fire" was shortened for AM-radio play, the album included the long version, along with the by-then notorious "The End," "Alabama Song" (a Weill-Brecht number about getting drunk and getting laid, Morrison's favorite pastimes, respectively), and other dark and smarmy takes on life's wretched vicissitudes.

For the Doors, their sudden arrival as pop darlings was some vindication for their treatment by the Whiskey's management, who by then had banned them for the patently offensive Oedipal drama enacted in "The End," which they continued to play even after they'd been told to drop it from the set. In similar fashion, the band would flout the rules set by Ed Sullivan for their appearance on that show in 1967, where they were asked to change the line, in "Light My Fire," "Girl we couldn't get much higher." They agreed to it and then didn't keep their promise, which is far more than the Rolling Stones can say about their experience with "Let's Spend the Night Together." Still, the Doors were forever banned from Sullivan, and the Stones did get another chance to appear. Who do you think won this moral battle?

Of course, none of that mattered much to the Doors. It didn't have to. Going big for them was a matter of pop knack *and* heavy psychological preening, and most of all it stemmed from continuing serendipity—the good fortune of timing and luck. But give them credit. They really did manage it, most of their music really does work, and their reputation has never stopped growing. In retrospect they rank as perhaps the greatest Los Angeles group of all, rising above the impressive company of Love, Steely Dan, X, Fleetwood Mac, even the Beach Boys and the Phil Spector groups. They somehow contained, and transcended, all the contradictions, paradoxes, and fascinations of sun-showered dread: their bright and catchy veneer launched the hits even as, in performance and toward the end of their lengthy album tracks, they revealed themselves as obsessed with sin, murder, and mayhem.

Or Morrison did anyway; the others just dug it until the troubles started. As the Lizard King, a weird take on Elvis, Morrison was always a potent sex symbol, convincing enough to carry off the hokum with a very real grasp on a very real nerve. Yet questions of credibility still remain, which begin with his pretensions to poetry. The Freudian conceits of "The End," which got them into so much trouble at the Whiskey-a-Go-Go, represent all their problems writ small: clocking in at 11:41, it's overblown, annoying, and contrived—but at times (such as the opening sequence of 1979's *Apocalypse Now,* not to mention any number of personal experiences that you and I have both had) it simply works.

Why it works is the mystery. Certainly it's related to Morrison's ability to convey the erotic attractions of death and murder. When Morrison intones, after a suitably portentous opening, "This is the end, beautiful friend," it's hard to know if the beautiful friend is someone he is about to murder, or if it is death itself. But even by then it already doesn't really, you know, matter—either way we're looking squarely into the void. And it's kind of sexy. But Morrison just keeps moving, finally escaping our ability to identify. In the end all we can do is try to get our minds around the awful contours of his vision. And still he keeps moving.

Morrison claimed to have had a dreamlike experience as a child involving slain Native Americans scattered across a desert highway, and later alluded (in the wake of Charles Manson) to having acted out the scenario himself, killing someone in the desert who had picked him up hitchhiking. True or untrue, it lends his obsessions authority. Whether it actually happened is not the point—he could imagine it, and convert it into pop music. At the peak of "The End," after he tells his mother that he's going to rape her, his scream of anguish is utterly convincing. All snickering from the peanut gallery, while fully warranted, finally amounts to little more than whistling past the graveyard at midnight.

But within just a few years, Morrison was already snared by the seductive vanities of his role as a rock star, sinking into alcoholism, gaining weight, and losing focus. He intended the Doors as a means to his end of becoming a poet, but fame had swallowed him whole and he could not cope with it. All the ensuing problems—his arrest for public obscenity in New Haven, his arrest for disorderly conduct aboard a plane bound for Phoenix, and finally his arrest in Miami for "lewd and lascivious behavior by exposing his private parts and by simulating masturbation and oral copulation"—all found their origins in alcohol, sadly enough, and not in any systematic aesthetic program of revolt. A brilliant man, drink reduced him to a pathetic buffoon.

Even so, the Doors' work still holds up, particularly their first album and the last three, 1970's *Absolutely Live* and *Morrison Hotel,* and 1971's *L.A. Woman,* which increasingly integrated all the elements, not just of Morrison's theatrical obsessions, but of an organically cohesive rock band—one that, with an effective turn to the blues, even seemed to hold the promise of a lifetime of graceful aging. But that was never in the cards for Morrison. No Neil Young or Lou Reed, even by the time of his Miami trial in 1970 he was already clearly a goner, having sacrificed far too much to the dark side of his spirit.

The circumstances of his demise remain another mystery of the Doors, their last (with Morrison gone the others, as it turned out, had little to offer—they were no New Order). Exhausted, Morrison had moved to Paris in April of 1971 to pursue his poetry, with no plans to return. He hung out there in relative obscurity until, on July 3, 1971, his body was found in the bathtub of his Paris apartment. The death was ruled the result of a heart attack, likely alcohol-related, but no autopsy was ever performed, and few people actually saw the body. Not that I want to fuel any rumors—there is not a doubt that Jim Morrison is dead. It's just that nobody really knows why. He was twenty-seven, and he was buried in Paris, where his grave has now become a pop mecca.

33

Guitar Heroes

DESPITE ITS hard-won status as icon, the electric guitar's central place in rock 'n' roll has never been quite as pervasive or assured as it sometimes seems. Chuck Berry made the first significant use of it—creating a set of now-classic riffs and licks that seem to stand as the very epitome of rock 'n' roll (all of them basically variations on the opening figure of "Johnny B. Goode"). In contrast, most of his contemporaries established themselves by rearing back and belting. They played the piano if they played anything. In the eighties the electric guitar gradually gave way to the beatbox, which now holds sway in pop music. Though the electric guitar still had its defenders at the beginning of that decade (hordes of them, in fact, account-ing to a large degree for R.E.M.'s base of support), it later came to be seen as the laughably retro stance of hopelessly out-of-it purists.

During the sixties and seventies, of course, it was a different story. Eric "God" Clapton's work with the Yardbirds, John Mayall, and especially Cream created the enormously compelling image of a guitar hero—the lone brave figure stepping forth from the welter of thunder and rhythm to con-front the screaming, adoring throng and symbolically wang his pecker. It was a gesture possessed of something essential and vital, and has itself be-come deeply etched into popular consciousness. Even now when you see people dancing unself-consciously to music they love you will see them making that characteristic gesture of striking chords on an electric guitar, even if the music itself has no guitars in it.

The first batch of guitar heroes were mostly steeped in the blues and tended to boast impressive chops. Many came from Britain's early-sixties blues scene, including Clapton, Jeff Beck, and Jimmy Page (all of whom played with the Yardbirds), and many loved to indulge in protracted, in-creasingly noodling solos (especially the denizens of San Francisco, such as Jerry Garcia and the Grateful Dead). The Rolling Stones' Keith Richards, by contrast, focused on texture and craft, using the electric guitar to deliver orgasmic power at carefully chosen moments. Jimi Hendrix managed to combine both strategies, and blew them both wide open.

As the sixties wore into the seventies guitar heroes came from everywhere, and endless noodling came to be the favored approach, which doubtless explains their eventual passing from favor. Still, Richards's legacy remains very much alive in the sampling and other careful inflections of rap and pop music today — it's exactly how Run-D.M.C. pulled off their stunt of taking Aerosmith's "Walk This Way" to number 4 in 1986. And you can depend on the fact that, into the foreseeable future, the electric guitar will never be gone for long from pop music. Those on the list below, however, are gone for good.

Duane Allman, died October 29, 1971, age 24
See Sha Na Na, Inc. (Allman Brothers Band).

Mike Bloomfield, died February 15, 1981, age 36
With Paul Butterfield, Electric Flag, super sessions, solo; from Chicago. For a time Mike Bloomfield, a white blues player with technique to spare, promised to be the U.S. answer to Eric Clapton as he contributed scorching work to Butterfield's band, to his own Electric Flag (which also featured singer Nick Gravenites), and to that peculiar sixties artifact, the supersession album (with Al Kooper and others). Perhaps Bloomfield's greatest moment was backing Bob Dylan at the Newport Folk Festival in 1965, where along with the rest of the band he was booed for selling out folk music. He also appeared on "Like a Rolling Stone" and other Dylan tracks from that time, and with his hero, Muddy Waters, on *Fathers and Sons*. In the seventies, as Bloomfield sank into a self-imposed obscurity based on his distaste for touring, he scored movies (including porn) even as he continued to record well received but poorly selling albums. He died in San Francisco from a drug overdose just after the release of his last album, *Living in the Fast Lane*.

Tommy Bolin, died December 4, 1976, age 25
With the James Gang, Deep Purple, solo; from Sioux City, Iowa. Bolin, a kind of pass-around lead guitar player, spent his career following in the footsteps of others. In 1973 he joined the James Gang for two albums after Joe Walsh quit. In 1975 he joined Deep Purple for three albums (two released after his death) after Ritchie Blackmore quit. During the mid-seventies he also recorded and released a couple of solo albums. He died in a Miami hotel room, reportedly of a heroin overdose.

Roy Buchanan, died August 14, 1988, age 48
With Dale Hawkins, Ronnie Hawkins, solo; from Ozark, Arkansas.
Buchanan was a much-praised white blues player who spent his life not living up to expectations, which, from his associations with Dale Hawkins
and Ronnie Hawkins (no relation), may have been somewhat inflated in the
first place. On the other hand, the Band's Robbie Robertson called him the
"finest rock guitarist I ever heard," and Buchanan claimed the Rolling
Stones asked him to join them in 1970. But nothing he released ever
matched the reputation. In the end he took his own life.

Charlie Christian, died March 2, 1942, age 25
Jazz player; from Dallas. Along with blues player T-Bone Walker, his boyhood friend in Texas, Charlie Christian revolutionized the electric guitar.
He was among the very first to play it, and all he did was experiment with
a single-string picking style—but that was enough. John Hammond discovered him in Oklahoma City. When Christian came to New York in 1939,
Benny Goodman hired him for his sextet. While there, Christian also
jammed with Dizzy Gillespie, Thelonious Monk, and others. But within a
year of arriving in New York, Christian had contracted tuberculosis. He
was hospitalized for it in 1941 and died six months later.

John Cipollina, died May 29, 1989, age 45
With Quicksilver Messenger Service; from Berkeley, California. Cipollina's
muscular, supple style frequently put Quicksilver a notch above such Bay
Area contemporaries as the Grateful Dead, the Jefferson Airplane, and
Moby Grape. Their output was relatively sparse, and wildly uneven, but
the best of it (on portions of their self-titled 1968 debut and 1969's *Happy
Trails*) was on a par with the very best of what was coming out of the San
Francisco scene of the time. The group suffered enormously from the presence of vocalist and founding member Dino Valenti, who was jailed for a
time in the mid- and late sixties after a drug bust but rejoined them in the
early seventies. Cipollina, a lifelong marijuana smoker, died of respiratory
ailments after years of session work in obscurity.

Steve Clark, died January 8, 1991, age 30
See Munching the Corpse.

Clarence Leo Fender, died March 21, 1991, age 81
Guitar designer, manufacturer; from Buena Park, California. Fender's guitar designs, including the Telecaster (originally called the Broadcaster) and
the Stratocaster, were among the very first solid-body electric guitars to be

mass-produced. They were a favorite of Jeff Beck, Eric Clapton, Jimi Hendrix, Buddy Holly, and many others. Fender died of Parkinson's disease.

Les Harvey, died May 3, 1972, age 25
With Stone the Crows; from Scotland. Les Harvey, the younger brother of Alex Harvey (see I Wanna Destroy), cofounded the impressive Scottish soul act Stone the Crows with Maggie Bell in 1969. The band won kind words from critics for their efforts but little more. Bell eventually went on to a solo career, and bass player Jim Dewar ended up with Robin Trower. In one of the most spectacular of all rock deaths, Les Harvey died by electrocution when he stepped on a live microphone wire during a performance at Swansea University. He was killed instantly.

Eddie Hazel, died December 23, 1992, age 42
See Super Dead.

Jimi Hendrix, died September 18, 1970, age 27
From Seattle. After Buddy Holly, Jimi Hendrix was perhaps rock's most enormous loss at the time he died. Hendrix arrived like a telegram from God, spent three years strutting astonishing chops with a gentle yet unmistakable top-this attitude, and in many ways set the tone and created the style, with Sly Stone, for the late-sixties U.S. counterculture. He died leaving behind only traces and remnants of his vast promise.

He'd spent a painfully shy adolescence learning to play guitar from listening to records by Muddy Waters, B.B. King, Chuck Berry, and Eddie Cochran. After leaving high school in 1959, he joined the army, from which he was discharged in 1961. Then he went on to a protracted period of paying his dues on the chitlin' circuit, backing Sam Cooke, B.B. King, Little Richard, the Isley Brothers, and many others. In 1964 he moved to New York and formed his own band, Jimmy James and the Blue Flames. They played Greenwich Village coffeehouses where the only acceptable fare at the time was blues. Hendrix obliged them, but already he was assembling the elements that later served him well: a roughshod improvising style that demolished and then restructured its own musical settings, sudden sustained passages of lyrical beauty, and a fascination with the pure, physical textures of sound, delivered at incredible volume, with feedback handled like it was a plastic art. Chas Chandler, formerly a bass player with the Animals, saw him in 1966, flipped, and moved him to London.

With Chandler as his manager, and bass player Noel Redding and drummer Mitch Mitchell as his band, the Jimi Hendrix Experience was born in 1967. Their first single was "Purple Haze," an in-your-face psychedelic statement that came right out of the void pulling no punches; there was never a doubt what it was about. Then the debut album *Are You Experienced?* followed, fulfilling all the promise of the single and then some. The pump now finally primed for him in the United States, Hendrix (with Paul McCartney pushing for him in the background) was booked to play the Monterey Pop Festival. There he made history, plain and simple, reviving an audience exhausted by the Who and triumphantly climaxing his set by torching his guitar. It was unbelievable, and unforgettable—the festival documentary has all the evidence. In perhaps the weirdest package in all of rock 'n' roll history, a tour opening for the Monkees was to follow. Chandler got him out of it by saying Hendrix had been banned by the Daughters of the American Revolution.

Though he was known for tricks like playing the guitar behind his back and with his teeth, and despite the antics at Monterey, Hendrix was never really much of a showman. Before long simply standing in one spot cranking out the most incredible sounds ever unleashed by a rock 'n' roll guitar player—and I mean *ever*—was not enough for the crowds he drew. Hendrix just shrugged his shoulders and retired to the comforts of the recording studio, eventually building his own, Electric Lady, in New York in 1970. By then he had released two more amazing albums, *Axis: Bold as Love* and *Electric Ladyland*. But that was still not enough for many of his followers, who applied pressure from all points: some wanted the big, big show, others called for a political stance, still others thought he should make some kind of public commitment to his black roots. For Hendrix, only in his mid-twenties, it was all too easy to lose direction, and he did. In his defense, he likely would have found himself again. Unlike, say, Elvis Presley, Hendrix was clearly capable of making his own decisions and seeing them through. Among his many impressive toss-off accomplishments, he opened up a significant branch of fusion. It was only too bad he couldn't stick around to direct it, and sadder still that he never got the chance to play with Miles Davis, who had his eye on him.

But the last two years of Hendrix's life are a chronicle of confusion as his managers, bands, and plans changed constantly. In 1969 alone the Experience disintegrated; he made his cosmically inspired early-dawn appearance at Woodstock with the Electric Sky Church, a group slapped together for the date (with one of the few decent performances to emerge from that tribal whatchamacallit); and he formed the all-black Band of Gypsies, with army buddy Billy Cox on bass and drummer Buddy Miles. In August 1970 he returned to Europe, fearing his reputation had dimmed there after his years in the United States. Shortly after, his girlfriend Monika Dannemann woke to find him dead beside her in their London apartment. Hendrix had been despondent in his last days and the coroner ruled it an open verdict, officially giving the cause of death as the now-classic (and much covered) inhalation of vomit during a heavily intoxicated sleep. Hendrix may have been despondent and confused, but the chances are that his death was an accident.

Freddy King, died December 28, 1976, age 42

From Gilmer, Texas. Freddy King was one of the great lyrical, gutbucket blues guitar players out of the mold of T-Bone Walker. During the fifties he played with LaVern Baker, Willie Dixon, Memphis Slim, and others. In 1961 he had a top thirty hit with the instrumental "Hideaway," which became a staple among surf music aficionados, along with "Teen Beat" and "Let There Be Drums" by Sandy Nelson, "Walk Don't Run" by the Ventures, and "Honky Tonk" by Bill Doggett. Five years later, however, King was back in Texas without a recording contract. For years he survived largely because of the appreciation shown him by British blues players (Eric Clapton covered his "Have You Ever Loved a Woman?" on *Layla*). Eventually King found opportunities to record again, but a lifetime of hard living finally caught up with him in Dallas, where he died three days after a Christmas show, from heart failure, a bloodclot, and internal bleeding from ulcers.

Paul Kossoff, died March 19, 1976, age 25

Cofounded Free; from England. Kossoff formed Free in 1968 when he and drummer Simon Kirke saw singer Paul Rodgers performing in an obscure British blues band called Brown Sugar. Alexis Korner gave them their name, but they worked out their trademark sound on their own, a combination of bone-crunching riffs, sudden open spaces, and Paul Rodgers's penetrating yowl (which was later plied for Bad Company, and still later for the Firm). It took Free a while to get a hit, but when they finally did it was a big one: 1970's "All Right Now," which went to number 4. But Kossoff's profound drug and personal problems kept the group in a continual state of flux and they were never really able to capitalize on their breakthrough. Today Kossoff may be best remembered for his trick of dying twice—first in 1975 with a thirty-five-minute heart and lung stoppage, followed seven months later by another that has held to this day. Both incidents were related to drug use.

Luther Perkins, died 1969

With Johnny Cash; from Battsville, Mississippi. Luther Perkins backed Johnny Cash in the Tennessee Two, with bass player Marshall Grant. The group came together in 1955, shortly before Cash signed with Sun, and continued into the following decade, after Cash had moved to Columbia. The group broke up in the chaos of Cash's drug troubles during that time. Perkins was a fine, understated player, with a rubbery blues-inflected style marked by a barbed-wire toughness. Cash's "Luther Played the Boogie," recorded in 1959 while the group was still together, covers the main points. He died in a house fire.

Merle Travis, died October 20, 1983, age 65
Singer, songwriter; from Rosewood, Kentucky. In the late forties, Travis designed what many consider to be the first solid-body electric guitar. After his friend Paul Bigsby built it, another friend, Leo Fender (see above), saw him playing it and borrowed it to design and build a similar one. The rest is, you know, history. A significant country figure as well, Travis wrote "Sixteen Tons," "So Round, So Firm, So Fully Packed," "Smoke, Smoke, Smoke That Cigarette," and others. He also appeared in movies. He died of heart failure.

Stevie Ray Vaughan, died August 27, 1990, age 35
From Dallas. The younger brother of the Fabulous Thunderbirds' Jimmie Vaughan, Stevie Ray had made himself a local legend on his own by the late seventies. In 1982 John Hammond took an interest, signing him to Epic and overseeing the production of two albums (1983's *Texas Flood* and 1984's *Couldn't Stand the Weather*). Then, as happens so often in any field of endeavor that can produce phenomenal phenomena of the suddenly perceived kind, everyone soon took an interest. The Rolling Stones auditioned him in 1982, David Bowie asked him to play on his 1983 commercial breakthrough *Let's Dance,* and purist critics everywhere raved at length. Vaughan's reputation was on the rise all through the decade—even 1986's de rigueur double-album *Live Alive* won effusive comment. He died in a helicopter crash returning from an impromptu one-off with Eric Clapton and Robert Cray in Wisconsin.

T-Bone Walker, died March 16, 1975, age 64
See Tombstone Blues.

Faces of Death 20:
Gunshot Suicides

Johnny Ace, died December 24, 1954, age 25
See The Ghost of Johnny Ace.

Joe Meek, died February 3, 1967
See Da Doo Ron Death.

Danny Rapp, died April 8, 1983, age 41
See The Day the Music Died: The First Death of Rock 'n' Roll.

Del Shannon, died February 8, 1990, age 50
See The Day the Music Died: The First Death of Rock 'n' Roll.

Larry Williams, died January 7, 1980, age 44
See Necro-Orleans.

Paul Williams, died August 17, 1973, age 34
See The Motown Morgue.

34

Drummed Out

DRUMMERS, NOT to indulge in too many clichés, are the soul and the heartbeat of rock 'n' roll, its largely unsung and most industrious heroes. If you're going to talk about a class system in rock 'n' roll, put a blue collar on the drummers. No one in music works harder—which may account in part for their current depletion and ongoing replacement by automation, namely the beatbox. But the beatbox really is a little more dependable and at least as inventive, if not nearly as flexible. And get this: for those who say it's the occasional mistakes committed by even the best drummers that makes their backbeat all the more warm, human, and valuable, some beatboxes now come with programs that automatically make mistakes at random. How about that?

It's obvious that no beatbox can ever replace the excitement of seeing a great drummer, like Keith Moon, thrash it out with all the stops opened, or of watching a brilliant drummer, like Charlie Watts, confine himself exactly to what works. Plus there's no way that a beatbox can ever be a responsive part of the complex equation that goes on between rock 'n' roll performers and their audience. But then again, no beatbox will ever have the ego to demand a twenty-minute drum solo, complete with Chinese gong, which may mean a happy end to any lingering temptations for updates of the "Toad" impulse. So the debate rages on.

No one in a rock 'n' roll band is quite so kinetically alive as the drummer, hidden behind his or her kit yet possessed of more presence throughout a good performance than anyone within hailing distance. All those on the list below have whacked their last snare and gone on to what we can only hope is a better world.

Carlton Barrett, died April 17, 1987, age 36
See Death inna Babylon.

John Bonham, died September 25, 1980, age 32
With Led Zeppelin; from England. "Bonzo," as he was affectionately called by friends and fans, was a classic of the seventies, known for his thundering drive, his legendary motel room antics, and his ability to absorb daunting quantities of alcohol. As a player, his reliance on the high-hat and cymbal harked back more to Cream's Ginger Baker than it anticipated the driving thump and scattershot snare of Metallica's Lars Ulrich or Slayer's Dave Lombardo, underlining Led Zeppelin's marginal influence on heavy metal today. Jimmy Page's first post-Yardbirds project may have seemed the epitome of heavy metal at one time, but in today's fast, bottom-throbbing anti-blues atmosphere, they don't even seem to belong at all. It's Black Sabbath, the Scorpions, and Motorhead who rule above all others, and Led Zeppelin now looks like just a decent blues band willing to take some interesting chances. For his part, Bonzo was always happy to take the big crashing four-four drum solo, but even more happy, sadly enough, to take a drink. After he left us in the approved vomit-choke fashion made so popular by Jimi Hendrix, the coroner investigating his death estimated that there was the equivalent of forty shots of vodka in Bonzo's system. Persistent whispers over the years have claimed that Jimmy Page's interest in Aleister Crowley and the occult had something to do with Bonzo's death, as well as the death in 1977 of singer Robert Plant's son Karac.

Karen Carpenter, died February 4, 1983, age 32
See Death Lite.

Eric Carr, died November 25, 1991, age 41
With Kiss; from Brooklyn. Eric Carr was the second drummer for Kiss, brought in in 1980 to replace Peter Criss. Where Criss had been a cat, in the group's pantheon of broadly made-up cartoon characters for its stage act, Carr was a fox. But shortly after Carr joined, the group ditched the makeup altogether, underwent periodic personnel changes—most notably, guitar player Ace Frehley left them in 1982—and toiled on, evidently wasting away into seemingly inevitable obscurity. But lo, in 1990 they had a hit single, the number 8 "Forever," and in 1991 a hit album, *Revenge*. Kiss was back. Carr, however, enjoyed only a taste of it, dying of cancer shortly after the release of *Revenge*.

Cozy Cole, died January 29, 1981, age 73
Jazz player; from East Orange, New Jersey. In 1958, Cozy Cole had a surprise million-seller with "Topsy II," which went to number 3. He called the follow-up, which stalled at number 27, "Topsy I," and the follow-up to

that, which never made it past number 36, "Turvy II." Presumably someone somewhere is still mixing "Turvy I." Cole, for his part, returned to jazz, where his long session resume includes dates with Jelly Roll Morton, Cab Calloway, and Louis Armstrong. He died of cancer.

Jimmy Hodder, died June 15, 1990, age 42
With Steely Dan. Hodder was the original drummer for Steely Dan, when they were still something like a regular group. He appeared on their durable first three albums, 1972's *Can't Buy a Thrill*, 1973's *Countdown to Ecstasy*, and 1974's *Pretzel Logic*. Then Walter Becker and Donald Fagen took over completely, making the group purely a studio-bound vehicle for their own ideas. The good times continued a while longer, but the music became increasingly rarefied and finally seemed to dry up altogether. Hodder drowned, but little else is known of his death.

Johnny Will Hunter, died 1976
With the Hombres; from Memphis. The Hombres started life as a touring act put together to support the studio-based hits of drag (as in hot rod) act Ronny and the Daytonas—the 1964 number 4 "G.T.O." was their biggest. On their own, the Hombres scored a hit in 1967 with the jokey, with-it "Let It Out (Let It All Hang Out)," which reached number 12. According to their organ player Billy B. Cunningham, who wrote it, the song was intended as a send-up of Bob Dylan's "Subterranean Homesick Blues," which they figured had to be a put-on itself. They also figured they could do at least as well, and they were right, in a way. Dylan's song, his first top forty hit, had only reached number 39 in 1965. Little is known of the details of Hunter's death.

Al Jackson, died October 1, 1975, age 39
With Booker T. and the MG's, sessions; from Memphis. For many years, Al Jackson was a session drummer for Memphis-based Stax-Volt, the record company that proved so key to the development of soul music. During the late fifties, Jackson played with Roy Milton and then Booker T. Jones drafted him for Booker T. and the MG's ("MG" for Memphis Group). They had a number 3 hit with "Green Onions" in 1962, but things otherwise went slowly for the group as they patiently waited for Jones to complete his high school and then college education. Jackson, meanwhile, appeared on sessions with such figures as Otis Redding (the MG's backed Redding at the Montery Pop Festival in 1967), Al Green, and others. Booker T. and the MG's, after scoring a couple of hits in 1969—"Hang 'em High," which went to number 9, and the number 6 "Time Is Tight"—finally broke up in 1971.

Jackson, along with bass player Donald "Duck" Dunn, tried to revive the group in 1973 with Bobby Manuel and Carson Whitsett, to no avail. Two years later Jackson was shot and killed outside his home when he surprised an intruder.

Howie Johnson, died 1988

With the Ventures; from Seattle. Johnson was the original drummer for the Ventures, recruited to support founders Don Wilson and Bob Bogle in 1960. He appeared on their first and biggest hit, the surprise "Walk—Don't Run," which went to number 2 in 1960 and set the standard for the group, who have made a career of delivering nimble instrumental tunes as catchy as they are driving. Though the Ventures' last official U.S. hit was the number 4 "Hawaii Five-O" in 1969, they've maintained a cult following through the years, particularly in Japan, where they have sold something like forty million albums. Johnson, however, has not been on hand for much of that. He left the group in the early sixties after an auto accident had limited his ability to play, and subsequently disappeared into obscurity.

Robbie McIntosh, died September 23, 1974, age 24

With Brian Auger's Oblivion Express, the Average White Band; from Scotland. McIntosh, like everyone in the impressive Average White Band, proved himself capable of an effective soul sound simply from having heard it on vinyl. After an apprenticeship with Brian Auger's Oblivion Express, he joined the Average White Band when they formed in 1972, and appeared on their number 1 instrumental hit in 1974, "Pick Up the Pieces." Then, at a party in Los Angeles later that year marking the end of their first U.S. tour, he inhaled poison, believing it to be cocaine. Bass player and vocalist Alan Gorrie, who took the same substance, would have died that night too but for the valiant efforts of Cher, who kept him awake while medical assistance was being sought. The group's next album, *Cut the Cake,* was dedicated to McIntosh.

Keith Moon, died September 7, 1978, age 31

See Who's Dead.

Jon Jon Paulos, died March 26, 1980, age 32

With the Buckinghams; from Chicago. Paulos drummed for the Buckinghams, an innocuous midwestern pop group who broke through in early 1967 with a British look and a number 1 hit, "Kind of a Drag." The song, released on the independent label USA, was kind of a fluke, but the group was quickly snatched up by Columbia, who assigned James William Guercio to the case. In preparation for his later work with Blood, Sweat and Tears and Chicago, Guercio got his feet wet with the horns'n'pop sounds of the number 6 "Don't You Care," the number 5 "Mercy, Mercy, Mercy," the number 12 "Hey Baby (They're Playing Our Song)," and the number 11 "Susan," all released in 1967. The Buckinghams never had another hit after that year. Guercio dumped them in 1968 and two years later they were history. Paulos went on to run a management firm for many years, but died from a drug overdose.

Jeff Porcaro, died August 5, 1992, age 38

With Toto, sessions; from Los Angeles. As a busy session player, Jeff Porcaro contributed to projects by Steely Dan and Boz Scaggs, among many others, incidentally writing two of Scaggs's most popular songs, "Lowdown," which reached number 3 in 1976, and "Lido Shuffle," a top twenty hit in 1977. In 1978 Porcaro got together with some high school friends who were also, by then, busy session players (including his keyboardist brother Steve), to form Toto, a glistening, sterile AOR band. They enjoyed enormous success, with top ten hits, the number 5 "Hold the Line" in 1979, the number 2 "Rosanna" in 1982, the number 1 "Africa" in 1983, and gold and platinum records up the ying-yang. (Later, Porcaro's brothers Joe, a percussionist, and Mike, a bass player, would also join the band.) When Porcaro died the first reports claimed his death was from an allergic reaction to an insecticide he was using in his garden, but it was later confirmed as drug-related.

Razzle, died December 8, 1984
See Munching the Corpse.

Doug Roberts, died November 18, 1981

With Jimmy Gilmer and the Fireballs; from New Mexico. Roberts was the second drummer for the Fireballs, coming in to replace Eric Budd in 1962. By that time they were Jimmy Gilmer and the Fireballs, after their producer Norman Petty (who also produced Buddy Holly, Buddy Knox, Jimmy Bowen, and many others) had put Gilmer and the group together. They hit with the biggest single of 1963 in the number 1 "Sugar Shack," which they followed with the top twenty "Daisy Petal Pickin' " the following year and, in 1968, in one last hurrah as the Fireballs again (though Gilmer was still their singer) with the number 9 "Bottle of Wine." Details of Roberts's death are scanty.

Dennis Wilson, died December 28, 1983, age 39
See Friends: Charles Manson and Dennis Wilson.

Ron Wilson, died May, 1989
With the Surfaris; from Glendora, California. The Surfaris had one and only one hit, but it was a monster: the surf classic "Wipe Out," which went to number 2 in 1963 and then returned to the charts three years later to reach number 16. As the drummer on that beat-crazy instrumental ditty, Wilson stands as the spiritual father, for better or worse, of one of the most cherished of all sixties conventions, the drum solo. Sadly, the fortunes of the Surfaris were never particularly good. They had to file suit to get their rightful share of the "Wipe Out" pot, even as they fought off a suit brought against them by a Los Angeles group claiming rights to their name—all of this while they were still in their teens. By the time everything was straightened out, surf-rock was over and they were on the oldies circuit. Wilson, who once set a record by drumming non-stop for 104½ hours, spent much of his life in dire poverty. He died from a brain aneurysm.

35

Super Dead

*I*N THE early seventies, black pop music took a profound and wonderful
turn. Following the lead of Sly Stone and Marvin Gaye, it suddenly transformed itself into something self-assured, emotionally felt, and clear-
sighted, much of it utterly gorgeous. Gaye's 1971 album *What's Going On*
and the singles it produced—"Mercy Mercy Me (The Ecology)," "Inner
City Blues (Make Me Wanna Holler)," and the title song, all top ten—stand
as perhaps the finest examples of this sweeping new maturity. Black pop
music boasted a sudden and complete mastery of studio technology on the
one hand and, on the other, a willingness to speak out with sensitivity on
issues of the day, with songs that demonstrated how much power could be
found in saying exactly what you meant.

For a year or two after that the airwaves were flooded with similar
sounds, all of them startling, original, and enduringly beautiful: Curtis
Mayfield's 1972 number 4 "Freddie's Dead (Theme from 'Superfly')" and
1973 number 8 "Superfly"; Isaac Hayes's 1971 number 1 "Theme from
Shaft"; the O'Jays' 1972 number 3 "Back Stabbers"; the Chi-Lites' 1971
"(For God's Sake) Give More Power to the People"; the Undisputed Truth's
1971 number 3 "Smiling Faces Sometimes"; the Staple Singers' 1971 "Respect Yourself"; War's 1972 "Slippin' into Darkness"; the Temptations'
1972 number 1 "Papa Was a Rollin' Stone"; and many more.

But by 1974, with the traumatic end of U.S. involvement in the Vietnam
War, the turmoil of Watergate, and the kidnapping of Patty Hearst, less
heavy fare became the first choice for U.S. pop consumers. In short order
many of the producers responsible for the great black pop turned to disco,
delivering up an opportunity to work it all out on the dance floor. If the
complex emotional release provided by the earlier hits was reflected in the
multileveled strategy of their studio mixes, the emotional release of disco

was simplicity itself, and purely physical. The release of those on the list below was pretty simple too, and quite permanent.

Linda Creed, died April 10, 1986
Songwriter; from France. Linda Creed was the lyricist for Thom Bell on some of his best projects, most notably with the Stylistics. She wrote the words for such hits as the 1972 number 9 "You Are Everything," the number 3 "Betcha by Golly Wow" from the same year, and the much covered "I'm Stone in Love with You," also from that year. All undeniably sappy, but like the Stylistics themselves they get under your skin. Creed cowrote her biggest hit, Whitney Houston's "Greatest Love of All," with Michael Masser. It reached number 1 the week she died of cancer.

Roger Lee Durham, died October, 1973, age 27
Singer, percussionist, with Bloodstone; from Kansas City. Funky Bloodstone scored big in 1973 with the lilting "Natural High," which went to number 10. The quintet had started ten years earlier as a vocal group called the Sinceres, and spent time as a show group in Las Vegas and Los Angeles before learning to play instruments. As Bloodstone, they took Jimi Hendrix's cue and moved to England in 1972. The pseudo-Brit strategy worked, and Bloodstone was soon scoring U.S. hits, with and without Durham, who died of unknown causes at the peak of the group's popularity.

Ronnie Dyson, died November 10, 1990, age 40
Singer, actor; from Washington, D.C. Dyson played the spade in the Broadway production of *Hair* and subsequently appeared in the movie *Putney Swope*. In 1970, with Thom Bell producing, he hit with the heavy relationship ballad "(If You Let Me Make Love to You Then) Why Can't I Touch You?," which reached number 8. The follow-up three years later, "One Man Band (Plays All Alone)," made the top thirty, but it was virtually the last ever heard from Dyson. He died of a chronic lung disease.

Marvin Gaye, died April 1, 1984, age 44
See The Motown Morgue.

Donny Hathaway, died January 13, 1979, age 33
Producer, arranger, songwriter, singer; from Chicago. Perhaps most famous for his duets with Roberta Flack, Donny Hathaway's brief career, sadly marred by mental illness, boasts a wide variety of activities. He worked as a producer and arranger with, among others, Curtis Mayfield

and the Impressions, Jerry Butler, the Staple Singers, Aretha Franklin, and Carla Thomas. In 1972 he sang the theme song for TV's "Maude." But it was the hits with Flack that really established him, most memorably with the 1972 number 5 "Where Is the Love" and the 1978 number 2 "The Closer I Get to You." The six years between them, however, were marked by Hathaway's tortured battles with his demons, during which time he accomplished little. He was working with Flack again when he ended his life by jumping from a fifteenth floor hotel window.

Eddie Hazel, died December 23, 1992, age 42

With Parliament-Funkadelic; from Plainfield, New Jersey. Eddie Hazel helped define funk—definitively, if almost anonymously—with his supple stylings for George Clinton's flagship operations in the seventies. He hooked up with Clinton in 1967, joining the Parliaments shortly after their top twenty "(I Wanna) Testify" and staying on through Funkadelic's 1974 *Standing on the Verge of Getting It On,* one of their finest. Hazel wrote and arranged most of that album, as well as stamping his sound indelibly into Clinton's mix. After a fling with Motown, which included writing the Temptations' top thirty "Shaky Ground," troubles with drugs landed him in prison for a year. He spent the rest of his life in obscurity, drifting in and out of sessions with Clinton. He died of complications from liver failure.

Don McPherson, died July 4, 1971, age 29

Singer, with the Main Ingredient; from New York. The Main Ingredient, which started as a soul group called the Poets, actually scored their biggest hits after McPherson's death, the 1972 number 3 "Everybody Plays the Fool" and its number 10 follow-up two years later, "Just Don't Want to Be Lonely." McPherson, the original lead singer, had been replaced by Cuba Gooding. McPherson died of leukemia.

William Powell, died May 26, 1977, age 35

Singer, with the O'Jays; from Canton, Ohio. The O'Jays formed as a black vocal quintet called the Mascots in 1958, but changed their name a few years later after Cleveland DJ Eddie O'Jay had lent them his support. For years they released singles that at best reached only the lowest ranks of the charts, any charts. But in 1967 they signed with Kenny Gamble's and Leon Huff's Neptune label and scored a couple of top twenty rhythm and blues hits with "One Night Affair" and "Looky Looky (Look at Me, Girl)." When Neptune folded in 1971 the group was reduced to a trio (Powell, Eddie Levert, and Walter Williams), but they hung on—despite offers from Motown and Holland-Dozier-Holland's Invictus—for the formation of

Gamble and Huff's Philadelphia International. It was worth the wait, as it turned out, because that's when the hits really started coming: the number 3 "Back Stabbers" in 1972, the number 1 "Love Train" in 1973, the number 9 "For the Love of Money" in 1974, and the number 5 "I Love Music (Part 1)" in 1975, among many others. The group had one more top ten hit, the number 4 "Use Ta Be My Girl" in 1978, but by then Powell was no longer with them. He had contracted cancer in the mid-seventies, quit touring after 1976, and died the following year.

Minnie Riperton, died July 12, 1979, age 31
Singer; from Chicago. A pop soul singer with a celebrated five-octave voice, Minnie Riperton's only hit came in 1975 with the number 1 "Lovin' You." But her background ran deep. She had received voice lessons as a child when the scope of her talent was uncovered, and then, at sixteen, opted for the pop route, going to work for Chess in the mid-sixties. There she sang with the Gems, backing such singers as Fontella Bass, Etta James, and others. A solo turn (as Andrea Davis) fizzled, and in 1968 she joined the psychedelic soul band Rotary Connection, staying with them for six obscure but well-regarded albums. By 1973, she had retired to raise a family but Stevie Wonder searched her out to ask her to join his touring group of back-up singers, Wonderlove. She did, and Wonder went on to produce the album for her that included "Lovin' You." Things were looking up but the following year, 1976, she was diagnosed with cancer, which eventually killed her.

Phillippe Wynne, died July 14, 1984, age 46
Singer, with the Spinners; from Detroit. Although the Spinners were formed in Detroit in 1957 and signed with Motown in the early sixties, Wynne did not join until 1972. By then the group, frustrated after many fruitless years as one of Motown's second-rank acts, was with Atlantic. Producer Thom Bell took an interest and, with Wynne out front, produced some of their biggest hits, including the 1972 number 3 "I'll Be Around," their 1974 number 1 duet with Dionne Warwicke, "Then Came You," the 1975 number 5 "They Just Can't Stop It (The Games People Play)," and the 1976 number 2 disco "The Rubberband Man." Wynne left in 1977 for a solo career, eventually finding his way into George Clinton's Parliament-Funkadelic aggregation. He died of a heart attack.

36

Alice Cooper's Cheese Theater of Cruelty

VINCENT FURNIER was born in Detroit, the son of a preacher, and raised in Phoenix. In 1966, when he was eighteen, a ouija board told him he was the incarnation of Alice Cooper, a seventeenth-century witch. Thus was the seed planted that would produce the one person most responsible for delivering the hysterically pitched theatrics of death and mayhem to rock 'n' roll. Usually, of course, it's David Bowie who gets the nod for bringing theater and androgyny to the party, but think about this for a minute. His was the studied, distant, cold presentation of a Meryl Streep or Robert Duvall, and, as he demonstrated clearly in the eighties, he may have shouted Art but he always, *always,* acted Business. Jim Morrison, similarly, was instrumental in introducing morbid excess to rock 'n' roll, but for all the seductive power of his dark obsessions he was tainted by the aura of a poseur: he considered himself a poet. And Ozzy Osbourne—well, not even Ozzy Osbourne takes Ozzy Osbourne seriously.

But Alice Cooper glowed hot like a weapon held to the face. He was a cartoon and knew it, revelled in it like a demented Jack Nicholson, chewing the scenery, throwing aside conventions and diving completely into his roles, pulling in everything he thought might work, and damn the torpedoes. Obviously he longed for commercial success, and he won it, but at every point in his career it always came on his own wonderfully ludicrous terms. No amount of appearances on the "Hollywood Squares" or as the golfing partner of celebrities could take his contributions from him. Indeed, they merely served to underline the scope of his achievement: delivering rock 'n' roll to the media circus, just as the media circus had become powerful enough to fell a president. If that power was subsequently co-opted and traded away by a president who was himself a media star, it was none of Alice Cooper's concern and hardly his fault. He remains the most believable rock star ever to appear as a game-show celebrity guest. It suited him as it suited no other, except perhaps Cher. If I have to tell you, that's praise.

And he managed it by chopping up plastic dolls and swinging from a noose on stage—though, in fact, that was only the most visible, memorable part of his claim on our attention. First there was his top forty radio success, which, beginning with "Eighteen," never strayed far from his intended audience, whoever it was at any given time. The top thirty "Eighteen," from 1971, and the 1972 number 7 "School's Out" stand as timeless teen classics, ranking with the best that rock 'n' roll has ever offered. By exhuming teen themes, lost for a time in the welter of post-Monterey rock, and reconnecting them to a new generation, he made them a tradition in their own right.

Then 1975's top twenty "Only Women" charted the weird course since taken to pop radio success by many a group of hard-rockin' heavy metal heroes, adopting the surprising (and, generally, unconvincing, though Cooper pulled it off) role of warbling sensitive male—see also the 1976 number 7 "Beth" by Kiss, the 1981 number 2 "Waiting for a Girl Like You" by Foreigner, the 1989 number 1 "I'll Be There for You" by Bon Jovi, and the 1989 number 4 "Patience" by Guns N' Roses. Maybe it was lame right down the line, but it went over big and has now for twenty years, and it started with Cooper. Call that tradition too.

But most likely, Alice Cooper is best remembered for his performances, which have always been elaborate productions, frequently misunderstood. The most characteristic and probably the best was 1972's "Killer" tour, promoting the album of the same name, which followed his band's first real success, *Love It to Death* (produced by Bob Ezrin, with "Eighteen"). Cooper showed an unerring instinct, as savage as it was calculated, for what would work onstage. The mascara ran from his eyes and corners of his mouth, the lipstick smeared into stubbly portions of his chin and upper lip as he chopped at baby dolls with an axe, slung rubber chickens around the stage, and, the climax, hung himself in an elaborate ritual. It was perfectly ridiculous but it struck deep chords. Fake hangings became a pastime among teens for a time, resulting in at least one fatality. Adults and parents everywhere were outraged, as they should have been.

But what remains now—the material on *Killer*—is laughable in its attempts to shock, and always was. That was the point. Listen to "Desperado" and tell me anyone can mean that seriously: "I'm a killer, and I'm a clown" (delivered with a perfect smarmy lounge demeanor); "Twenty dollars will make you die" (that's some kind of way-lowball pricing structure there, which cannot be accounted for even by inflation); "You're as stiff as my smoking barrel" (no comment). That was also the album that gave us "Dead Babies," inspired by a series of mildly vulgar jokes popular at the time. But, above all else, the album rocks irresistibly, which only made the stage act all the more hilariously credible.

Still, if the wild antics never left Cooper's shows, their impact did wane steadily. It's not easy to maintain a balance between action entertainment figure and cultural avatar, particularly when it was accomplished in the first place almost accidentally. Cooper's job was finished almost as soon as it began. Even by 1973's *Billion Dollar Babies* he was fading from view, his shuck becoming just a little too obvious (though it set him up perfectly for TV). Kiss blasted him off the map a few years later, and since then a continual series of up-the-ante metal bands have come and gone (by the late seventies and beyond they were all metal, though Cooper, child of a gentler age, was not, really). His influence is apparent in such latter-day developments as Gwar, who spray stage-blood and stage-jism on audiences eager for it, occasionally going to jail for their efforts. A handful of the so-called death-metal bands (Deicide, who perform covered in a goo of pig's blood, comes to mind) also owe him a nod of thanks.

And Cooper himself is hardly out of it yet, though he is now clearly something of a leftover. Even as recently as 1989 he scored a top ten hit, with "Poison." The tour supporting it proved he'd lost little of his edge and, more important, that all was right with the world still: it featured a section where he slit open a woman's stomach and pulled a baby from it. Call that tradition too.

Faces of Death 21:
Miscellaneous Violence

Electrocuted

Les Harvey, died May 3, 1972, age 25
See Guitar Heroes.

Keith Relf, died May 14, 1976, age 33
See Transatlantic Tombstone Blues.

John Rostill, died November 26, 1973, age 31
See Beatles Bugouts.

Stabbed

Meredith Hunter, died December 6, 1969
See Gathering Moss with the Rolling Stones.

King Curtis, died August 13, 1971, age 37
See Blow, Big Man.

Sal Mineo, died February 13, 1976, age 37
See The Day the Music Died: The First Death of Rock 'n' Roll.

Drowned

Johnny Burnette, died August 1, 1964, age 30
See The Day the Music Died: The First Death of Rock 'n' Roll.

Jimmy Hodder, died June 15, 1990, age 42
See Drummed Out.

Brian Jones, died July 3, 1969, age 27
See Gathering Moss with the Rolling Stones.

Shorty Long, died June 29, 1969, age 29
See The Motown Morgue.

Billy Murcia, died November 6, 1972, age 21
See I Wanna Destroy: The Final Death of Rock 'n' Roll.

Dennis Wilson, died December 28, 1983, age 39
See Friends: Charles Manson and Dennis Wilson.

Poisoned

Bobby Fuller, died July 18, 1966, age 22
See The Day the Music Died: The First Death of Rock 'n' Roll.

Robert Johnson, died August 16, 1938, age 27
See Hellhound on His Trail.

Tommy Tucker, died January 22, 1982, age 49
See Twitch and Shout: Rhythm and Blues Deaths.

37

Death Lite

WHILE ROCK 'N' ROLL has always stood for energy and power, its ranks have long been riddled with easy-listening turncoats. For every Little Richard there has been a Pat Boone, for every Leonard Cohen a Judy Collins, for every Johnny Rotten a Steve Strange. Don't act surprised. There's a lot of money at stake here and plenty of people who don't want to jump around in an excited frenzy every time they switch on the radio or play an album—and many, indeed, who would prefer never to be challenged by pop music at all. And let's get real. Those people include you and me too. If there isn't *someone* on the list below you like, even just a little bit when you're away from your friends, alone in your room or car, then I think you're a liar, or as dead as any of them. If those below pose very few challenges, we may nonetheless spend the rest of our own lives pondering why on earth we listen to them on the radio, buy their albums, and flat out enjoy their music.

Bobby Bloom, February 28, 1974
Singer, songwriter. Bobby Bloom was a one-hit wonder with a long pedigree, including a stint as Captain Groovy on "The Bubblegum March" by Captain Groovy and His Bubblegum Army. But he is best remembered for his island-inflected number 8 hit in 1970, "Montego Bay," cowritten with popmeister Jeff Barry. They followed it with "Heavy Makes You Happy," which the Staple Singers covered and took to the top twenty. Then obscurity swallowed him. In 1974, he was killed in an accidental shooting, though details about it are scanty and some reports have suggested suicide

Karen Carpenter, died February 4, 1983, age 32
Singer, drummer, with brother Richard as the Carpenters; from New Haven, Connecticut. Karen Carpenter and her older brother Richard reeled off

a seemingly endless stream of saccharine hits in the early and mid-seventies. The best was the 1971 number 2 "Superstar," written by Leon Russell and Bonnie Bramlett, or maybe it was the 1970 number 2 "We've Only Just Begun," or maybe it was 1977's "Calling Occupants of Interplanetary Craft." The worst? You heard it, you name it. Karen's voice had a poignant clarity matched by few pop singers, but sadly it was put almost exclusively to the service of maudlin tripe. Somebody should have told her about Cole Porter. In the late eighties, director Todd Haines embalmed her in a biography picture that, from all reports, is sensitive and powerful. But it was made with Barbie dolls and voice-overs, which led to its subsequent suppression by the Carpenter family. Karen died of heart complications related to her long-standing anorexia nervosa.

Harry Chapin, died July 16, 1981, age 38
Singer/songwriter; from New York. Chapin is likely best remembered for his bittersweet story-song hits of the early and mid-seventies, most notably the top thirty "Taxi" from 1972 and the number 1 "Cat's in the Cradle" from 1974. But, behind the scenes and elsewhere, he accomplished much more. In 1969 he collaborated on a silent documentary about boxing, *Legendary Champions,* which was nominated for an Oscar. After his singing career was launched, Chapin devoted much of his energies to numerous causes, chiefly battling world starvation. In the mid-seventies he cofounded the World Hunger Fund, raising over $5 million, and until his death more than half of his concert schedule (which averaged over 200 dates a year) was devoted to benefit performances. After his death, his manager, Ken Kragen, established the Harry Chapin Memorial Fund, dedicated to continuing Chapin's efforts. Four years later Harry Belafonte asked Kragen to head up the project that eventually became known as USA for Africa. Chapin died on the Long Island Expressway in an auto accident.

Bill Chase, died August 9, 1974, age 40
Trumpet player, with Chase; from Boston. Bill Chase started as a big-band jazz trumpet player, but in the early seventies, as Blood, Sweat and Tears and Chicago were riding high on the charts, he jumped on the jazz-rock bandwagon and put together his own brassy aggregate, which he named after himself. Chase scored a top thirty hit, 1971's "Get It On," and won accolades from the jazz magazine *Downbeat.* But after two albums and a tour they broke up. He was on the comeback trail with a new Chase when he plummeted to his death in a small airplane in Minnesota on the day that Nixon resigned from office. Three other members of his band died in the same accident: Walter Clark, John Emma, and Wallace Yohn.

Brian Cole, died August 2, 1972, age 28
Bass player, singer, with the Association; from Tacoma, Washington. Cole was a founding member of those venerable pioneers of soft-rock, the Association. He was with them for all the big hits, including the controversial 1966 number 7 "Along Comes Mary" (thought by some to be about marijuana), the 1966 number 1 "Cherish," the 1967 number 1 "Windy," and the 1967 number 2 "Never My Love." In 1972, with the group's fortunes well on the wane, Cole died of a heroin overdose, prompting the group to break up. They have since re-formed and may now be found on the oldies circuit.

Barbara Cowsill, died January 31, 1985, age 56
Singer, with the Cowsills; from Newport, Rhode Island. Barbara Cowsill was Mom in the Cowsills, the sixties family group who provided the prototype for the Partridge Family. The Cowsills included kids Bill, Bob, Dick, Paul, Barry, John, and Sue, and were managed by their nonperforming Dad, William "Bud," who was a retired Navy officer. Their hits were actually pretty good, including the 1967 number 2 "The Rain, the Park and Other Things," the 1968 number 10 "Indian Lake," and the classic "Hair," from the musical, which they took to number 2 in 1969. Shirley Jones, let alone Florence Henderson, had nothing on Barbara Cowsill. The details of her death are obscure, but kids Bob, Paul, John, and Sue have since reunited to tour again.

Jim Croce, died September 20, 1973, age 30
Singer/songwriter, truck driver; from Philadelphia. Jim Croce was a mustachioed, cigar-smoking, East Coast working-class folkie who suddenly crashed the pop charts in the early seventies. Two of his biggest hits—"You Don't Mess Around with Jim," which went to number 8 in 1972, and "Bad, Bad Leroy Brown," a number 1 hit the following year— were uptempo soundalikes of only marginal interest. Croce accomplished more with his ballads: the 1974 number 9 "I'll Have to Say I Love You in a Song," the 1973 number 1 "Time in a Bottle," and especially 1972's top twenty "Operator (That's Not the Way It Feels)" were surprisingly poignant, affecting tunes. At the peak of his fortunes he died in an airplane crash that also killed his guitar player, Maury Muehleisen. Crocodile tears and enormous sales followed, but even (maybe that should be particularly) in death Croce never seemed quite suited for the role of a legend.

Percy Faith, died February 9, 1976, age 67
Orchestra leader; from Toronto. Percy Faith signed on with Columbia and Mitch Miller in 1950 and immediately started turning out big schmaltzy

hits, just the way Miller liked it. Faith's biggest, and perhaps his schmaltzi-est, was "Theme from 'A Summer Place,' " the memorable theme from an otherwise lame 1959 movie. The song stayed at number 1 for nine weeks early in 1960, and for many years afterward teens could be heard picking out the melody on pianos everywhere. Faith never came close to that kind of success again, but early in 1976 he recorded a disco version of it, which might be the next best thing. A month later he died of cancer.

Vince Guaraldi, died February 6, 1976, age 46
Piano player, composer; from San Francisco. The Vince Guaraldi Trio scored a minor hit in 1963 with the first chart version of "Cast Your Fate to the Wind," a folk-tinged beatnicky kind of syrupy instrumental ballad they took to number 22. Two years later a British orchestra, Sounds Or-chestral, took it into the top ten. Shortly after, Guaraldi stumbled on to the gig that made his career: scoring Charlie Brown TV specials with wonder-fully affecting kiddie music. He died of a heart attack.

Terry Kath, died January 23, 1978, age 31
Singer, with Chicago; from Chicago. Singer Terry Kath cofounded and spent all of his career with the mega-successful jazz-rock ensemble Chicago. You'd need a slide rule to calculate the dimensions of their success since 1970, but let's just say they've scored at least nineteen top ten pop hits over the years and leave it at that, so we don't have to regurgitate any titles and their associated memories. Kath's death, which harks back to Johnny Ace himself, has already become the stuff of urban legend. A gun collector, and ever the practical joker, he's said to have shot himself in the head at a party thinking the gun was not loaded. Other stories paint a more grim picture, with Kath playing Russian roulette in a variety of settings, including alone at home, and at the breakfast table with his family present. Whatever the specific details actually may be, he died by his own hand with a gun under lurid circumstances. The group went into shock but were shortly rallied by Doc Severinsen, and subsequently returned to their hit-making ways.

Bobby Scott, died November 5, 1990, age 53
Piano player, singer, songwriter; from Mount Pleasant, New York. Bobby Scott primarily confined himself to jazz throughout his career, where he es-tablished himself as a respected composer. But he did score a top twenty hit early in 1956 with the inoffensive "Chain Gang" (no relation to the Sam Cooke song) and, a few years later, wrote "Taste of Honey" as the theme for a play; later the song became one of Herb Alpert's biggest hits (after it had already been covered by the Beatles). Scott also wrote "He Ain't Heavy,

He's My Brother," a number 7 hit for the Hollies in 1970, discovered and was the first to record Jesse Colin Young, of the Youngbloods, and worked with Marvin Gaye late in Gaye's career. He died of lung cancer.

"Sir" Walter Scott, died circa December 27, 1983
Singer, born Walter Northeis, Jr., with Bob Kuban and the In-Men; from St. Louis. "Sir" Walter Scott sang for Bob Kuban and the In-Men, a mid-sixties St. Louis-based eight-piece ensemble whose sound was roughly in the horns'n'pop vein of the work of producer James Guercio (the Buckinghams, Chicago). They hit once and only once, in 1966, with "The Cheater," which went to number 12 warning of the dangers of a seduction artist. The group never came close to matching it again, and eventually fell into obscurity and disbanded. Nearly eighteen years later, two days after Christmas in 1983, Scott left his home to buy a battery for his car, and was not seen or heard from again for over three years. In April 1987, his body was discovered in a cistern in St. Louis. He had been bound and killed, shot in the back execution-style. His widow and her lover were indicted for the murder. Now *that's* irony.

Tom Sellers, died March 9, 1988, age 39
Producer, formed the Assembled Multitude; from Wayne, Pennsylvania. Sellers put together the musicians (many of whom would go on to join MFSB) for the Assembled Multitude, a studio concoction that churned out orchestrated covers of the progressive-rock standards of the day, including the top twenty "Overture from Tommy (A Rock Opera)" from 1970, their only hit, along with "Woodstock" and chestnuts from "Jesus Christ, Super-star." Before that, in the late sixties, Sellers played briefly in a band called Gulliver with Daryl Hall. He died in a house fire.

Spanky and Our Gang
From Chicago. Spanky and Our Gang came in on the wave of folk-rock that swept the nation in the mid-sixties, thanks to Bob Dylan, the Byrds, and others. The group—just barely folk, and certainly not rock—were not with-out their charms, as they proved in a series of top forty confections, each as sweet and creamy as the next: the number 9 "Sunday Will Never Be the Same" from 1967, along with the top twenty "Lazy Day" from later that year, and 1968's "Like to Get to Know You," among others. Two of their guitar players, however, didn't make it: Malcolm Hale died in 1968, and Lefty Baker, born Eustace Britchforth, died some time after that of an en-larged liver. Details about their deaths are scanty. During the eighties, Spanky, whose real name is Elaine McFarlane, went on to take the role of

Mama Cass Elliot when the Mamas and the Papas re-formed. She was known affectionately, if revoltingly, as "Mama Spanky."

Jud Strunk, died October 15, 1981, age 45

Singer, banjo player, comic; from Jamestown, New York. Strunk was a sort of folkie oddball who scored a number 14 hit in 1973 with the feather-weight "Daisy a Day." MGM gave him the shot as much as anything because he was a regular that year on TV's "Laugh-In" (then in its own death throes). But he got the hit anyway. Then he receded into oblivion. He was killed in an airplane crash.

38

Sideshow Radio

*T*wo songs from 1971 offered astonishing evidence of the depths rock 'n' roll fans seemed eager to plumb in the wake of the brutalizing events of the sixties and their growing sense of grim powerlessness. Or perhaps I should say the heights those fans seemed eager to climb, since the stunning attack on convention these two songs produced has rarely been matched on the radio. If neither was an out and out spectacular success — "Timothy" by the Buoys reached number 17 in the spring of 1971, and the harrowing "D.O.A." by Bloodrock reached only number 36 a few months earlier — the fact remains that they did reach the top forty, both of them, which must be counted a genuine victory of some kind.

In their way, they were the beginning of something that was neither rational nor cynical. It was rather a joyful, nonjudgmental embracing of sensory experience, that was, in effect, taking the freedoms demanded in the sixties to their logical and natural conclusions. "D.O.A.," in particular, looked forward to the savage renaissance of horror in movies that began in 1973 with *The Exorcist* — a renaissance that lasted nearly fifteen years, during which the spectacle of meaningless death was evoked again and again, with brutal rhythm, until finally desensitization allowed anyone still willing to look a glimpse of both the erotic beauty and even the humor of that spectacle (though 1990's *Henry: Portrait of a Serial Killer* brought all that full circle). In the early eighties, a few postpunk bands, notably the Cramps, tried to reclaim those darkly joyful excesses of horror, as did Slayer, who merely subtracted the joy.

But there is nothing the slightest bit loud-hard-fast about "D.O.A.," which takes on the funereal ambience of driver-training films like *Signal 30* that are still, the last I heard, shown to teens shortly before proms as a shock inducement to follow safety precautions. With its gloomy texture and gruesome details, "D.O.A." simply pushes this ambience to the furthest extreme. Here, death may be an unfortunate fact, but it is merely a fact, and the starting point for what follows. It neither condemns nor celebrates thrill-seeking, nor does it seem particularly concerned about anything that's going on here—it doesn't, in fact, have much of a point of view at all. It's just looking.

Clocking in at a most seventies 8:25 in its long, definitive album version, the song's scene is the back of an ambulance, whose sirens blast on the chorus (they had to be edited from the initial release because too many listening in their cars were pulling to the side of the road). The gothic, mannered, hoarse-voiced singer (Jim Rutledge) has just been involved in an accident—hard to tell if it's plane or auto—and he describes the experience in excruciating detail: "Something warm is flowing down my fingers," "I try to move my arm and there's no feeling/And when I look I see there's nothing there," "The girl I knew has such a distant stare." Then the bridge and guitar solo. The ending is something of a cheat ("God in heaven, teach me how to die"), but you can't have everything. It's a well-known fact there are no atheists in foxholes, and as ham-handed as they may have been about it, Bloodrock was dealing with nothing but death, eyeball to eyeball.

In contrast to the dire strains of "D.O.A.," the Buoys' "Timothy" was cheerful pumping bubblegum whose scenario, cannibalism among friends trapped in a mine (Timothy appearing as the meal), was as vacuously calculated as it was repellent, leaving it more a camp artifact than anything. Yet it is still sufficiently horrific to remain oddly disturbing, even in the midst of its broad shtick—"Joe said that he would sell his soul/For just a piece of meat," indeed. In its time it became something of a cult favorite, as zany "Timothy for Lunch Bunch" clubs formed on college campuses (with Scepter's promo people involved from behind), rather than the controversial object of banning and general cause celebre for which its writer Rupert Holmes (more famous nearly a decade later for "The Pina Colada Song" and "Him") had hopes. But its disappearance from all airplay today, even on oldies stations, speaks loudly of its residual power, as peculiar as it is ridiculous.

Two other songs from the period also merit mention, if only in passing. They had neither the teeth nor the enduring ability to shock of the two above. But they certainly rank as sideshow radio. Terry Jacks's "Seasons in the Sun," a number 1 tearjerker about a man dying from cancer, was a hit in 1974 just as the United States was giving up the ghost in Vietnam. And Bobby "Boris" Pickett and the Crypt-Kickers' "Monster Mash" was rereleased in 1973, no one quite knows why, and reached number 10—after its 1962 release had already gone all the way to number 1.

39

Hustled: Disco Deaths

DISCO DOES not suck. After punk-rock, it was the most interesting development in pop music to come out of the seventies—and at this point, that's not just an opinion any more. While it's true that much of disco is formularized and calculated (believe me, searching secondhand stores for the gems can be unrewarding work), I'd like to know any branch of pop music in which that's not the case. It's also true that the trademark four-on-the-floor beat, that famed and much reviled disco thumpa-thump, quickly grew monotonous. And okay, it was somewhat distressing to see such artists as the Rolling Stones, Rod Stewart, and Blondie wholeheartedly jumping on a bandwagon.

On the other hand, "Miss You," "Do Ya Think I'm Sexy," and "Heart of Glass" represent some of the greatest sonic possibilities of disco, which at its best utilized studio technology *and* respected the need to shake a booty. That's rock 'n' roll and that was disco's strength, delivering glorious cascades of lush, pounding, utterly irresistible sheets of sound that worked on and off the dance floor, and incidentally, returned the music to the nightclubs where it belonged. Just think—the Trammps could deliver up a ten-minute-plus tour de force, "Disco Inferno," and you never had to sit through an interminable guitar solo. You didn't even have to sit. If anything, you wished the guitar solo that occupies some forty-five seconds or so of the mix was just a little longer and more fiery, the better to shake it all the harder.

By the time of the Trammps' hit, however, disco was already in decline. When it first emerged, in the early seventies, it came from Philadelphia and New York studios with a sound that was basically just quick, up-tempo soul adapted to the technological innovations of the studio (most notably multi-tracking). Then KC and the Sunshine Band, in Florida, and producer Giorgio Moroder, in Munich—Donna Summer was his most famous client—began to tart it up. Moroder is probably the big-thump culprit, but even so the deadening throb took over slowly. On 1975's "The Hustle," perhaps the first disco anthem, it's still not in evidence, nor did it appear on KC's big hits of the mid-seventies ("Get Down Tonight," "That's the Way [I Like It]," "[Shake, Shake, Shake] Shake Your Booty," etc.). Even when the Bee Gees pushed disco over the top, in 1976 and 1977, four-on-the-floor was not mandatory.

But alas, by 1978, in the wake of *Saturday Night Fever,* it was, and producers were in complete control of it, churning out mountains of vinyl with mechanical beats over which they layered whatever they felt like. It's not surprising that a strong reaction to it set in, but let's get some perspective here. I mean, you have to wonder if those who were busy burning records and raising banners had the slightest clue about the ecstasies of rhythm and motion. Or if they were even listening to the likes of Chic, who always boasted a spry, nimble, and penetrating guitar sound. Ask yourself this simple question: Would *you* want someone who says disco sucks for a sex partner?

Those on the list below do not have to ask such questions, for they are no longer of this world. If they lived a bad life, they are doubtless in hell now, where the Devil and his minions have never quite got the hang of BPM's and smooth segues. If they lived a good life, God Himself may be working the 'tables—and holding.

Neil Bogart, died May 9, 1982, age 39

Record company executive. Hustler Neil Bogart gets the credit (if that's the word) for creating bubblegum in the sixties and Kiss in the seventies, as well as for launching the Queen of Disco, Donna Summer. With his Buddah label, along with production team Jerry Kasenetz and Jeff Katz, he gave us 1968's number 1 "Green Tambourine" by the Lemon Pipers, number 4 "Yummy Yummy Yummy" by the Ohio Express, and number 4 "Simon Says" by the 1910 Fruitgum Co., along with subsequent hits by Melanie, the Brooklyn Bridge, and many more. He adapted neatly to the changes of the next decade, abandoning Buddah and forming Casablanca. Then, with Kiss providing dependable cash flow, he ventured into disco, signing the Village People, whose "Y.M.C.A." reached number 2 in 1979, and, most importantly, Donna Summer.

At first, Summer's work with Giorgio Moroder did much to define disco's style and substance, with such classics as the sixteen-minute mouth-breather "Love to Love You Baby," the shortened version of which went to number 2 in 1976, "Last Dance," number 3 in 1978, and a very weird version of "MacArthur Park," a number 1 hit later that year. But with such forays into rock as "Hot Stuff" and "Bad Girls," both number 1s in 1979, she turned out to be a genuine pop star of the first rank. Though Bogart and Summer eventually parted company (she sued him to get off the label), they had helped each other—and Bogart, at any rate, had covered all bets. In the early eighties he was similarly positioned again, rescuing Joan Jett from obscurity on his new Boardwalk label and releasing her "I Love Rock 'N Roll," which went to number 1 in 1982. But, just as Jett's Tommy James cover, "Crimson and Clover," was reaching the top ten, Bogart died of cancer.

Andy Gibb, died March 10, 1988, age 30

Singer, youngest brother of Bee Gees members; from Australia. In 1977, at the onset of the Bee Gees' disco surge, Andy Gibb made a spectacular debut with three consecutive number 1 pop hits, each a little more lame than the one before: "I Just Want to Be Your Everything," "(Love Is) Thicker than Water," and "Shadow Dancing." His next three releases made the top ten, but then a cocaine problem—due, he said, to his break-up with TV's "Dallas" star Victoria Principal—bore down on him, and in the early eighties his life went into disarray. The hits dried up, he was fired from hosting TV's syndicated "Solid Gold," and one opportunity after another slipped away from him. In 1985 he entered rehab. In 1987 he declared bankruptcy. In 1988 he died of an inflammatory heart virus, evidently unrelated to drug use.

Van McCoy, died July 6, 1979, age 35

Producer, singer, songwriter; from Washington, D.C. Van McCoy is best remembered as a disco artist because of his number 1 hit in 1975, "The Hustle," a genuine artifact of the era. But his musical lineage actually goes all the way back to vocal groups. In the early sixties he performed in a Frankie Lymon and the Teenagers-type group, the Starlighters, and then moved around the industry for a time, finally hiring on with Scepter (home of the Shirelles, Dionne Warwick, and the Isley Brothers) as a studio hand. He worked for Jerry Leiber and Mike Stoller as a staff writer, and went on to write a few pop hits, including the top twenty "Baby, I'm Yours" for Barbara Lewis in 1965. He also wrote songs recorded by Aretha Franklin, Tom Jones, Peaches and Herb, Gladys Knight and the Pips, and others. During the early seventies, he worked with the Stylistics, which led to his association with producers Hugo and Luigi and the disco success that branded him and set a standard he never matched again. He died of a heart attack.

George McCrae, died January 24, 1986, age 41

Singer; from West Palm Beach, Florida. George McCrae was a soul singer who scored a number 1 pop hit in 1974 with the disco "Rock Your Baby," which practically amounted to the beginning and end of his career. The song was written and produced by Harry Wayne Casey and Richard Finch, later more famous as KC and the Sunshine Band. The next year McCrae's wife Gwen scored with the soundalike "Rockin' Chair," which went to number 9. The McCraes also recorded duets but eventually were divorced. McCrae died of cancer.

Steve Rubell, died July 25, 1989, age 45
Nightclub entrepreneur. In 1977, with his partner Ian Schrager, Steve Rubell opened Studio 54 in Manhattan, and in short order it became the world capital of disco, attracting celebrities by the fistful: Andy Warhol, Michael Jackson, Margaret Trudeau, Truman Capote, Cher, and countless more. So exclusive was it at its height that not even the celebrities were guaranteed entrée. Bouncers stood at the door enforcing a strict dress code and handpicking participants for the nightly party, while inside the beautiful people gyrated to the strobe and the rubber thump 'neath the silvery mirror-ball, or retired to dark corners for sex or cocaine. It was the wild life's last sensational hurrah, before AIDS and crack. Studio 54 closed in 1979, when Rubell and Schrager were indicted on income-tax charges and spent thirteen months in prison. After their release, they opened the Palladium, a faint echo of its predecessor. Rubell died of complications from hepatitis and septic shock.

Sylvester, died December 16, 1988, age 41
Singer, born Sylvester James; from Los Angeles. Sylvester was a disco singer from Los Angeles who traded on a campy image. He emerged from San Francisco in the early seventies, decked out as a transvestite with a glitter-rock act. His weird assortment of covers, including Neil Young's "Southern Man" and Procul Harum's "A Whiter Shade of Pale," didn't catch on and he disappeared — only to reappear five years later. Harvey Fuqua breathed new life into him as a disco star with the top twenty "Dance (Disco Heat)" in 1978. He was backed by Martha Wash and Izora Rhodes, who later became Two Tons o' Fun, then the Weather Girls, and he also appeared in Bette Midler's 1979 vehicle, *The Rose.* With the Village People and the Bee Gees, Sylvester was a prime symbol of disco and fell hard when the music did. He spent most of the eighties in obscurity, and finally died from AIDS-related troubles.

Faces of Death 22:
AIDS

Freddie Mercury, died November 24, 1991, age 45
See Sha Na Na, Inc.: The Second Death of Rock 'n' Roll.

Sylvester, died December 16, 1988, age 41
See Hustled: Disco Deaths.

Ricky Wilson, died October 13, 1985, age 32
See I Wanna Destroy: The Final Death of Rock 'n' Roll.

40

Death inna Babylon

THE HISTORY of reggae, the rock music of a parallel universe, is as cryptic as it is organic, marked at every step by gnarled twists and turns. It begins with Rosco Gordon, a U.S. bluesman from Memphis. In 1952, his "No More Doggin' " was picked up on Jamaican radios from broadcasts out of New Orleans. Along with other rhythm and blues tunes from the likes of Louis Jordan, Johnny Ace, and Fats Domino, it was much loved in Jamaica. But something about the funny beat in that Gordon tune, a back-to-front rhythm that emphasized the first and third beats, seemed to catch completely the imagination of Jamaican musicians, who had been weaned on forties "mento," a more typical Caribbean musical style drawing on both the island sounds of calypso and rhumba, and African spirituals.

During the late fifties and early sixties, U.S. pop music paled and Jamaican musicians were forced to fall back on their own resources. They began to develop a quick, bouncy, infectious sound called "ska." Most of it featured Gordon's funny beat, along with rhythm and blues arrangements and song structures drawn from mento. With its heavy reliance on sound systems, ska also gave rise to "toasting," a yammering style of shtick that focused on the DJ's participation and prefigured rap, and "dub," which emphasized the almost psychedelic electronic acoustics that could be produced by manipulating the soundboard. In 1964, ska enjoyed its only hit in the United States: Millie Small's "My Boy Lollipop," which went to number 2.

Then, in the mid-sixties, as rock and soul came to prominence in the United States, Jamaican music once again began to supplement its style with outside influences. Essentially all the innovations of ska were retained, but they were slowed down for the heavier exercises of "rude boy," and then slowed down even more for the sultry and sensual "rock steady," which dominated in the late sixties. That, in turn, gave way to a brief return to a looser, quicker sound, called "poppa-top." In 1969, Desmond Dekker and the Aces scored the second major Jamaican hit in the United States with the number 9 "Israelites," a poppa-top number that looked toward the changes reggae was about to bring.

The chief distinction of reggae, which emerged in the early seventies, was the willingness of its proponents to address political issues. Most by then subscribed to Rastafarianism, the puritanism of a parallel universe, which preaches a millenarian vision and requires its followers to lead ascetic lives. Nonetheless, many Rastafarians are inveterate marijuana smokers (just as many Catholics are wine drinkers), which provides the other thread that ties most reggae musicians. Otherwise, reggae is a rich and mixed bag; music of uncommon power and warmth, encompassing an enormous variety of elements from the musical backgrounds that shaped it.

It's unlikely this chapter would be included—as, indeed, would reggae be included in any pop music reference—if it weren't for the contributions of Bob Marley. Nevertheless, if Marley almost single-handedly vaulted Jamaican pop music onto the world stage, others were there to provide the setting, and others came after him to maintain its vitality. Those below are dead now. May Jah be with them all, and with you.

Carlton Barrett, died April 17, 1987, age 36
Drummer, with Bob Marley and the Wailers. Carlton Barrett was assigned to the Wailers in 1969, along with his brother Aston "Family Man," shortly after the Wailers' founding threesome of Bob Marley, Peter Tosh, and Bunny Livingston had joined forces with producer Lee "Scratch" Perry. The Barretts had previously played with Perry's Upsetters, but ended up staying with Marley for the rest of his life. They established themselves among the elite of reggae's players, and came to be considered one of the finest rhythm sections existing, along with Sly Dunbar and Robbie Shakespeare. After Marley's death, they spent the eighties free-lancing. Carlton was shot to death outside his home in Kingston, but little else is known of the incident.

Don Drummond, died April 21, 1971
Trombone player, with the Skatalites. Drummond led the Skatalites, a Jamaican session group that appeared in one way or another on practically everything recorded on the island in the mid-sixties. He has been credited with inventing ska, the infectious fast-beat dance sound that prefigured reggae. Whether he actually did or not, a good many enduring island stars spent time in his band, including Roland Alphonse, Tommy McCook, Johnny Moore, and Jackie Mittoo. Those who hired the Skatalites for sessions included the Wailers, the Maytals, the Heptones, Justin Hines, and

more. Drummond died after suffering many years from mental illness, but specific details about his death are obscure.

Leslie Kong, died 1971, age 38
Producer. The Chinese-Jamaican Leslie Kong was one of the earliest and most influential producers in Jamaica. His career, brief as it was, nevertheless spanned the eras of ska, rock steady, and reggae. He got into the business at the urging of Jimmy Cliff, shortly after Kong had expanded his ice cream shop into a record store. Kong produced Cliff's "Dearest Beverley" in 1962 and went on to work with many others. In 1968 he produced Desmond Dekker and the Aces' "Israelites," the fluky first U.S. reggae hit in 1969. He also worked with Bob Marley, the Wailers, the Maytals, the Melodians, and Ken Boothe. With his career still on the rise, he died of a heart attack.

Bob Marley, died May 11, 1981, age 36
Reggae singer, songwriter; from Rhoden Hall, Jamaica. Bob Marley, like Bob Dylan, never had a lot of hits—not a single one in the U.S., in fact. And his albums didn't sell that well either, despite (maybe because of) his prodigious ability to churn them out one after the other. But he stands as one of the giants of reggae, and rock, and pop music—indeed, he is one of the most influential and warmly regarded figures in all of popular culture. Marley's affecting presence in performance helped establish him as an internationally renowned superstar. He was particularly beloved in Britain and Africa, but there is likely no corner of the world that has not been touched by him somehow.

Born in a small rural Jamaican community, he ran away to Kingston in 1959, when he was just fourteen. It was the time when ska and then rock steady and ultimately reggae were about to explode. At seventeen he met Jimmy Cliff, who introduced him to ice cream shop owner Leslie Kong, who in turn produced his first singles. Then, with Peter Tosh and Bunny Livingston, Marley formed the Wailers in 1964 as a vocal group and hooked up with producer Coxsone Dodd, who helped them get "Simmer Down," "Put It On," "The Ten Commandments of Love," and others right. But there was little money to be found there—the Jamaican music industry was in its formative stages and shot through with corruption. Royalties were practically nonexistent. The Wailers folded in 1966, and Marley moved to Wilmington, Delaware, where his mother had moved three years earlier, and found work in an auto factory. That, however, turned out to be too much monkey business for Marley, and a year later he returned to Jamaica, where he signed a songwriting deal with Johnny Nash (who six years later had a number 12 hit with Marley's "Stir It Up"), re-formed the Wailers, and took another tilt at music.

By the end of the decade he was committed to Rastafarianism. In 1969, he fell in with producer Lee Perry, who taught the Wailers to play their own instruments and brought in the rhythm section from his studio band the Up-setters (brothers bass player Aston "Family Man" Barrett and drummer Carlton). Island signed the Wailers in 1972—the label, which had been delivering Jamaican music to a world audience since 1962, knew what they had in Marley. The first album, 1973's *Catch a Fire*, was promising. The follow-up later that year, *Burnin'*, delivered on that promise, artistically and commercially, the latter helped in part by Eric Clapton's cover of "I Shot the Sheriff," which became a number 1 hit in the United States in 1974. The Wailers' overseas tour in 1973 made further inroads for the group, who were now clearly on the rise. But after the tour, Tosh and Livingston left, unhappy with the increasing focus on Marley. Undaunted, Marley restructured the group in 1974, adding a trio of female backing singers, the I-Threes, which included his wife Rita, and pushed on.

Like Mick Jagger and Keith Richards in 1968, Bob Marley in 1976 was suddenly transformed into something brilliant and significant. Unlike Jagger and Richards, however, Marley's breakthrough clearly had more to do with God than Satan. Any more questions about his sudden prominence may be referred to the albums themselves. Nearly all of his prolific output holds up, track by track, boasting gorgeous melodies and endless hooks. Live, by all reports, he was even better, his performances positively charismatic, memorable events for anyone who saw them. Rastafarianism lent him credibility as a social leader, and Marley's statements on public issues were taken seriously. Late in 1976 he was the victim of an assassination attempt, which he survived. Wounded but not slowed, he continued recording and performing, and his reputation continued to grow steadily, and was still growing at the end of his life. During his 1980 tour of the United States, he collapsed. Shortly after that he was diagnosed with brain and lung cancer. Seven months later that was what killed him.

Peter Tosh, died September 11, 1987, age 42
Reggae singer, songwriter; from Westmoreland, Jamaica. Tosh cofounded the Wailers in 1964 with Bob Marley and Bunny Livingston, but quit and went solo in 1973 after Island made Marley the focus of its promotion. Tosh always had a decidedly keener and more bitter edge than Marley, and was even more politically outspoken as well: in 1978, at a concert for 30,000 in Jamaica, Tosh directly addressed the prime minister, who was in attendance, railing at him from the stage to legalize marijuana, and

proceeded to smoke it then and there. (Later that year he was arrested on another charge, incarcerated, and beaten nearly to death by Jamaican police.) Tosh turned out a steady stream of records through the late seventies and early eighties, and frequently toured. In 1978 he recorded with Mick Jagger and toured with the Rolling Stones. He toured with Jimmy Cliff in 1982. He was shot to death in his home by a burglar.

Faces of Death 23:
Diseases with Proper Names

Lew DeWitt, died of Crohn's disease, August 15, 1990, age 52
See Country Corpses.

Clarence Leo Fender, died of Parkinson's disease,
March 21, 1991, age 81
See Guitar Heroes.

Woody Guthrie, died of Huntington's disease,
October 3, 1967, age 55
See Just Us Dead Folk.

Leadbelly, died of Lou Gehrig's disease, December 6, 1949, age 60
See Just Us Dead Folk.

Ronnie Mack, died of Hodgkin's disease, 1963
See Beatles Bugouts.

41

The Grateful Dead's Long, Strange Spinal Tap Trip

DESPITE TEMPTING fate with its name and lifestyle, San Francisco's pioneering psychedelic group the Grateful Dead has remained largely free of incident over the course of its long career. Except for one tiny detail—finding a keyboardist who can stay alive. Like the fictional (I think) Spinal Tap, with its series of drummers who succumbed to spontaneous combustion one after another, members of the Grateful Dead have been forced to suffer through a series of untoward deaths by whoever they assign to the ivory duties. Of course, it's never been quite as spectacular as spontaneous combustion, but still: they just keep *dying*.

It started with the burly Ron McKernan, known as Pigpen, who was in at the inception of the group, along with guitar players and singers Jerry Garcia and Bob Weir. Pigpen, who also sang, played with Garcia and Weir in the mid-sixties in the bluegrassy Mother McCree's Uptown Jug Champions, and then in the Warlocks, a rock band with drummer Bill Kreutzmann and bass player and singer Phil Lesh. In 1965 that group changed its name to the Grateful Dead, though none suspected the ultimate dimensions of what they were starting.

Pigpen, at any rate, stayed with them for their greatest and perhaps most significant triumphs through the sixties—the notorious acid tests in San Francisco in 1966, their rise to the top of the heap of psychedelic bands (by a process of elimination as much as anything), the invention of their spacy, lengthy style of performance, and the sudden, surprising focus in their two albums from 1970, *Workingman's Dead* and *American Beauty,* which together provided the foundation for their subsequent career as a performing band with a cult following.

Pigpen never let the group get too far from his first musical love, the blues, which was the cornerstone for most rock bands of the time. A section of the Dead's concerts was devoted to highlighting him on a long tune or two. Looking at it now, with the benefit of hindsight, it was perhaps not the most comfortable fit—his "Turn on Your Love Light," for example, which takes up a whole album side on 1970's double-album *Live Dead,* doesn't hold a candle to "Dark Star," which takes up another side. But he meant well. He had a serious drinking problem, however, which finally killed him, on March 8, 1973, after he'd spent the previous two years mostly incapacitated from complications of a liver disease. He was twenty-seven when he died.

While Pigpen was still ailing, the group had tinkered with its sound slightly, adding Keith Godchaux as a second keyboardist (with Pigpen, when he was available) and also bringing in Godchaux's wife Donna on backup vocals. After Pigpen's death, the couple was formally ordained as members of the Dead, and went on to record and tour with the group through much of the seventies. That was the period when the band was clearly settling in for the long haul, focusing on its live shows and establishing the loyalties of its most rabid followers, called Deadheads, who often trekked after the group from town to town on its tours. The Godchaux's term ended in 1979, when they were asked to leave because of unspecified musical differences. A year later, on July 23, 1980, Keith died in an auto accident in Marin County. He was thirty-two.

Brent Mydland came in to replace him and remained with the group through the eighties, a period that saw it go from a firmly established phenomenon to a full-blown institution, as a new generation swelled the ranks of Deadheads even further. But on July 26, 1990, Mydland was found dead in his San Francisco apartment from drug complications. He was thirty-seven. A very brave man named Vince Welnick, formerly of the Tubes, has taken his place. If Welnick has any sense at all, he will take Prince's advice and spend this decade partying like it's 1999.

Over the years, it hasn't been just the procession of keyboard players that has brought the Grateful Dead close to the face of death. They did play at Altamont, after all, which gave rise to one of their standards, "New Speedway Boogie." Since the mid-eighties, Jerry Garcia has suffered severe health problems, only some of them related to a long-standing heroin addiction he recently licked. And, in a celebrated case, a newly minted Deadhead, nineteen-year-old Adam Katz, was murdered under mysterious circumstances outside a Dead concert in New Jersey's Meadowlands Sports Complex on October 14, 1989.

None of these details, however, has quite the beguiling pizzazz of the curse of the Dead keyboardists.

42

Stop Your Sobbing

THE PRETENDERS, like the Allman Brothers Band before them in the seventies, stand as the one great doomed rock band of the eighties. With their leader Chrissie Hynde's ties to the Kinks' Ray Davies—and more importantly with her own uniquely potent sensibility—they also stand as the most significant bridge across the punk-rock chasm, tying the best of sixties rock culture with the best of eighties postpunk rock to produce a look and sound and attitude that drew on rock's past and helped to define its future. If Elvis Costello somehow replicated and reanimated Buddy Holly and Bob Dylan, Chrissie Hynde managed the same stunt with John Lennon. Lennon's anger and pain, his poignant sentimentalism, his overweening charm—they are all alive in Hynde.

Hynde had come to the rock 'n' roll wars with a long and impressive pedigree of self-invention. An Ohio native, she spent the seventies bouncing back and forth between London and Akron, putting in time as a rock critic for *New Musical Express* and as a clerk in Sex Pistols impresario Malcolm McLaren's specialty shop. Before forming the Pretenders she had played with Mick Jones, later of the Clash; Masters of the Backside, who would go on to become the Damned; someone named Johnny Moped; Chris Spedding; Johnny Thunders; and Nick Lowe.

Once she finally settled in with bass player Pete Farndon, guitar player James Honeyman-Scott, and drummer Martin Chambers, as the Pretenders in 1978, they went to work quickly. Their self-titled debut album, released in January of 1980, was a positive revelation. Driven by a powerful backbeat, textured by astonishing guitar interplay that was slicing and pithy yet never flashy or indulgent, it was music defined above all else by Hynde's corrosive complexities of the heart—bitingly sarcastic one moment, as on "Precious" or "Tattooed Love Boys," achingly sweet the next, as on "Kid" or the top twenty hit "Brass in Pocket."

But it may have been "Stop Your Sobbing" that turned the neatest trick of all, taking as its starting point the instantly hoary punk-rock convention of including one (and only one) cover song on album releases. In Hynde's treatment of the old Kinks number, gushing pathos played off flinty bitterness in a tidy package, clocking in at 2:38. It clearly signalled the arrival of a startlingly original new rock 'n' roll voice who seemed capable of drawing on its deepest sources. Hynde and the Pretenders looked to be as equal to the task of achieving greatness as the Clash or Elvis Costello. Perhaps more so, because, unlike them—though it took some time to see the dimensions of all of them—Hynde was no eclectic, but a visionary, the very best strategy for making the long haul.

There was no stopping her but death could slow her down considerably, and it did, in a sequence of events nearly as rapid as the mechanisms of her spitfire mind. After 1981's *Pretenders II,* the disappointing follow-up to the debut, bass player Pete Farndon, at one time a love interest of Hynde's, was booted from the group for habits that had resulted in a heroin addiction. But two days after Farndon was fired, it was the *other* guitar player, James Honeyman-Scott, who died—on June 16, 1982, in his sleep, of a heroin overdose, aged twenty-five. Hynde and drummer Martin Chambers were suddenly all that was left of the group. Nearly a year later Farndon, who had never been invited back though there had been occasional talk of it, died of a heart attack resulting from drug complications, aged twenty-nine. During this troubled period Hynde became pregnant with a child by Davies.

Something about the extremes of joy and pain during this time seemed to cement her resolve. With an iron will so powerful you could almost see it, she centered herself and regrouped. In 1984, with bass player Malcolm Foster and guitar player Robbie McIntosh (no relation to the Average White Band's drummer of exactly the same name, who died in 1974), she released the astonishing *Learning to Crawl,* every groove and note of which is devoted to what she had been through. "My City Was Gone" recounts the pains of her losses in a succinct industrial metaphor, appropriate to a punk-rock star, while "Time the Avenger" measures her newfound respect for the rigors of life, and "Back on the Chain Gang," a number 5 hit in 1983, sounds a bittersweet note of cautious optimism. "Watching the Clothes" recalls the romantic sentiments of Lennon's "Watching the Wheels," and underlines their unfathomable connection. And once again her cover song was chosen carefully: "Thin Line Between Love and Hate," a beguiling, chilling hit from 1971 by the Persuaders, a New York soul group.

By then, if there'd ever been a question, it was clearly Hynde and Hynde alone who was the Pretenders. Her 1986 outing, *Get Close,* along with subsequent releases, have seen continual personnel changes and have been increasingly uneven. But her best material ("Don't Get Me Wrong," "I Remember You," "Hymn to Her") continues to be music marked by a trial-hardened spirit that nonetheless remains willing to risk and love. Death may have proved Chrissie Hynde's most uncompromising opponent in an obstacle-strewn career filled with heartache, but she has proved herself equal to it, and has overcome all of its harsh impositions, save loss.

43

I Wanna Destroy:
The Final Death of Rock 'n' Roll

BY THE mid-seventies rock 'n' roll clearly was not feeling well. The big business interests that were by then in complete control of it had, as its market surveys dictated, taken the jukeboxes and AM-radio formats and sock hops and tiny smoky clubs, from which rock 'n' roll was originally made, and transformed them into double-live greatest-hits record albums and FM-radio and enormous arenas playing host to enormous crowds and enormous caravans with forty-three tons of equipment transported painstakingly from site to site, city to city—night after night, day after day, year after year. Target-marketing and market segmentation became increasingly important in an approach to the business that has not stopped or indeed even slowed yet. The first signs of trouble were in the proliferation of hyphen-rock, which began in the mid-sixties with "folk-rock" and eventually led to such designations as country-rock, blues-rock, acid-rock, art-rock, jazz-rock, Southern-rock, progressive-rock, glitter-rock, hard-rock, soft-rock—and, finally, punk-rock.

Don't get me wrong. None of this necessarily resulted in any lack of good music or great moments. The immediate transformation of rock 'n' roll after the Beatles, in the era of folk-rock, produced music of astonishing depth and endurance. When I tote up my list of favorite albums—Bob Dylan's *Highway 61 Revisited,* Van Morrison's *Moondance,* the Velvet Underground's *Loaded,* the Beatles' *Rubber Soul,* the Beach Boys' *Pet Sounds,* the Rolling Stones' *Beggars Banquet*—most of them are from the mid-sixties. And all through the seventies (and indeed through the eighties), as hyphen-rock gradually wore into postpunk, there has always been much more worthwhile music than might be supposed from the generalized grumping. There has always been a reason to go to the record shop, the CD mart, the club, the hall, the arena: Marvin Gaye, Al Green, Neil Young, the Allman Brothers Band, Fleetwood Mac, Miles Davis, Joni Mitchell, Mott the Hoople, Bob Marley, Steely Dan, Todd Rundgren, Gram Parsons, Richard and Linda Thompson, Patti Smith, those amazing productions of Thom Bell, the Ramones, Roxy Music, David Bowie, Iggy Pop, Nick Lowe, Graham Parker, Brian Eno, Chic, the Clash, Prince, Michael Jackson, Bruce Springsteen, the Replacements, and many more—believe me, many more.

But as the seventies wore on, none of it—save, eventually, punk-rock, and then only temporarily—came to mean much of anything beyond a kind of glorified lifestyle choice. Already, with the advent of heavy metal on the one hand and disco on the other, the splintering of the forces that together brought rock 'n' roll into the world in the first place was becoming evident. What was terrific about the first wave of rock 'n' roll was that no one could pick out any part of it to hate. People had their quirks of taste, of course (me, I've never gone for the Everly Brothers), but all of it was seen as coming from the same place, that incredible womb from which Elvis Presley crawled circa 1954—and I'm not talking about Gladys here. Similarly, in the sixties the Beatles provided a unity for everything that was happening. In the late sixties, some divisiveness began to be felt—the Beach Boys, for example, were largely despised by those embracing the rock culture of San Francisco—but for the most part the Beatles' eclectic, wide-ranging tastes served the times well, as Elvis Presley's eclectic, wide-ranging talent had done a decade earlier. Much that was offered was still offered sincerely, and still accepted.

But as the seventies wore on the splintering spun out of control. "Disco Sucks," which is a lie, became a motto around which a fair segment of rock fans rallied. James Taylor and his sensitive singer/songwriter ilk were despised by those who preferred to down 'ludes or suck on a bottle of Southern Comfort and rock out. Long songs were brutally truncated to short versions deemed suitable for AM-radio airplay, effectively separating the "true fans" from the "dilettantes." (True fans, by implication, were those who sat still for long rambling jams complete with drum solos, while dilettantes were those who expected craft, nerve, and quickness.) Some listeners were tired of heavy relevance, and claimed political issues had no place in pop music, which was "just" "entertainment"; others had a widely assorted collection of axes they yearned to grind at length and for which they expected advances and royalties. In 1974, the Righteous Brothers, who had once given us the mind-boggling "Unchained Melody," now wrung their hands over the fatalities of rock 'n' roll and sang, "If there's a rock and roll heaven/Well you know they got a hell of a band." It was a number 3 hit. More than ever rock 'n' roll had become a Sara Lee product—everybody didn't like something, but nobody didn't like rock 'n' roll—available in the freezer case of your neighborhood record store.

In the confusion that followed Watergate and the end of U.S. involvement in the Vietnam War, and then the end of the Vietnam war itself, there was not a lot in American life that made sense—except as an arena for getting yours, even while the worst recession since the Depression began to set in and gas prices soared at sickening rates after the OPEC oil embargo late in 1973. By 1975, a year that produced such lasting number 1 pop monuments as Barry Manilow's debut "Mandy," the Carpenters' anemic cover of "Please Mr. Postman," and Olivia Newton-John's "Have You Never Been Mellow," rock 'n' roll was clearly moving toward a mushy middle ground. Within five years, its audience was primed for an unthinking acceptance of rock 'n' roll as nostalgic fodder for commercials. (You surely have your own favorites—mine was the Rascals' "Good Lovin'," whose exuberant refrain was turned into a tepid "Group Health" for the health services provider. But the Nike commercial that used the Beatles' "Revolution" before Michael Jackson, who "owns" it, put a stop to it—that was pretty good too.)

The victory was complete. Rock 'n' roll had been purchased by and deeded to a popular culture in thrall to business and advertising interests. All that remained was to officially put it to death—which was exactly the point at which things became very interesting again for a time. Punk-rock arrived from Britain swinging truncheons, spewing venom, and taking no prisoners (at least not until they gave themselves ever-lengthening breathers to sign the contracts proffered by major-label record companies). It declared the final death of rock 'n' roll even as it breathed life into the drying husk of the music industry. It reclaimed the most important elements of rock 'n' roll—its unifying spirit, its place in small clubs and on independent labels, its role as three-minute songs released on seven-inch singles (and, by implication, to be heard on the radio; though by that time radio was controled by an industry that rejected punk-rock; the Sex Pistols' "God Save the Queen," for example, was at once so popular and so vilified that it reached the number 2 position on the U.K. charts in 1977 literally as a blank space, while in the United States the Sex Pistols didn't even know anyone who had ever been in the charts).

The origins of British punk-rock are complex, related to the failing economy of Britain and the rise of Margaret Thatcher's conservatism, among other factors. But it was inspired in no small measure by the ruckus started in the mid-seventies in New York by the likes of the New York Dolls, Patti Smith, and the bands clustered around CBGB: the Ramones, Richard Hell, Television, Talking Heads, and Blondie. Much of that, however, as artful and winning as it was and remains, was still groping for its place, largely rejecting any kind of explicitly political stance. Inspired by the Velvet Underground, their concerns and their priorities were primarily aesthetic. It was not what has come to be understood by the term art-rock, which usually refers to the bombastic pomp of groups like Genesis, Yes, King Crimson, or Emerson, Lake and Palmer, but it was art-rock nonetheless. Richard Hell, his shirt yanked open on the cover of his 1977 debut album to reveal, scrawled on his chest, "You make me —— ," was making a calculated aesthetic point (and with that gesture, along with the title song from the album, "Blank Generation," he almost got away with naming a generation). That was also the impulse behind Patti Smith's cover of Van Morrison's "Gloria," with the famous drawled opening, "Jesus died for somebody's sins/But not mine." And behind the Ramones' studied stoopid tough guy pose, with the short songs, searing attack, and shared last name. (Let's not even talk about Talking Heads, okay?)

The Sex Pistols and Elvis Costello and even, to some extent, the Clash and the Jam (along with such bands as X-Ray Spex, the Adverts, the Slits, Swell Maps, the Pop Group, and many others) were making "statements" as carefully wrought as their New York counterparts. But they were up to something else as well—they were attempting no less than a total seizure of power, an insurrectionist act that only gained credence from its obvious absurdity. Above all else that is what the British punk-rockers wanted; to reclaim rock 'n' roll's power to frighten, provoke, force issues, and, ultimately, change lives and life itself. The New York axis, which came to be called new wave (already a derisive term by the early eighties), had no such agenda. In the end, like all good nihilistic Americans, they got off on their own powerlessness; they found in that their liberation, or the illusion of it anyway. (Kris Kristofferson, of all people—but who better?—had embalmed the idea earlier in the decade in a now famous bathetic couplet: "Freedom's just another word for/Nothin' left to lose.")

It was their powerlessness that enraged the British punk-rockers and pushed them forward. Perhaps the closest any U.S. group came to the unholy, earth-shaking fury of the British punk-rockers was Cleveland's Pere Ubu, who emerged from a similar kind of blasted urban and economic landscape, which they aggressively worked into their music as texture, and thrust into the faces of their followers—hoping, like everyone who adopted the punk-rock/new wave mantle, for a radio hit. For many years, in fact, the idea that punk-rock was going to take over the radio and the charts, if not the world, seemed a perfectly reasonable assumption; after Elvis and the Beatles, clearly something had to come along to fill the widening void at the center of rock 'n' roll. And much of it, new wave and punk-rock alike, fit all the requirements—with songs that were quick, catchy, and memorable, and would play well as counterpoint to soft-drink commercials, jabbering disc jockeys, and rioting in the streets. As with the music of Elvis and the Beatles, punk-rock promised, above all else, that it would always command attention, and that people would always care about it, even if they hated it.

Then, as it continued not to happen, the whole idea began to seem a little ridiculous, a little childish and vain and silly. And finally, for the most part, it was forgotten, except for the occasional question that arose: Why did we ever think *that* belonged on the radio? Nearly fifteen years after its moment, however, just when the rest of the industry was least expecting it, punk-rock did finally storm the citadel, as Nirvana—a punk-rock band if ever there was one—took their 1991 album *Nevermind* to the very top of the charts, and its single, "Smells Like Teen Spirit," a song as inspiring as it is incomprehensible and without a shred of compromise to it, to number 4 on the pop chart. It was an amazing moment, and heartening evidence that though rock 'n' roll has basically gone on to meet its maker (whichever one that is) the earthly and unearthly forces that created it are still alive and with us.

In their time, the Sex Pistols and Johnny Rotten were something genuinely new and different. They knew it, or Rotten knew it, as deeply and completely as he knew their time was limited (the only point their otherwise savvy manager Malcolm McLaren missed). When they leaped onto the scene they wasted no time. In the very first single, late 1976's "Anarchy in the U.K.," after the insane cackle Barry McGuire should have indulged himself with over ten years earlier, Johnny Rotten announced, "I am an antichrist/I am an anarchist/Don't know what I want,/But I know how to get it." And, in something little more than a year, the Sex Pistols gnawed away at the foundations of rock 'n' roll until it fell in rubble about them. Then they broke up midway through their first U.S. tour, early in 1978, and nothing in rock 'n' roll was ever the same again.

It's not easy to convey their impact at the time. When they reached the United States in 1977 and their shows began to raise controversy and even to be banned, it was impossible to imagine what could be going on. At the time, in the aftermath of Vietnam and Watergate, riots and political assassinations, and with the advent of publicly sanctioned pornography (the appearance of the vagina, or at least the "pubic triangle," in *Playboy* and *Penthouse,* along with the illicit hit movie of the day, *Deep Throat*) and brutally explicit horror (launched by *The Exorcist*), it seemed that all possible excesses of expression had been reached. Really. There seemed nowhere else to go. What could a rock band possibly do that would be offensive? Yet the Sex Pistols *were* frightening somehow. Those names that seem so casually goofy now—Johnny Rotten, Sid Vicious, the Sex Pistols—were portentous as hell back then. The fury was undeniable, and so was the vision. As with Elvis and the Beatles (particularly John Lennon), it was impossible to tell if it was God or Satan behind them. It raised some wonderful questions: Could it be that They had been *collaborating* all along? Could it be that the afterworldly Cold War had ended just as the earthly one was getting underway?

Whoever was responsible for them, the Sex Pistols did their work and went, as William Burroughs has said of similar actions in a different context. When the group was finished, it was finished, leaving behind a legacy whose shape is still so pervasively unclear that it simply goes by the term "postpunk." Johnny Rotten and the Sex Pistols were a moment out of time, analogous in their way to the Big Bang of the universe. And just look at how popular music has been expanding infinitely since them. I mean that literally, without irony. I don't know about you, but everybody I talk to has been confused about the "direction" (the word really must go inside quotes) of pop music since, oh, about 1979. Nothing has made sense—radio formats, album charts, tour schedules, movies appearances, MTV—nothing. Everything that seemed so right at first (contemporary hits radio, or music videos) ended up doubling back on itself, and finally seemed the worst waste of time, while those things that at first seemed the most ridiculous (Prince, or Madonna) ultimately became the most compelling.

Of the major forces in what took the place of rock 'n' roll in the eighties—let's say, just for the heck of it, that they were Elvis Costello, Husker Du, Chrissie Hynde, Michael Jackson, Madonna, Metallica, Prince, Public Enemy, R.E.M., and Bruce Springsteen (I'll give up Costello and Hynde if you give up U2)—each has its strengths and sources, and each, for the most part, has its center. But nothing, finally, binds them. It's not like the Elvis Presley, Chuck Berry, Little Richard, Jerry Lee Lewis, and Buddy Holly of the fifties; nor the Beatles, Rolling Stones, Animals, Who, Kinks, Hollies, and Herman's Hermits of the mid-sixties; nor the Jimi Hendrix, Cream, Doors, Jefferson Airplane, Grateful Dead of the late sixties; nor even the Neil Young, Van Morrison, Bob Marley, Marvin Gaye, Al Green, Patti Smith, Roxy Music of the seventies, though by then a pattern of splintering had clearly set in.

Basically, when Johnny Rotten howled, "I wanna destroy," he was perfectly serious about it, and what's more, as events proved, perfectly capable of it. But he didn't destroy rock 'n' roll—he just, true to the cliché, made the time-honored comment about the emperor's new clothes and let the rest take care of itself. Rock 'n' roll was dead but nobody cared. They wept for Elvis Presley and John Lennon, but they still had the records (that would be taken care of in another decade or so) and the legs on which to dance to them. If the community that conceived and nurtured it was demolished, what did that matter? From there it was just the shortest possible step to the ascendance of Ronald Reagan and one of the most vicious administrations in U.S. history. Next stop: Bitburg, 1985.

Set to Autodestruct

Lester Bangs, died April 30, 1982, age 33
Rock critic; from Escondido, California. Bangs was a daffy, gentle, acerbic wit who pushed back the boundaries of rock criticism throughout the seventies. Many of his ideas—such as the trash aesthetic and the related debunking of technique as a criteria of judgment—have lasted to this day. He was the first to popularize the term "heavy metal" (which he pulled from the confluence of a William Burroughs novel and a Steppenwolf song) to describe the thundering sounds of Steppenwolf, Led Zeppelin, Alice Cooper, and Black Sabbath. Starting in 1971 he lived in Detroit and worked with Dave Marsh at *Creem,* where together they made it the irreverent model for a flood of later punk-rock and heavy metal fanzines. In 1976 Bangs moved to New York and lived as a free-lance writer, contributing some of his greatest and most significant work to the *Village Voice* (including his eulogy to Elvis Presley, in which he said good-bye to you). In the early eighties a couple of book deals—biographies of Blondie and, with Paul Nelson, of Rod Stewart—kept him going, and he also formed and played in his own bands, an abiding aspiration. He died from complications of a Darvon overdose, probably accidental.

Stiv Bators, died June 4, 1990
Singer, born Steve Bators, with the Dead Boys; from Cleveland. Basically a second-rate pastiche of Iggy Pop and Johnny Rotten, Bators even so was capable of the Dead Boys' memorable signature song "Sonic Reducer." As a kind of punk-rock star he moved to New York, won notoriety among the CBGB set (thanks in large part to being managed by CBGB owner Hilly Kristal), and became involved for a time with Bebe Buell, an unmistakable indication that he had arrived. He relocated to England in the early eighties and, setting up camp in the territory abandoned by Joy Division, helped form the Lords of the New Church, a kind of punk-rock supergroup specializing in goth-rock, which also featured players from Sham 69, the Damned, and the Barracudas. He was run over by a car in Paris. He walked away from the accident—according to the rumors, because he was so inured to pain—and died later of the injuries.

Chris Bell, died December 27, 1978, age 27
Singer, guitar player, with Big Star; from Memphis. Chris Bell went to high school with Alex Chilton in Memphis but they didn't play in a band together until after Chilton scored a handful of top forty hits with the Box Tops. Together, as Big Star, they wrote most of the material for 1972's debut *#1 Record,* to this day a major influence—along with the work of the Raspberries, Todd Rundgren's Nazz, and others—on what would come to be called power pop: sweetness-and-light melodies offset by crunching electric guitar chords and a sour view of life, now a staple of the pop lexicon. Bell left soon after to pursue a solo career and spent some time in Europe, where he recorded a very fine album, *I Am the Cosmos,* that was not released until 1992. Late in 1978, back in Memphis again, Bell drove his car into a telephone pole on his way home one night and died instantly.

D. Boon, died December 23, 1985, age 27
Singer, guitar player, born Dennis Dale Boon, with the Minutemen; from San Pedro, California. Boon was the de facto leader and guiding force of the much overlooked Minutemen, an articulate and prolific southern California hardcore trio whose songs, in the beginning, rarely ran longer than a minute, hence the name. Never at a loss for political or musical savvy, they made a project of deconstructing all forms of popular music within reach, particularly drawing on blues, funk, and bop, and throwing them back as ingenious if harsh shards of sound in the service of leftist doctrine. It worked astonishingly well over album after album. Boon died in Arizona in an auto accident.

Darby Crash, died December 7, 1980, age 22
Singer, born Paul Beahm, with the Germs; from Los Angeles. Darby Crash fronted the Germs, an early Los Angeles hardcore unit who appeared in Penelope Spheeris's *The Decline of Western Civilization.* Not surprisingly, the spike-haired singer took the Sex Pistols as his starting point, combining the charms of both Johnny Rotten and Sid Vicious with savage conviction. One of his best stunts involved throwing himself flat to the stage, tearing his shirt off, and proffering a magic marker to the crowd, who then adorned him with graffiti: "Fuck You," swastikas, "Pat & Patty," and so forth. He killed himself after a pretty good first album on Slash, reportedly in tribute to Sid Vicious—the suicide, that is, not the album. It was a heroin overdose.

Ian Curtis, died May 18, 1980, age 23
Singer, with Joy Division; from England. Ian Curtis sang and provided the lion's share of vision for Joy Division, a bleak quartet named for prostitutes

in Nazi concentration camps. In their few years together the group won only scattered notice, but their two impressive albums, *Unknown Pleasures* and *Closer,* both from 1980, along with an even more impressive single from that year, "Love Will Tear Us Apart" have remained important touchstones since their release. Their dark take on life and its travails has provided an enduring influence, affecting the work of most of Britain's early and mid-eighties goth-rockers, as well as industrial-dance pioneers from both England and Chicago. As it turned out, Curtis was articulating the real thing. Just four days before the group was scheduled to begin their first tour of the United States he hanged himself. The group, however, carried on, eventually winning an enormous following as New Order.

Rick Garberson, died July 15, 1979
Drummer, with the Bizarros; from Akron, Ohio. The Bizarros were a promising group who emerged from the same generalized Ohio scene that also produced Devo, Chrissie Hynde, and Pere Ubu in the late seventies. They chipped in a tough, razorish punk-rock sound long on lyrical fulminations, most of which never amounted to anything, commercially or critically. Their raw guitar stylings did look forward in some ways to the more fully realized angular grating of Gang of Four's Andy Gill. Garberson died from carbon monoxide poisoning, later ruled accidental, but little is known of the specific circumstances.

Martin Hannett, died April 18, 1991
Producer; from England. Hannett is most famous for producing the dour records of Joy Division, but he worked with many others inside the British punk-rock and postpunk scene as well, including the Buzzcocks, New Order, Magazine, and even, very early in their career, U2. He managed to keep a hand in all along, working in the late eighties and early nineties with such latter-day British groups of interest as Happy Mondays, the Stone Roses, and Kitchens of Distinction. He died asleep in his chair at home, from health problems related to many years of drug abuse.

Alex Harvey, died February 4, 1982, age 47
Singer; from Scotland. Alex Harvey was no punk-rocker, having first broken in during Britain's skiffle rage in the fifties (as "The Tommy Steele of Scotland") and then living on the fringes of the British blues scene during the early part of the following decade. But when he finally found his moment and grabbed on tight for the ride, it was with the Sensational Alex Harvey Band in the early seventies, a glam-rock outfit contemporary with Slade and Mott the Hoople. As part of his stage act, Harvey brandished a

can of spray paint and used it liberally; the set list included covers of songs by the Coasters and Tom Jones, along with something called "There's No Lights on the Christmas Tree, Mother; They're Burning Big Louie Tonight" (references to a version of which may be found in the classic rock 'n' roll movie from 1956, *The Girl Can't Help It*). Where do you put a guy like this, except in proximity to the New York Dolls? By the time punk-rock had arrived Harvey was past forty and suffering health problems related to drugs and other hazards of the rock-star lifestyle. He died of a heart attack.

Hollywood Fats, died December 8, 1986, age 32
Guitar player, born Michael Mann, with the Blasters; from Los Angeles. Hollywood Fats played with the Blasters very briefly in the mid-eighties, replacing Dave Alvin who had left to join X. His nickname must have been based on something—he was not with the group long before he died of a heart attack.

Peter Laughner, died June 22, 1977, age 24
Guitar player, rock critic, with Pere Ubu; from Cleveland. Peter Laughner was, with David Thomas, the cofounder of the seminal U.S. art-punk band Pere Ubu in 1975. At the time, both were rock journalists, Laughner with *Creem*. Laughner played guitar and contributed to the songs on the group's first two singles, including "30 Seconds Over Tokyo" and "Final Solution," two of their best. In 1976 Laughner, a legendary drug abuser, left Pere Ubu to form his own group, Friction, from which little if anything was ever heard. He was dead by the time Pere Ubu's impressive debut, *The Modern Dance*, was released in 1978; the album included one of his songs, "Life Stinks," and another, "Humor Me," that was dedicated to him. He died of acute pancreatitis.

The New York Dolls
From New York. The New York Dolls emerged in the post-rock pre-punk early-seventies welter of glam-rock, championing trash, androgyny, old-fashioned rock 'n' roll, drugs, and fun. They were much loved as a live act but somehow the point never quite made it to vinyl. Still, they knew their place and worked it well—singer David Johansen looked back to Mick Jagger and forward to Axl Rose, while his compadre Johnny Thunders did the same with Keith Richards and Slash. They had that seductive, unruly, swaggering poise about them; that much, anyway, has survived.

As with the Glimmer Twins (and as may happen yet with Rose and Slash), it was ultimately the guitar player who earned the most credibility and won the most enduring status as a legend. Of course, that legend has all too often been related as much to heroin addiction as to guitar playing, but still, Johnny Thunders (born John Genzale) was an incredibly ferocious performer when he was on the beam. And he was otherwise about as aimless as it gets. The Replacements' sardonic, hardly prescient "Johnny's Gonna Die" from 1981 covers the main points. In the mid-seventies, after the Dolls broke up, Thunders cemented his reputation with Richard Hell in the Heartbreakers (no relation to Tom Petty's group of the same name), consistently reeling off memorable knockout performances, even through the nod. Punk-rockers everywhere—particularly British punk-rockers—loved it and flocked to see him for years. But in the end, his body was found in a New Orleans hotel room, dead of a drug overdose, with alcohol and methadone nearby in the room. It was 1991, and the question was not why he died but how he had lived so long. He was thirty-eight.

Billy Murcia, the original drummer for the New York Dolls, didn't last long. On the group's first tour of England in 1972, he mixed alcohol and drugs and suffered an overdose. All night long, reportedly, his girlfriend worked to keep him awake and alive—evidently she never thought to seek medical assistance—walking him continually around their hotel flat, putting him into a bathtub of cold water, and forcing black coffee into him. To no avail. The official cause of death was suffocation. He had drowned on the coffee, or choked, more likely, though "drowned," which reportedly appears on the death certificate, tends to dignify just a little the whole sorry episode. He was twenty-one.

The Dolls' long-term drummer, Jerry Nolan (a Charlie Watts in his own fashion), who came in to replace Murcia, stayed with the group until the end, then went on to join Thunders and Hell in the Heartbreakers. Nolan died in 1992 of a stroke after undergoing treatment for pneumonia and meningitis, aged forty-five.

Nico, died July 18, 1988, age 48
Singer, born Christa Paffgen, with the Velvet Underground, solo; from Berlin. Nico was a singer and fashionable person from Berlin best remembered for her ghostly, affecting contributions to the Velvet Underground's debut, *The Velvet Underground & Nico,* including "Femme Fatale" and "I'll Be Your Mirror." In 1959, she'd wangled a small role in Fellini's *La Dolce Vita* (1960), and used it as a springboard to a modeling career, which in turn gave her an entrée to Brian Jones and Jimmy Page who helped her cut a single, "The Last Mile," in 1965. Then she moved to New York and met Andy Warhol, appearing in his *Chelsea Girls* (1966) and eventually becoming associated with the Velvet Underground through him. After the Velvets' first album she left for a solo career, which started with 1968's *Chelsea Girl,*

featuring contributions from Lou Reed, John Cale, Bob Dylan, and Jackson Browne. Browne, with whom she was involved for a time, also performed with her, along with Tim Hardin and Tim Buckley. Two more albums were produced by John Cale, who played all instruments except Nico's by-then trademark harmonium. In 1974 Cale produced *The End,* which featured a memorable cover of the Doors' Oedipal epic and such musicians as Roxy Music's Brian Eno and Phil Manzanera. But nothing made a dent commercially, and Nico spent the rest of her life dragging her harmonium around on intermittent essays of clubland, where she continued to be a focus of interest among punks and others who had cut their teeth on the Velvet Underground. Sadly, more often than not they would call for "Heroin" from back corners all through her sets. A few more albums were released toward the end of her life, most of them recycling Velvet Underground and David Bowie chestnuts. She took a spill from her bicycle while vacationing in Ibiza and died from a resulting brain hemorrhage.

Malcolm Owen, died July 14, 1980

Singer, with the Ruts; from England. Owen led the Ruts, a late-seventies British punk-rock group shot through with strains of reggae, with his full-throated yelpings reminiscent of the Clash's Joe Strummer. Reportedly the foursome was a terrific performing act. They eventually continued as a trio, called Ruts D.C. (for da capo, "from the beginning"), after Owen's death. Owen died of a heroin overdose, in the bathtub at his mother's home.

The Pretenders

See Stop Your Sobbing.

George Scott III, died August 5, 1980

Bass player, with James Chance, John Cale, the Raybeats, 8 Eyed Spy; from New York. George Scott was a free-lance bass player in New York's late seventies punk-rock scene. He first emerged as one of James Chance's Contortions, and was later one of Chance's Blacks in James White and the Blacks. Still later he collaborated with Chance and others on the soundtrack to a Diego Cortez film, *Grutzi Elvis.* Scott also played with John Cale on Cale's 1979 "Sabotage" tour and with the twangy surf-oriented Raybeats. Perhaps his best project was 8 Eyed Spy, Lydia Lunch's post-no wave outing with guitar player and saxman Pat Irwin. The group petered out shortly after Scott's death, about which little is known.

Will Shatter, died December 9, 1987, age 31

Singer, bass player, born Russell Wilkinson, with Flipper; from San Francisco. Shatter was a vocalist and one of two bass players for Flipper, perhaps the heaviest rock band of all time. They emerged in the early eighties, in the heyday of West Coast hardcore, playing as slow as the others played fast, yet every bit as loud, effectively quadrupling (at least) the sonic impact quotient. How anyone ever left their shows alive is not known. Their first album, *Generic,* was their best, though all the others had at least a little something to recommend them. The group was continually in flux throughout the eighties, but after Shatter died of a heroin overdose it was basically over for good.

Snakefinger, July 1, 1987
Guitar player, born Phillip Lithman; from Texas. As Lithman, expatriated to London in the early seventies, he brought his country and bluegrass background to the lively pub-rock outfit Chilli Willi and the Red Hot Peppers, who were contemporary with Brinsley Schwarz and Ducks Deluxe. After they disbanded in 1975, he headed back for his homeland and ended up in San Francisco working with the Residents, with whom he took a memorable turn on their cover of "Satisfaction." Then came his solo bid as Snakefinger. It was a broad leap from bluegrass strummin' to avant-PoMo, and more often than not the seams showed: "Even with copious musical and technical input from the Residents, he just isn't that weird," *Trouser Press*'s Ira Robbins and Robert Payes complain. He died from heart problems.

T. Rex
From England. T. Rex was an important part of the glitter-rock scene that preceded and in many ways prefigured punk-rock. The band started life in the late sixties as a hippie acoustic duo called Tyrannosaurus Rex, with Marc Bolan (born Feld), ever the focus of the group, and percussionist Steve Took. Lovely flower children, they were inspired by the work of J.R.R. Tolkien—unicorns and gnomes figured prominently. Their earliest outings were produced by Tony Visconti who also stuck with Bolan through much of the seventies and produced David Bowie as well. In about 1970 they expanded to a quartet, shortened the name, and plugged in. Success beyond their wildest dreams ensued, in a business story in which everything went right for several years. They became huge in England, pushed forward by an ever-rising swell of popularity called "T. Rextasy," with some eleven consecutive U.K. top ten hits, including four number 1s. Most of them came from 1971's *Electric Warrior* and 1972's *The Slider.* In 1973 Ringo Starr produced and directed a documentary that detailed the whole thing. In the United States, meanwhile, only the 1972 number 10 "Bang a Gong (Get It On)" managed anything close to what was happening in England,

mostly because the band never put together a sizable U.S. tour at the right time.

In 1975, with the Bay City Rollers in ascension in Britain, Bolan called it quits with T. Rex, left his wife for soul singer Gloria Jones, who had sung behind him for two years, and came to the United States for a brief rest. He was back in England the next year, putting together a new T. Rex and taking them on the road with punk-rock band the Damned as their opening act. By 1977 his touch for hits had become suddenly sporadic at best, but he continued to record and perform. His glitter-rock stint, which had lent him a certain amount of punk-rock credibility, helped him stay afloat toward the end. He took a turn as a guest pop journalist for the U.K. *Record Mirror,* writing a weekly column, and hosted a late-afternoon TV variety show called "Marc," which showcased David Bowie, the Jam, Generation X, and many others. Then, in the early morning of September 16, 1977, as Bolan and Jones were returning home with Jones driving, their car went off the road and crashed into a tree, seriously injuring Jones and killing Bolan, which effectively ended T. Rex. He was thirty. Took, who had been dissociated from Bolan for more than a decade, choked to death in 1980, aged thirty-one. Steve Curry, the group's bass player during the glory years, died in 1981, aged thirty-four.

Rob Tyner, died September 17, 1991, age 46

Singer, born Robert Derminer, with the MC5; from Detroit. Tyner provided an effective set of snarls, yelps, and howls for the MC5, a strident Detroit-based quintet who may arguably be considered one of the first (along with the Fugs) real punk-rock bands. In 1968 they played the Chicago riots. Their outspoken manager John Sinclair, leader of the White Panther Party, was jailed for marijuana possession in what later became a sizable cause célèbre. The group's debut album, 1969's live *Kick out the Jams,* was controversial and eventually became the source for another cause célèbre for its use of the word "motherfucker" in the title song. Some record stores refused to carry it. Their label Elektra did all they could to mollify everyone, publicly defending the band even as, behind the scenes, they insisted the group record a cleaned-up version of the song, which went out on later pressings. Then, perhaps gun-shy from their experience with the Doors, Elektra finally threw up their hands and dropped the band altogether. The MC5 went on to Atlantic and released two more albums, one produced by Jon Landau, before disbanding in the early seventies. Tyner struggled as a photographer and in various musical projects, solo and with others, the rest of his life. In 1990 he released an album, *Bloodbrothers.* He died of a heart attack.

Sid Vicious, died February 2, 1979, age 21

Bass player, born John Ritchie, with the Sex Pistols; from England. Distinguished by an utter lack of musical talent and possessed only of a lust for fame, Sid Vicious in many ways fit the void-inflected role called for in the Sex Pistols far better than the departing Glen Matlock, who left them toward the end of 1976 for the Rich Kids, Iggy Pop, and other projects. Unfortunately, it had been Matlock who brought the greatest ability to write songs to the group, directing their efforts as they brewed up their two greatest moments, "Anarchy in the U.K." and "God Save the Queen." But, well, they must have figured it's the chance you have to take. If the Sex Pistols' outlook for continuing to catch the attention of pop music fans was somewhat compromised, their public profile was already basically in place. And the music itself by that time was well beside the point, as for the most part it always had been.

Sid Vicious, little more than a criminally disturbed child, played his assigned role with relish. He suffered injuries onstage, bled through performances, doggedly pursued heroin addiction, and in general lived his life in a brutally demented haze. For him, sadly, it was no role. He became a Sex Pistol in early 1977, shortly after the group had appeared on live British TV and said the word "fuck," creating enormous sensation and outrage thoughout the country. The world awaited the Sex Pistols with outstretched arms, from which dangled handcuffs and syringes. At that point the Sex Pistols were the apotheosis of punk-rock, representing all it could ever become. Every step they took inspired hundreds more to follow. The truth is that it was not the Velvet Underground whose every sale inspired another band but the Sex Pistols. By the time their only album, 1977's *Never Mind the Bollocks, Here's the Sex Pistols,* was certified gold, in 1988, it's not out of the question that 500,000 punk-rock groups had come and gone worldwide. But the Pistols themselves had self-destructed ten years earlier, breaking up within a year of Vicious joining, after international bannings, houndings, and a glorious period of seemingly endless general foofaraw that finally culminated in their sixth U.S. date in San Francisco on January 14, 1978; at which point Johnny Rotten declared the group finished, reclaimed his given name (John Lydon), and left for New York. Guitar player Steve Jones and drummer Paul Cook flew to Rio de Janeiro for a vacation. The group's manager and mastermind Malcolm McLaren returned to London.

Sid Vicious had himself a drug overdose and was hospitalized—not for the first or, God knows, the last time. Recovering, he stayed in the United States with his girlfriend Nancy Spungen and together they became the fun couple of that year. They were arrested on drugs charges, but they were never slowed for a moment in their pursuit of, um, whatever it was they were pursuing. For a time Vicious tried to establish a solo career, which was at once pathetic and horrific, and always fascinating. But the superstar status he longed for was never in the cards for him. On October 11, 1978, nine months after the demise of the Sex Pistols, he was arrested for murder in the stabbing death of Spungen. It was likely that he killed her but evidence indicates she goaded him to it. McLaren bailed him out of jail but a few months later Sid Vicious had himself another overdose, and this time he did not survive.

Ricky Wilson, died October 13, 1985, age 32
Guitar player, with the B-52's; from Athens, Georgia. Wilson was a co-founder of the utterly charming B-52's, pioneers of the now ubiquitous new wave junkstore chic, which they crossbred with stepped-up Carolina beach grooves for the sole—and perfectly splendid—purpose of dancing all night. Their first single, 1979's "Rock Lobster," was an irresistible cartoon sensation, as was the self-titled debut album that gave it a context and all that followed. By 1983's *Whammy!,* Wilson and drummer Keith Strickland were providing the bulk of the music but the band's charms, though still in place, were beginning to wear thin. Since Wilson's death, his contributions have been sorely missed, despite the band's surprise resurgence in the late eighties. But let him explain the salient facts by which he should be remembered: "Hi, my name is Ricky and I'm a Pisces. I love computers and hot tamales." He died of AIDS.

Munching the Corpse:
The Utter Assurance of Death's Future

O KAY, FINE, never mind: rock 'n' roll did not die in 1977. What else are we going to call Bruce Springsteen and the Replacements and R.E.M. and Nirvana and a host more from the past fifteen years? But still, as the music industry's first sizable recession since World War II settled over it like a gray pall in the late seventies, stifling its flexibility (such as it ever was), and as the unmistakably chilling effects of the Reagan administration and a hegemony of conservative interests settled over the country at the same time, and MTV ("where the commercials are the entertainment") became the focus of youth culture, rock 'n' roll became more and more a calculated consumer choice rather than a spontaneous cultural force. Maybe that's not death to you, but to me it's an awful lot like artificial life support.

Then, as the wearyingly insane eighties rolled along, with the biggest peacetime military build-up in history, with a national debt of similar dimensions, and with—the facts show it—wealth being systematically concentrated into the hands of the few, rock 'n' roll consumers by necessity became discriminating shoppers, carefully allocating their leisure dollars. Death was happy to take its place as just another option in the record and CD bins, and among the hundreds of choices facing nightclub, theater hall, and arena booking agents alike. Naturally, it was an option that many took, selecting the model and color of their choice. The list below includes some of those for whom death was a concept, followed by a section listing those who opted for the real thing.

Death as Comment

Steve Albini
Graduating in the early eighties from Hellgate High School in Missoula,

Montana, Steve Albini moved to Chicago and emerged as one of the most infuriatingly provocative rock critics in print, most of his work appearing in such criminally overlooked fanzines as *Forced Exposure* and most of it championing music that is uncompromisingly primitive, violent, and sexually disturbing. He was like a heartless Lester Bangs, and quickly established himself as a writer you might hate but will always read. During the mid-eighties, Albini led his own band, Big Black, whose 1987 swan song, *Songs About Fucking,* stands as the apotheosis of all that he reveres. His next band was called Rapeman, but now he devotes most of his energy to producing.

Aztec Camera

A postpunk outfit from Scotland led by singer/songwriter Roddy Frame, Aztec Camera mostly devoted itself to pop music with neo-folkie inflections. Much of it was hit and miss—sparkling when they were on, but more often flat and inert. In 1984, they covered Van Halen's daffy mega-hit "Jump," and transformed it from a dance-floor whoop into an unforgettable suicide note. First they slowed it down and put the focus on Frame strumming an acoustic guitar. Toward the end they opened it up into a terrifying metal screech from Malcolm Ross's feedback-distorted Hendrix turn. In between, Frame moans home the point: "You might as well jump."

Nick Cave

In the mid-eighties Australian Nick Cave emerged full-bloomed from his band of many years, the Birthday Party. With the Bad Seeds, he completely indulged his fascination with the superficial trappings of U.S. blues, gospel, and sixties rock, and proved himself up to every challenge with relentlessly dark, dank, ominous music. Cave idolizes Leonard Cohen, but he genuflects before Elvis Presley. On "Tupelo," from 1985's *The Firstborn Is Dead*, he spliced John Lee Hooker's somber textures with W.B. Yeats's doomed sensibility (e.g., "And what rough beast, its hour come round at last/Slouches towards Bethlehem to be born?") for an astonishingly penetrating treatment of Elvis's birth.

The Cramps

The Cramps are heirs to the legacy of Screamin' Jay Hawkins and the Crazy World of Arthur Brown—pure camp, but at times Satan himself may be spied among the crowd, clutching a drink, leering, and roaring at their antics. They came out of New York in the late seventies, at the time of new wave, but their music hews close to a ragged rockabilly sound and their lyrics continually evoke Louisiana swamps and female sexuality, in the service of an incoherent yet hair-raising vision: "Goo Goo Muck," "Can Your Pussy Do the Dog?," "I Ain't Nuthin' But a Gorehound" from *Smell of Female,* and many more. What do you think these songs are about? Led by Lux Interior, who preens as a demented Elvis Presley while his wife, Poison Ivy Rorschach, provides the scintillating, obscene focus of their live act and album cover art, the Cramps draw people in any way they can, including crazy covers: "Surfin' Bird," "The Crusher," "Strychnine." The whole thing is pretty funny but once you stick around awhile, they've got you.

The Cure

After Joy Division, perhaps no single band was more important to the development of Britain's early eighties preponderance of goth-rock than the Cure, which has essentially boiled down to the two-man enterprise of Robert Smith and Laurence Tolhurst. Goth-rock—purely British, a kind of overweening, majestically pretentious keyboard/beatbox stew, aimed at recalling a feeling of *Wuthering Heights* but more often updating Yes—was a staple all through the eighties, and lingers still. (Others to look for in the genre include Depeche Mode, Erasure, Spandau Ballet, the Psychedelic Furs, Gary Numan, mid-period Ultravox, and the Cocteau Twins.) But as depressed and overflowing with a doomy atmosphere as the Cure managed to be in the early eighties, the subsequent twists and turns of their career and their overall longevity have made it clear that at bottom they are professional entertainers. And goth-rock, in the long run, has turned out to be more about unexamined narcissism and self-pity than good and evil or life and death. But we all knew that in the first place. Right?

Death Metal

In the late eighties, death metal emerged from two separate breeding grounds: one in England, calling itself "grindcore" and finding its focus in Earache Records, and the other in the Tampa Bay area of Florida, with producer Scott Burns heading up the attack. Though the two scenes developed separately, they are remarkably similar. Both look to the ever-impressive Motorhead and Slayer as their starting points, delivering seven-ton attacks at impossibly fast speeds. Slayer, in fact, and the unparalleled deathly grandeur of their 1986 *Reign in Blood,* may fairly be considered the beginning of it, though their origins in turn reach back to the early eighties. The bands come with names like Death, Napalm Death, Pestilence, Carcass, Deicide, and Atrocity, and feature vocalists whose sounds issue from the lower registers and the very back of the throat, diverging from the high-pitched screech school of mainstream metal. And their lyrics are so brutal: "Mangled body, flattened corpse, stench of rot/Hammered carnage, crusted thing, maggots breed," goes one song by Sadus, "Good Rid'Nz." Or, from "Forgotten Genocide" by Cerebral Fix: "Captured, taken, tortured in a cell/Beaten to death, no skin or bone/Raising an eyelid to the sight of death/Crushing blow of an angry fist/Feel the snap of a fragile limb." Clinical, you might call it. Typical titles include "Reek of Putrefaction" by Carcass and "Chopped in Half" by Obituary, and as a rule taboos are hunted high and low, systematically flushed out, and annihilated. Deicide's Glen Benton, who claims to have killed people, has an upside-down cross burned into his forehead and is happy to explain at mind-numbing length exactly why he is a bona fide Satan worshipper. His fearsome foursome often drench themselves in pigs' blood before performances. It's all a little bit ludicrous and sick—and the best of it, such as Slayer, is genuinely frightening to behold. But likely enough most of it is on a par with the infamous Gwar, who are something of the Kiss of death metal. Gwar performs in masks and costumes with elaborately staged theatrical scenarios that are uniformly resolved in mayhem and carnage. Arms and heads are lopped off and spew blood (it's advisable to stay back of the first thirty rows or so at their shows) or, alternately, religious figures such as priests are raped, and the rapist's cannon (which, of course, is literally about that size) spews jism. Whether this sounds intriguing or abhorrent to you—there's rarely a middle ground—Gwar's performances are surprisingly hackneyed and ineffective.

Diamanda Galas

Diamanda Galas, a performance artist from Los Angeles with a huge, near-operatic singing voice, has devoted herself to an epic of enormous proportions, "The Plague Mass," since her brother died from AIDS in 1986. Galas's ability to focus her rage is astonishing. Drawing lyrically on such sources as the Bible's Old Testament and Baudelaire, and sprawling now across several albums, her work is harrowing, moving, and difficult—and quite possibly the most hallucinatory and powerful music you are ever likely to hear.

Ministry

Led by the prolific Alien Jourgensen, otherwise an extremely busy producer in Chicago, Ministry weathered an early period as a tepid early eighties goth-rock outfit before emerging as one of the finest and most ferocious practitioners of industrial dance. On the breakthrough *The Land of Rape and Honey,* from 1988, and its follow-ups, 1989's *The Mind Is a Terrible Thing to Taste* and 1992's *Psalm 69,* it's rarely clear what exactly is going on, but the atmosphere is decidedly unnerving. And that dance beat under-neath it inviting you to shake your booty is only one of the tricks used to make you like it. It's like anxiety with a beat—and you *can* shake your booty to it, if you can loosen up your booty with all that menace bearing down on you.

My Life with the Thrill Kill Kult

Another product of Chicago, My Life with the Thrill Kill Kult emerged circa 1989 with an industrial-dance surface that has gradually modulated into almost pure disco, all of it in the service of Satan. Their 1989 "Kooler Than Jesus" CD single, which clocks in at well over forty minutes, features such lengthy workouts as "Nervous Xians" and "The Devil Does Drugs" (sample samples: "Sympathy for the Devil," " . . . and this is for the dentist!"). By the time of 1991's vastly overlooked *Sexplosion!* they were locked in to the rubberband-beat and the focus had turned all the way to sadomasochistic sex-for-sale. In performance the edge remained. At one point, an anatomically correct (if exaggerated) Jesus on the cross is brought to the stage and ritually used for sexual purposes.

Nine Inch Nails

With the release of the debut *Pretty Hate Machine* in 1989, Nine Inch Nails quietly insinuated itself as a major force in nineties industrial dance. And it was mostly accomplished by word of mouth—with virtually no promotion, the thing stayed on the albums chart for months, and then years; it finally went gold, and then platinum. But it's no wonder it didn't get airplay. Trent Reznor, a studio wizard who essentially is the band, is no happy camper and he's all too willing to go into the details at length. On a 1992 EP tease (which itself spiked to number 7 on the albums chart the week it was released) for the long-awaited follow-up, the most airworthy song was called "Happiness in Slavery." Reznor has since rented the former home of Roman Polanski and Sharon Tate in Los Angeles (see Friends: Charles Manson and Dennis Wilson), where he is completing the album.

Ozzy Osbourne

Britisher Ozzy Osbourne's greatest accomplishment was to form Black Sabbath in the late sixties, considered by many today to be the first heavy metal band of any significance—he stands as something like the Bill Haley of metal. The concept was to create music for people on downers. It had to be loud and simple to reach through the anesthesia, heavy and visceral to actually touch a nerve. Voila! "Paranoid," "Iron Man," and a series of lugubrious albums rife with gestures of bloodletting and Satanism. But it's hard to figure Osbourne. On the one hand he's clearly a commercial animal, diligently working his gold mine, but on the other he seems to take some of the shtick seriously, though he frequently denies it. Back when he first emerged, he was not nearly as much fun as Alice Cooper, that's for sure, nor was he anywhere near as smart as the Rolling Stones. And if it was all purely superficial, it still led to hellish problems. In 1981, after he'd left Black Sabbath for a solo career, Osbourne took a turn as a geek, becoming legendary for biting the head off of a live dove during a meeting with label executives. A few months later a fan at a show in Des Moines, Iowa, tossed him a dead bat and he bit the head off that too. Oops—a rabies scare ensued, and the Ozz had to undergo the lengthy, painful treatment, after which he gave up that particular bit in his act. In 1982 his guitar player Randy Rhoads died in a freak plane accident (see Unavailable for Comment), and in 1986 he was sued by the parents of a teen suicide because of his song "Suicide Solution." Nothing much slowed him, however, and in 1989 he scored a number 8 hit with Lita Ford, "Close My Eyes Forever." He's clean and sober now, and the latest word is that he plans to retire. Wonder what the Devil will have to say about that.

The Plasmatics

During the late seventies and early eighties, all decked out in mohawks and leather, the Plasmatics tried very hard to be good old plain entertainment, in a punk-rock kind of heavy metal way, but there was always something a little insidiously psychotic and scary about them. Lead mannequin Wendy O. Williams ("W.O.W."), a one-time porn star and live-sex performer, took to the stage with only duct tape or shaving cream covering her nipples. Standard parts of the act included smashing televisions with a sledgehammer, blowing up cars, and wielding a chainsaw on the guitars. It always seemed like it was supposed to signify something, but it never quite did. Their manager, Rod Swenson, kept them busy with Evel Knievel-type publicity stunts, such as driving a brakeless car over a cliff into the Hudson River—Williams leaped from it at the last minute, and the whole thing, of course, was filmed and distributed to local news stations around the country. Early in 1981, while touring, Williams was arrested on obscenity charges in Milwaukee and, the next night, on the same charges in Cleveland. That helped stoke the publicity machine, but when the Plasmatics started releasing their pathetically lame albums later that year it was all but over. The band signed to Capitol in 1982 and fizzled. Williams went on to a solo career and eventual obscurity.

Unavailable for Comment

Cliff Burton, died September 27, 1986, age 24

Bass player, with Metallica; from Los Angeles. Burton was the original bass player for Metallica, whose significance among eighties metal bands, along with Slayer and Queensryche, cannot be understated. Taking their cue from Motorhead, Metallica stripped away the bombast of seventies metal and substituted speed, producing a sound at once heavy and quick. If the pyrotechnics, particularly of guitar player Kirk Hammett, sometimes drifts toward noodling fusion, they always manage to retain an edgy drive courtesy of their locomotive rhythm section. The 1986 album *Master of Puppets* was the last on which Burton appeared. He was killed in a bus crash in Sweden.

Steve Clark, died January 8, 1991, age 30

Guitar player, with Def Leppard; from England. Clark played guitar for Def Leppard, a mainstream metal band of the eighties who were nearly (but not quite) as cursed as they were successful. They first emerged from England's metal new wave of the late seventies, with Iron Maiden, Saxon, and others, and then went on to mega-platinum status, most of it due to their success in the United States. Their breakthrough albums were 1981's *High'n'Dry* and especially 1983's *Pyromania,* which took a year in ten studios to complete, but paid off. In 1984 drummer Rick Allen lost his left arm in an auto accident. Everybody adjusted and the group soldiered on. Other projects encountered other difficulties, almost without exception, but earned back their investments, also without exception. Clark's life-style finally caught up with him, however, and he died of alcohol-related respiratory failure, just a week before Iraq was engaged in war by the United States.

Nigel Preston, died May, 1992

Drummer, with the Cult; from England. Preston was one of the many drummers passing through the Cult (shortened from Death Cult, shortened from Southern Death Cult), who made a career logging the territory originally cleared by Joy Division and the Cure before turning to metal in the late eighties. Preston joined in 1983, as something like their third drummer, after leaving Sex Gang Children. In turn, he left the Cult in 1985, and little is known of his activities after, nor of his death.

Razzle, died December 8, 1984

Drummer, with Hanoi Rocks, born Nicholas Dingley; from England. Razzle was recruited to play in the Finnish Hanoi Rocks after they had relocated to England in 1982 and lost their original drummer, Gyp Casino. The group was basically metal, but came with a bluesy tinge, a glittery overlay, and dim hopes to fill the void left by the New York Dolls, nearly ten years after the fact. Ex-Mott the Hoople players Ian Hunter and Overend Watts lent them a hand, but in the end the group's reach far exceeded their grasp, and they never lived up to expectations—their fans' or their own. Pals with members of Motley Crue, Razzle died in an auto accident involving Motley Crue singer Vince Neil. Neil, as a result, was charged with vehicular manslaughter, spent just under three weeks in jail, and was required to donate community service and give a series of lectures at high schools and colleges on the dangers of drinking and driving. Which of course he did. Rock on, dude.

Randy Rhoads, died March 19, 1982, age 25

Guitar player, with Quiet Riot, Ozzy Osbourne; from Los Angeles. Randy Rhoads, who was in on the formation of Quiet Riot, enjoyed his greatest success after he'd left them in 1979 for Ozzy Osbourne. With the Ozz, he was on hand for the renowned, much-loved chewing up of birds and bats, and also appeared on the first gold albums: 1980's *Blizzard of Ozz* and 1981's *Diary of a Madman*. Rhoads went out in memorable fashion, horsing around on Ozzy's private airplane with two others—Ozzy's hairdresser and the pilot, who was at the controls—for the benefit of those below on the tour bus. On their final swoop, the plane wing nicked the bus, spun out of control, and crashed into a nearby house. All on board were killed.

Stefanie Sargent, died June 28, 1992, age 24

Guitar player, with 7 Year Bitch; from Seattle. Sargent was a founding member of 7 Year Bitch, a promising grunge outfit from Seattle who, like many, struggled for years with little to show for it but a small, rabid local following. In 1992, their break seeemd to loom on the horizon after a well-received appearance during the New Music Seminar in New York led to a sudden spate of interest from both press and major labels—no doubt due in part to the surprising success of the Pacific Northwest's Nirvana earlier that year, along with the homegrown-going-national "riot grrrl" movement. Sargent returned home to Seattle and celebrated, which led to her accidental death from a heroin overdose.

Bon Scott, died February 19, 1980, age 33

Singer, with AC/DC; from Scotland, via Australia. Most of the members of AC/DC moved from Scotland to Australia in 1974 for a long slow climb to metal favor that lasted the rest of the decade. Their first albums were produced by guitar players Angus and Malcolm Young's older brother George with Harry Vanda, who were both ex-Easybeats (scoring in 1967 with the top twenty "Friday on My Mind"). AC/DC finally hit their stride and subsequently struck multi-platinum bonanzas when Angus began to iterate metal's unconscious homosexual themes and got into short pants—they broke big with 1979's *Highway to Hell* and never looked back. But Scott enjoyed the big time just a little too much, and before long he had died from the altogether too familiar choking on his vomit in an intoxicated sleep.

Hillel Slovak, died June 27, 1988, age 25
Guitar player, with the Red Hot Chili Peppers; from Haifa, Israel. Slovak, raised in Hollywood, was an original member of the Red Hot Chili Peppers, whose gestures were all frat-boy outrage even as their music—in the spirit of their times, the mid-eighties—yoked together elements of metal and rap. Slovak, who provided the Hendrix-inspired fireworks, had survived on the fringes of weird for much of the decade, with and without the Peppers (in the early eighties he played with James Chance). As the band coalesced they found themselves working with such figures as George Clinton and Michael Beinhorn, Bill Laswell's partner in Material. Shortly after the release of their third album, *The Uplift Mofo Party Plan,* Slovak died of a heroin over-dose. Shocked, the band went into eclipse for a time, but eventually regrouped and took their stuff to the highest points of the chart.

Trouble T-Roy, died July 15, 1990, age 22
Rap artist, born Troy Dixon, with Heavy D. and the Boyz; from Mt. Ver-non, New York. Trouble T-Roy was a member of Heavy D.'s posse, a dancer and stage presence with Heavy D. and the Boyz, who scored a top twenty hit in 1991 with "Now That We Found Love." He died when he took a fall from the theater balcony after a show in Indianapolis.

Andrew Wood, died March 19, 1990, age 24
Singer, with Mother Love Bone; from Columbus, Minnesota. Wood was a comer in Seattle grunge circles in the late eighties. He sang with Malfunk-shun before forming Mother Love Bone in 1988 with guitar player Stone Gossard, bass player Jeff Ament, and others. He had licked a heroin habit and cleaned up over three months before the release of their Polydor debut, *Apple.* But evidently he went looking for another taste on the eve of the

band's breakthrough, and died from an overdose. A month later the album was released, as scheduled, but the tour was canceled. Gossard and Ament went on to form Pearl Jam. They also appeared, with other Seattle players (including members of Soundgarden), on the tribute to Wood, 1991's *Temple of the Dog*, which went into the top ten of the albums chart in 1992.

About the Author

Jeff Pike is a freelance writer whose work has appeared in *Billboard*, the *Utne Reader*, and the *Seattle Times*. He lives in Seattle.